Routledge Revivals

Supplies Management for Health Services

First published in 1979, *Supplies Management for Health Services* looks at the characteristics and problems of hospital suppliers and examines the way in which the hospital and the National Health Service deal with supplies problems and relations with suppliers. Beginning with a description of the National Health Service and its supplies organisations and the role of the Department of Health and Social Security in this field, the book then reports on the detailed studies made over two years of the supplies problems of ten London area health authorities and ten London manufacturers of medical equipment.

The NHS situation is then contrasted with the supplies situation in three non-health organisations and with the health supplies situation in France and West Germany. The final part of the book analyses the information obtained, proposes a means of assessing supplies systems, and evaluates the NHS situation. This is followed by the realistic proposals for reform, advocating a system similar to that used in British defence services, based on a central procurement agency, close cooperation with private manufacturers, and manufacture by government where necessary. This book will surely interest students of economics and global health.

Supplies Management for Health Services

Stanley Hyman

Routledge
Taylor & Francis Group

First published in 1979
by Croom Helm

This edition first published in 2022 by Routledge
4 Park Square, Milton Park, Abingdon, Oxon, OX14 4RN

and by Routledge
605 Third Avenue, New York, NY 10017

Routledge is an imprint of the Taylor & Francis Group, an informa business

A Library of Congress record exists under ISBN: 0856647071

ISBN: 978-1-032-24811-0 (hbk)
ISBN: 978-1-003-28023-1 (ebk)
ISBN: 978-1-032-24812-7 (pbk)

Book DOI 10.4324/9781003280231

SUPPLIES MANAGEMENT FOR HEALTH SERVICES

Stanley Hyman

CROOM HELM LONDON

Croom Helm Ltd, 2-10 St John's Road, London SW11

British Library Cataloguing in Publication Data

Hyman, Stanley
Supplies management for health services.
1. Medical care – Great Britain 2. Medical supplies 3. Materials management – Great Britain 4. Medical instruments and apparatus.
I. Title
658.7 RA395.G6

ISBN 0-85664-707-1

Printed in Great Britain by
Billing & Sons Limited, Guildford, London and Worcester

CONTENTS

FOREWORD

This is a report of a study undertaken with the help of a grant from the Social Science Research Council and of the resources of Middlesex Polytechnic (1976-78) and Portsmouth Polytechnic (1977-78).

The objectives of the study, as defined in the 1975 application for funds, were:

1. to discover the characteristics and problems of those firms whose primary goal is to supply hospitals with the goods and services necessary for their activities;
2. to examine the ways in which the hospital and the National Health Service deals with its supplies problems and relations with suppliers;
3. to seek solutions to the problems of suppliers and hospitals through changes in the organisation and procedures of both, based on insights that may emerge through examining both the industry and the hospital service as parts of a single system;
4. to observe empirically the processes whereby new needs of hospitals become apparent and the ways in which suppliers satisfy them;
5. to contribute to the development of organisation theory.

In order to achieve these objectives, the co-operation of ten area health authorities and ten manufacturers of electro-medical equipment located within Greater London was sought and obtained and they were visited at quarterly intervals over eighteen months. Comparative studies were also proposed so as to avoid unwarranted assumptions about NHS supplies; help was obtained from British Airways, the Greater London Council, and ICI Limited. Studies and visits were also carried out in France and West Germany in order to learn about their health care supplies systems. These comparative studies were much more superficial than the primary NHS studies but they have proved to be useful.

All these studies were carried out by a part-time research assistant, Mrs P. Day, a part-time secretary, Mrs V. Gittus, and by my participation in the midst of many other commitments. The project was based on Middlesex Polytechnic throughout, but I left in July 1977 to take up a post in Portsmouth Polytechnic and continued to direct the project from there. The study could not have been completed without the extraordinary dedication of Mrs Day and Mrs Gittus who worked well beyond formal requirements and showed exceptional initiative and responsibility. I am most grateful to both of them for all their efforts. I, of course, am solely responsible for the shortcomings of the study.

I should like to stress that the objectives of the study have compelled us to ignore many interesting avenues. This is *not in any way* a study of the National Health Service, the Department of Health and Social Security, nor of any of the health authorities or firms that co-operated with us. It is not a study of pharmaceutical drugs or the pharmaceutical industry as they have been studied thoroughly by others. It is a study of some supply problems in the NHS viewed from the perspectives of both the Service and the suppliers. We were not equipped to undertake comprehensive studies of all organisations involved in all NHS supplies and, if through making unavoidable general statements, I have been inaccurate, I apologise and trust that our aims and limited resources excuse our shortcomings. This can only be a small contribution to a vast subject of growing importance and I hope that many others will build on this limited foundation. It appears to be the only study of its kind and I hope the normal indulgence shown to pioneers will be extended to us. It should be remembered that we did not have access to many parts of the NHS. The heart of the study is a report on visits totalling about 300 hours. A vast number of people have helped us in our work, especially in the DHSS, the NHS, the ten suppliers and those employed in the comparative organisations we studied. We have endeavoured to report accurately, to respect confidences and to give acknowledgement where we have been allowed to do so. I would ask all of them to accept my most sincere thanks and my hope that the outcome may seem a justification for the time they gave us.

Stanley Hyman
August 1978

Part One

THE NATIONAL HEALTH SERVICE

1 THE STUDY OF HEALTH SERVICE SUPPLIES

This book reports on a research project that investigated the problems associated with supplying the British National Health Service with the goods and services it requires. The general problem of procurement is magnified in the National Health Service.

There is no single central buying organisation but a large number of independent regions and areas (and hospitals within areas) covering a range of purchases now valued at about £600 million pounds. While that represents only about 8 per cent of the total annual NHS expenditure, it is a vast amount of money and the ways in which that money is spent must be a matter of concern; it can affect the welfare of patients and is part of public expenditure.

Good procurement necessitates consideration of the needs and problems of suppliers, and thus concern about the effectiveness of the complete procurement process. There is a single system, involving both the NHS and its suppliers. The system perspective increases the objectivity of this study as we have not been biased towards the narrow interests of either buyer or supplier.

The project has been based on a detailed study of ten area health authorities in three Thames regions of the National Health Service and of ten manufacturers of electro-medical equipment. Although they represent only a small part of total purchasing—perhaps 3 per cent—these products are distinctive to the NHS, whereas the majority of purchases represent such items as food, clothing, and building maintenance expenses that are used by many organisations, industries and social services.

A study confined to health services supplies would lack opportunities for comparison and appraisal and the project has therefore compared the NHS supply situation with that in one large private firm, one local government authority, one nationalised industry, and with the hospital supply situation in France and West Germany. This has been an ambitious programme, particularly as the bulk of the work has been done by a part-time research assistant and a part-time secretary over two years, and it has been impossible to be comprehensive. Most of the twenty-three collaborating organisations were visited once every three months, first to discuss the general supplies situation then to investigate particular problems identified at earlier interviews by observation and discussion. The French and German studies have been based largely on literature surveys, correspondence, previous market research studies, and a series of visits to French and German organisations.

Origins

The project originated in a study concerned with the general problem of efficiency in organisations. That began at Kingston Polytechnic in 1967 and involved a series of visits to two each of five different kinds of organisation by a team of specialists in finance, personnel, marketing, general management, and operations management. Although each visit was brief and the assessment crude, it was possible to rate the organisations in terms of assessed efficiency and thus to identify the best and the worst. Those two organisations were studied in the light of a hypothesis that efficiency was a function of the external relationships of an organisation, and not primarily of its internal organisation. Some initial evidence was obtained that indicated the correctness of the hypothesis.[1]

One type of organisation investigated was the hospital, and the team found it extremely difficult to come to an initial assessment on the efficiency of the hospital. A number of attempts have been made by researchers to formulate a procedure for making an objective assessment of hospital effectiveness. One obvious method is to consider costs but that is unhelpful when the purpose of the hospital is to preserve or improve health. One can conceive of a hospital with no current costs—perhaps an empty hospital—but one failing to fulfil its proper function. If patient care becomes the criterion of efficiency, most studies have been concerned with the length of time patients have had to stay in hospital for particular illnesses or operations. Those studies are certainly important but inadequate until one knows the subsequent fate of the patient. If he is sent home too soon and drops dead the next day, the hospital is not efficient, but it might claim that its statistics demonstrate its efficiency in getting patients home more quickly than anybody else.

As the team had no specialist knowledge of the hospital, it decided to study one particular aspect of hospital activity where its collective industrial experience might enable it to make a justified judgement—the purchasing of hospital supplies from industry. An initial enquiry demonstrated the complexity of the subject and led to a pilot study in the Kingston Hospital Group in 1969-70 which was financed by grants from the Nuffield Provincial Hospitals Trust and the then South West Metropolitan Regional Hospital Board (out of private funds). That study involved some investigation of suppliers' problems. It was a useful pilot study but the scale of its operations and the difficulties of undertaking the project indicated the need for further work. The reorganisation of the National Health Service in 1974 may have changed the situation radically but no related studies have appeared. An application was made for a grant to the Social Science Research Council and the project started in April 1976.

Related Studies

There is now a wide range of studies of hospitals, health services, and the British National Health Service in particular. They are well documented and a number of books exist reviewing relevant knowledge, some of which are listed in the bibliography. Most of the studies are specialised, concentrating on specific problems or procedures of the NHS, with a view to improving performance. Another range of studies are 'broad brush' reviews of knowledge and problems, such as Brian Abel-Smith's *Value for Money in Health Services.* Robert Maxwell's study of *Health Care: The Growing Dilemma* in nine major countries is painstaking and most informative, analysing expenditure in those countries and demonstrating enormous economic problems associated with satisfying different and future health requirements.

One range of studies by Professor R. Revans has been concerned with several dimensions of hospital life. His books on *Morale in Hospitals* and *Communications in Hospitals* are pioneering in many senses and undoubtedly will influence the future management of hospitals.

So far as procurement is concerned, the literature appears to be divided into (a) highly technical studies about particular products, and (b) anecdotal articles that expound at some length and with considerable repetition the remembered problems of NHS supplies officers. Very few of the existing studies are rigorous and analytical and a great deal of valuable knowledge is being lost through the failure to adopt systematic procedures for learning about the experience of many successful supplies officers.

None of the existing studies (apart from my report on the Kingston project) appears to be concerned with the twin problems of the NHS and the supplier. Stringent separation has led to the absence of enquiries into the total procurement process that to be successful must incorporate the needs of both of the principal parties. Such studies have not been made because most investigators tried to meet the immediate problems of one party. As a result, many of the really important and difficult problems have been left on one side.

Studies of Supplies

The field of study of what is variously known as purchasing or supplies management, or procurement management, is somewhat meagre, particularly in Britain. The Institute of Purchasing and Public Supplies has for many years led the way in the training of managers concerned with purchasing, and it publishes useful journals. It has not undertaken research to any extent, and its library is small. The situation in the USA is different, with many journals and books reporting on problems and on research projects, and many professional institutes and university courses are devoted to the subject. In Britain, serious academic study has been slight, with useful initiative being taken by the Administrative Staff College in the form of the work of Dr David Farmer.

In industry, both public and private, buying is still a poor relation of production and marketing, and many opportunities for sensible economies and quality improvement continue to be missed. The salaries of purchasing managers appear to be comparatively low, and the procedures of many firms in respect of buying, contracts and payments does not seem to be satisfactory. There are some outstanding exceptions but these tend to be associated with large organisations. British Airways has some of the most advanced procedures now in use and they could be matched with similar success stories elsewhere. But good purchasing seems to be very dependent on the abilities of individuals, without the general theory and status associated with such areas as accounting and engineering that form such an important part of organisation effectiveness.

This is not a specialist study of procurement management—a suitable umbrella term to cover the whole process—and no expertise is claimed in this field. We have looked at the work of purchasers and suppliers and attempted to assess it objectively without being able fully to appreciate all the burdens of the individuals on both sides because we have not worked as the professional has done. However, through an association now extending over ten years, I believe that I have obtained an appreciation of the difficulties and successes of procurement. The loyalty and energy that most people concerned with NHS supplies devote to their work is outstanding, especially when much of it must be repetitive and dull. The project should be seen as a study of procurement management and as a study of the relationship between the private and public sectors in what is called 'the mixed economy'. These issues are important to political and financial management in general and need analysis and discussion. The final part of this book aims to contribute to that debate.

Organisation Theory

The implications of this study for the theory of organisation are considerable, especially in respect of inter-organisation relationships. This is a relatively new facet of organisation studies, and the recent book edited by William M. Evan[2] does indicate a degree of progress in a vital but generally neglected field. When the organisation is studied from the outside instead of internally, many new considerations emerge. Internally, an organisation appears to be a collection of individuals, resources, and conventions that bind it together into an entity isolated from the rest of the world. Viewed from the outside, the organisation appears to have one or a few very distinctive characteristics, and many more common to a wide range of organisations. The common needs of organisations may be better met by each organisation having closer links with general common service suppliers, and then concentrating on its truly distinctive needs and abilities.

Notes

1. S. Hyman, 'How to Be efficient', *Management Today*, June 1968.
2. William M. Evan, *Inter-organisation Relations*, Penguin, London, 1976.

2 ASSESSING SUPPLIES SYSTEMS

The proper focus of attention in the consideration of health is the welfare of the individual and the availability of doctors and nurses. But the work of medical staff is dependent on the provision of a vast range of products and services that make it possible for expertise to be properly applied and used. Thus the emotion and drama of medicine has to be translated into many more mundane activities, such as the process of deciding what goods and services should be bought and then obtaining them in appropriate quantities and qualities and at optimum prices. Hospitals have to be designed, built, equipped and kept running on a twenty-four hour basis every day of the year. In addition to hospitals, there are numerous clinics and other medical centres, nearly all of which are in Britain operated by the NHS out of public funds. In other countries, there are varying mixtures of public and private provision of health services, and one estimate indicates that probably 60 per cent of the world's population are now served by public medical services. Most informed opinion suggests that this proportion will increase over the next few years and that possibly by the end of the century the proportion of totally private medical treatment will be infinitesimal on the scale of world population. Whether medical services are private or public, they will still require the goods and services ancillary to medical practice.

The significance of health service supplies increases with the awareness of rising demand for health care throughout the world. One authoritative study shows that a country which had spent 3½ per cent of its national product on health in 1950 was spending 6 per cent of a much larger gross national product by 1969. In that year the United Kingdom spent about 4½ per cent of GNP and the United States about 6½ per cent. That 2 per cent difference costs the United States 19,000 million dollars. In the United States the annual health expenditure per person was about 400 dollars in 1972 but that would pay for only about two days of acute hospital care, including physician's fees. In Britain and in most other countries, approximately 70 per cent of health service expenditure goes on salaries and wages. The remainder goes on hospital building and the supplies of medicines, medical equipment and dressings of all kinds.

Bearing in mind the very low standards of health care in developing countries, it is obvious that the future demand for doctors and other trained medical personnel is going to be enormous and far beyond the resources now available, or likely to be available, to produce fully trained doctors to the standard now considered normal in advanced countries.[1]

The Nature of Supplies Management

The work of supplies managers in most organisations is largely concerned with routine purchasing of standard requirements. From one perspective, it appears to be a dull bureaucratic paperchase that requires little initiative or ability. At the other end of the scale, the chief buyer for a large organisation may be spending millions of pounds a year and concentrating his efforts on discovering new and better products from more reliable suppliers and at better prices, a search that may take his interests all over the world. For most organisations, procurement lies somewhere between these two extremes, but there can be no doubt that successful purchasing requires considerable knowledge built up over many years of experience, based on a critical and scientific analysis of needs and opportunities.

Purchasing is not a crafty activity aimed at securing bargains. Every buyer knows that such purchases can be made, and from time to time should be made, without any adverse consequences, but if the organisation is known to be interested solely in such 'bargains' it is unlikely to be offered sufficient sound products at reasonable prices that it truly requires. Hospitals in the past and certainly before the National Health Service began, were known as suitable places to sell off second-rate fruit and vegetables because they were cheap and the hospitals were poor. Traces of that tradition are still to be found.

Thus an unexpected development of buying has been the need to establish good relationships with suppliers. Older generations saw the supplier as the enemy and believed that anyone offering goods for sale must be slightly dishonest and lacking in concern for the welfare of the customer. That unfortunate tradition is disappearing in parallel with the growth of good marketing, which is based on the principle of seeking to establish a high enough reputation to obtain repeat orders over many years. Thus there is no place for 'get rich quick' techniques when the buyer and the supplier are both concerned with satisfying needs that will recur for very long periods of time.

Purchasing is a perfectly reasonable relationship between supplier and buyer and it does not have to involve the dishonesty that many appear to assume is the hallmark of private business. Nor does it mean that the buyer can continue to act without consideration for the personal and economic problems of the supplier, while expecting him to guarantee more to the buyer than he even asked for.

The major steps in the process of purchasing are:

1. *Identifying a Need.* The buyer or the potential buyer has to become aware of the need to purchase a product or service. In most cases this will be obvious, as with the daily need for food in a hospital. On the other hand, the provision of familiar services, such as catering in a hospital, can descend into an unimaginative continuation of methods that ignore new techniques which could lead both to economies and better diet. So there are obvious needs that the buyer is aware of and there are underlying needs that an incompetent buyer may not appreciate until someone points them out. This is of course done by many suppliers looking for additional sales. Such attention may be irrelevent or unwelcome, or descend occasionally to dishonesty, in terms of offers and claims made, but a supplier can be a very useful source of new knowledge to a buyer.
2. *Specification.* Having identified a broad need, purchasing cannot take place effectively until a very precise description has been made of the product or service needed to meet identified requirements. Thus there is little point in a hospital asking a shop to supply a bed until it has worked out exactly what kind of bed, for what purposes and for what patients the hospital bed is needed. The answer to that question required many months of study by a group from the King's Fund. Specification is needed for very common products in daily use as well as for the most sophisticated and unusual equipment and machinery. Specification requires the collaboration of the ultimate user with the purchasing officer, and perhaps an expert scientist, often in consultation with one or more potential suppliers who should possess their own expert staff and considerable relevant experience.
3. *Price.* Whilst anyone may be able to buy anything at a price, the competent buyer has to be able to buy at the best available price. That does not necessarily mean the cheapest price because the cheap product is unlikely to possess the durability and quality that the buyer requires if he has specified his need with precision. In addition to trying to find the best possible price for the specified product from all available sources, the buyer has to consider the further reductions in price per unit that may be possible by buying in large quantities and over long periods. Of course, the apparent price advantage has to be compared with the real additional direct and hidden costs that may be associated with long-term buying agreements.
4. *Contract.* Some kind of agreement is involved in every sale of goods and some exchange of advantages for money takes place. But usually

both parties have in mind a whole host of considerations and requirements that should be written down and agreed between them so as to minimise and possibly avoid misunderstanding, bad feeling, and disappointed expectations. Thus a contract should not only specify the product but also the price, delivery, packaging, servicing and any other relevant aspect of the purchase and use of the product over long periods of time.

5. *Delivery.* Delivery needs to be stated with clarity in view of the many misunderstandings that arise over this issue. Where it is important for precise dates to be stated and agreed, they must be worked out with care by both sides and no worthless promise should be given by any party if the kind of trust necessary to long-term business is to be built up. Penalty clauses are frequently inserted into contracts in order to ensure observation of undertakings but if a supplier has a monopolistic power, then any such contract enforcement clause may not be honoured, as in the case of the Post Office and telecommunications equipment manufacturers. Delivery involves decisions about places for delivery as well as dates and the number of delivery points can cause very great difficulties to the supplier and increase his costs unreasonably. On the other hand, many buyers assume that the supplier realises that deliveries will have to be made to a number of points and are astonished at the bad feeling that wide delivery networks create. Once again, the fullest possible definition of requirement in a contract is the best way of ensuring that the proper consideration is given to this issue in formulating prices, and it may well be that a supplier is estimating for more extensive delivery than a particular customer requires.

6. *Quality.* It is vitally important in every purchase for the quality to be specified and to be honoured and monitored. There are many ways in which this can be done, and in some cases it will be necessary to examine each unit supplied in order to ensure that it meets the specification. But in most instances random examination of samples is enough. Having agreed whether it is universal or sample, both parties need to decide where the inspection should take place. Sometimes it will be sensible for the buyer to appoint someone to undertake quality control on behalf of both parties within the supplier's organisation.

7. *New Products.* The development of new products is clearly a vital necessity to the health of any economy. The needs met by old products may diminish or disappear and new needs emerge. A static economy could not remain prosperous. On the other hand, there can be an excessive number of innovations that appear to lead to unnecessary additional expenses. The optimum policy may emerge from a joint exploration of

needs by supplier and buyer, but the need for initiative for change and invention will remain, and the lead will normally come from the supplier. If he is sensible, he will build his plans on a calm appreciation of the position of potential buyers.

8. *Staff.* The provision and training of adequate purchasing staff is a vital necessity for a satisfactory supply system and we need to assess the NHS supplies activity partly on the basis of its staffing policy. This involves a consideration of the qualifications, training, and experience of those concerned with buying for the Health Service, and careful assessment of the national organisation of purchasing. Whatever system of staffing operates, there are very complex difficulties in view of the range of specialised equipment and services needed by a health service, and it is necessary to appreciate the range of specialist staff available, in addition to the supplies officers, in forming any judgement of adequacy.

9. *Authorised Buyers.* One of the problems facing supplies officers in the NHS is the existence of a wide range of people authorised either to requisition supplies which the supplies officer has to obtain or to buy directly without consulting the supplies officer. The relationship between the supplies officer and medical staff, catering officer, pharmacist, and nursing officers can be of considerable importance in this respect. Some authorised buyers may lack scientific knowledge that would justify their status. For example, nursing staff are usually consulted about interior decorations and the design of crockery, but it remains to be proved that a nursing qualification carries with it the knowledge necessary to make sensible decisions outside nursing.

10. *Stores.* A proper system for the receipt, custody, and issue of stores is an essential part of a supplies system and one which it is relatively easy to assess objectively. There are indications that the NHS lacks adequate storage facilities and systems, partly because of inadequate investment ever since 1948 in this area of work. But the issue concerns the provision of central stores as opposed to a large number of small ones, and this needs to be carefully examined and evaluated.

An Ideal Supplies System

Before one can make an assessment of an existing phenomenon it is necessary to have clear bases for judging it. Some concept of the perfect procurement system is likely to help such an analysis and provide a basis for assessing the present achievement. This is different from a pure exercise in daydreaming, and there can be no assumption that it will be easy to move from the present to what is apparently perfect. The aim is more modest: it is simply to begin to design a method of measurement in broad terms that will enable us perhaps to identify major problems before further examination.

On the basis of the ten major steps in purchasing identified above, the ideal NHS purchasing system should perhaps resemble the following: 1. *Identifying a Need.* A suitable procedure should exist whereby current purchasing was regularly reviewed in order to assess the appropriateness of the goods and services being purchased in terms of their age, cost, maintenance problems, and use. Such a service also ought to be carrying out a regular series of surveys about the chief activities of the NHS hospital or clinic in order to assess whether the activities are being satisfactorily met by existing products, and hence identifying areas for concern, leading to the search for substitutes, or new products. At the third level of sophistication, the assessment process should be examining the most costly activities carried out by staff and buildings to see whether there are opportunities for replacing at least some of their work by manufactured products or processes. Obvious areas concern automated patient records, measurement of patient conditions, and appropriate extensions of bio-engineering that would permit the knowledge of automation and computers to be applied to medical and surgical processes where appropriate. While such an assessment service should operate throughout a national health service, there would need to be an integrated national assessment service that would be able to give priority to investigating the needs of the greatest common use and cost. But it need not be and should not be purely an economising process—it would lead to innovations in products and procedures that may well increase some costs, and that would be justifiable if in turn it helped to increase health standards, either through prevention or cure; 2. *Specification.* There would be a carefully organised process of defining with the greatest possible relevant precision the characteristics of the product or service that was being sought. This involves a consideration of the information requirements of both the NHS and the supplier in order to avoid misunderstanding. Making specifications is the job of an expert and the specialist with technical knowledge must be guided by the expert in making useful statements about the uses to which the product or service is to be put and hence the form and substance it should take. Whenever possible, specifications already in existence outside of the NHS should be used, and careful consideration should be given to existing products in order to avoid the cost of manufacturing for an assumed special need. Such a procedure is only justified for goods or services likely to be required in large numbers and over a long period,

and hence many small local purchases should be exempted.
3. *Price.* In order to decide whether the price asked for a product is reasonable, the buyer must have knowledge of prices being quoted elsewhere within his area and country and in other countries, and he should be able to make his own informed estimate of total production costs. Computerisation makes collection and dissemination of such information possible, either through a dispersed information network or through a process of central checking on proposed contracts before they are authorised. It is essential to match price for quality and other key aspects, such as service and delivery, and the specification should enable this comparison to be made if the needs of the potential supplier in quoting prices is taken into account in designing the specification.
4. *Contracts.* The chief needs of both parties having been defined by assessment of purpose, specification, and pricing, the formal legal contract should become a much simpler process of negotiation. A contract to be meaningful at law and useful in practice must define quantities to be purchased over stated periods, at different prices, to given delivery points. Any other arrangement is unlikely to constitute a contract in law nor to have value to either party. As there are potential advantages in price for larger quantities purchased, the contract service should be organised on a national basis, and possibly an international basis, with provision for delegation to regions or areas where the nature of the purchase or the product makes this sensible.
5. *Delivery.* Given that the NHS is a national organisation, delivery of its supplies needs to be organised on a national basis, at least in respect of large contracts for standard products. Moreover, in view of the need to keep costs down to a minimum, the possibilities of joint delivery by several suppliers would be a basic activity of the buyer and the optimum delivery system would take into account the needs of both supplier and buyer in order to optimise economic advantages. This suggests a network of stores throughout the country and the assessment of whether the NHS should maintain its own national system of area stores or whether it should endeavour to share stores with other public bodies and with some suppliers, would require regular evaluation.
6. *Quality.* The twin dangers of buying at too low a quality and at too high a quality indicate the need for a regular review of specified qualities and a process of monitoring the experience of users. Such a monitoring system would be carefully designed by specialists and based on proper statistics.
7. *New Products.* A satisfactory supplies system would involve considerable effort at identifying the need for new products. In many instances,

such needs would emerge from the earlier stages in the supplies system and would link up with a carefully organised research and development service which in turn would work with approved manufacturers, sharing research staff wherever possible, and basing its activities on development contracts, as used particularly in the defence industries.

8. *Staff.* The earlier requirements demonstrate that a satisfactory supplies system requires a staff of well educated and trained people with extensive provision for their development and updating of knowledge. They would have to be capable of exercising independent judgement on the requests for purchases received throughout the NHS. Supplies staff should be protected from re-organisations of the NHS structure that are not normally relevant to supplies but can lead to upheavals in the employment and career prospects of supplies officers.

9. *Authorised Buyers.* A satisfactory supplies system implies the existence of a few authorised buyers who would be required to take very careful advice from specialists and whose decisions would be carefully monitored by administrators and users. There seems to be no justification for having a range of buyers except where the authorised buyer negotiates a process of delegation that relieves him of routine paperwork—although such routine paperwork should be radically reduced as a satisfactory supplies system evolves.

10. *Stores.* As stores are a key element in a supplies system, they must be carefully designed with all appropriate modern equipment. Particular attention should be paid to the needs of the delivering supplier and to the needs of porters who are going to take goods from the stores to the user.

It is against this background of the role of supplies in the NHS and the criteria of a satisfactory supplies system that we can begin to examine and evaluate the provision of supplies in the British National Health Service in 1978.

Note

1. R. Maxwell, *Health Care: the Growing Dilemma*, 1975. Britain's percentage of GNP for the NHS was 6 per cent in 1976: a total of £6,531 million.

3 THE MINISTER AND NATIONAL HEALTH SERVICE SUPPLIES

The National Health Service Act 1946 laid down the framework for the National Health Service that came into force in July 1948. It involved the transfer to national ownership of most hospitals whether voluntary or supported by local and central government funds and the introduction of a comprehensive health service for general practitioner services, optician services, pharmaceutical services, and dental treatment. It evolved out of a national insurance scheme for health that originated in 1910. Earlier provision of assistance against illness can be traced back through a long history, particularly since the growth of hospitals after the Reformation. The Act did not prohibit private medical practice, private hospitals and private medical insurance, but after thirty years of the introduction of the National Health Service only about 5 per cent of the population did not use it. The total number of beds in private hospitals is about 10,000, as compared with about 500,000 in the NHS.

The NHS is a vast activity, involving considerable expenditure of all kinds. About 70 per cent of its expenditure goes on salaries and wages of medical and non-medical staff. The remaining 30 per cent covers all the costs of maintaining buildings, feeding patients, supplying them with medicines and all forms of medical needs and equipment.

Although the NHS exists under that title, it should not be conceived as a national service run by a ministry. The Department of Health and Social Security has a Secretary of State who is responsible by law to Parliament for the provision and administration of a national health service. But no legislation gives him the power to control the activities of hospitals, clinics, doctors, or any other medical or non-medical personnel in the NHS. Under the reorganisation of 1974, the NHS operates through fourteen regional hospital boards and ninety area health authorities in England, the Welsh Health Authority and eight area health authorities in Wales and fifteen health boards in Scotland. Each of those one hundred and twenty-eight entities is legally independent.

The simplest authoritative description of health service organisation is in *Britain 1976: An Official Handbook*:

> The general form of the organisation established in 1948 to administer the National Health Service persisted until April 1974 when a major

reorganisation took place. The health ministers – the Secretary of State for Social Services in England, and the Secretaries of State for Scotland and Wales – have a broad responsibility for all aspects of the health services in their respective countries, and a duty to make provision to meet all reasonable requirements for hospitals and other accommodation for health services; for medical, dental, nursing and ambulance services; for facilities for the care and after-care of the sick; for the provision of a contraceptive service; and for any other services needed for prevention, treatment and diagnosis of illness.

The organisation responsible for the provision of these health services is three-tier in England, and two-tier in Scotland and Wales. Within each of the three countries the health departments (the Department of Health and Social Security in England, the Scottish Home and Health Department in Scotland, and the Welsh Office in Wales) are responsible for strategic planning, while area health authorities in England and Wales, and health boards in Scotland, are responsible for area planning and operational control of all health services in their area. In England only, because of its greater size and population, there is an intermediate tier of regional authorities responsible for regional planning and certain central services . . .

They are all statutory agencies of central government and co-operate closely with local authorities responsible for social work, public health, education and other services. In general the areas covered by area health authorities and health boards correspond with those of the new major local authorities established in England and Wales in 1974 and in Scotland in May 1975.

Area authorities and health boards have wide discretion to determine the pattern of services best suited to their area, and most have deputed the day-to-day running of services to health districts which usually contain a district general hospital and have a population of between 150,000 and 300,000, though some are considerably larger.

The health authorities and boards consist mainly of unpaid part-time members. The chairmen and members of the regional authorities and health boards, and the chairmen of the area health authorities are appointed by the health minister concerned after consultation with professional, local authority, university and other interests. The members of the area health authorities are appointed by the regional health authorities in England, and the health ministers in Wales except for some members appointed by the corresponding local authorities, and at least one nominated by the university concerned. Area authorities in areas containing a teaching hospital are known as area authorities (teaching) and in addition to two university nominees contain at least two members with experience of medical teaching.

Medical and dental schools are not under the control of the health ministers but it is their responsibility to provide hospital clinical facilities for the training of medical students. The universities are responsible for the provision of teaching.

There is statutory provision for professional advisory committees and the authorities have a duty to consult with these committees. At the national level the main standing advisory bodies are the Central Health Services Council in England and Wales, and the Scottish Health Service Planning Council in Scotland. In Scotland a Common Services Agency organises those services that can be provided most efficiently by one agency.

Public representation in the re-organised service for England and Wales is provided by district community health councils. These consist of about 20-30 members, half of them appointed by local government councils and the rest mainly on the nomination of voluntary bodies interested in local health services. They are not involved in management but act as a channel of communication between health authorities and the public.

In Scotland local health councils have been set up by the health boards to represent the interests of the public, and to report on questions relating to the health service in their area or district.

The Secretary of State can, of course, refuse to supply them with finance but he can only do so to the extent that enables the NHS to continue: he is responsible for seeing that there is a health service but he is not responsible for running each particular unit of it. At the same time, he is answerable to the House of Commons for the NHS and any detail of day-to-day activity can form the basis of a question from a Member of Parliament that he is obliged to answer. In that respect in particular, the Secretary of State for Health and Social Security is in a different position from that of other ministers responsible for a nationalised industry or public corporation: it is now clearly established that Parliament cannot question them on specific activities, such as the reason why a particular train ran late or why a particular telephone call could not be made.

Any explanation for this somewhat untidy system of administration lies in history. The number or location of hospitals in the country was until 1948 unco-ordinated. Each hospital was the result of some local initiative, frequently a charitable act either by an individual or by a religious foundation. With the growth of social legislation in the nineteenth century, local government authorities became involved with the provision of hospital facilities and their growth then became a factor of finance and rates on a purely local point of view. The outbreak of the second world war in 1939 led immediately to a national hospital service designed to cope with the anticipated large number of casualties from air raids. In fact, for most of the war the number of such casualties was small but the nucleus of a national health service was established and did not disappear until formally transformed into the NHS after the 1946 Act.

The 1946 Act kept public health facilities separate from the hospital and general practitioner services, and local government authorities remained responsible for public health and the school medical services. In the following twenty years there were criticisms of this separation, and eventually prolonged discussion took place that led to the 1974 restructuring that now operates. Instead of separate services and different administrative structures, there is now the straightforward three-tiered organisation of the ministry, the regional health authorities, and the area health authorities. Most areas are divided into districts and that has led to a number of complex administrative set-ups that have been the subject of more recent criticism. Many reforms are under discussion, and in 1975 a Royal Commission on the National Health Service was established, largely as a result of a dispute concerning pay for doctors. The wide terms of reference of the Royal Commission is likely to involve a reconsideration of the existing arrangements.

Supplies Organisation

The Secretary of State for Health and Social Security is responsible for the general provision of goods and services needed to enable the NHS to function.

Prior to the 1974 reorganisation of the NHS, the DHSS issued a circular that provided an outline of the Department's policy on health service supply matters. It said:

> 1. The immediate need is to maintain existing services and while the information set out in the following paragraphs is designed to achieve this the intention is also to make clear the supply responsibilities of the Department, Regional Health Authorities (RHA) and Area Health Authorities (AHA).
>
> 2. RHAs and AHAs must plan their supply organisations to accord with national policies for which the Department's Supply Division has ultimate responsibility. The main points of this policy are set out below:

NATIONAL SUPPLY POLICY

3. Supply Division of the Department of Health and Social Security has ultimate responsibility for all Health Service supplies and in consultation with representatives of RHAs and AHAs as appropriate will:

(1) determine appropriate levels and methods of contracting and purchasing for certain commodities and equipment and keep these levels and methods under review;
(2) determine storage and distribution policies;
(3) arrange evaluations of supplies and equipment and sponsor trials of new developments particularly in the medical supply field;
(4) prepare national specifications where appropriate;
(5) arrange central contracts where this is appropriate;
(6) be responsible for the preparation of a National Health Service supply vocabulary;
(7) rationalise supplies procedures;
(8) consider appropriate staffing structures for supplies organisations;
(9) advise on the application of computer services in the supplies field;
(10) continue to arrange and finance such research projects as may be needed;
(11) provide guidance and information to the Health Service;
(12) liaise between the Health Service and industry;
(13) produce standard equipment lists for capital schemes;
(14) approve equipment estimates for major capital schemes;
(15) arrange as appropriate for training supplies staff;
(16) monitor the performance of the supplies organisation.

The circular went on to examine storage policy, contracting and other minor matters (DHSS reference R/N1020/18 of 29 June 1973).

After the formation of the NHS in 1948 the then Ministry of Health considered the advantages which might be gained by large-scale buying, and by early 1949 central contracts had been placed by, or on behalf of, the Ministry for a range of supply items. At the same time, hospital management committees were encouraged to consider making joint contracts for commodities not covered by central contracts. Several committees of enquiry into supplies had reported in the 1950s but no major reforms were proposed.

In 1964, when total expenditure on goods and services on the revenue account amounted to £145 million, a committee was appointed to review the organisation for the purchase and distribution of goods and services in the hospital service in England and Wales. The (Hunt) Committee published its report in 1966 and this was accepted as a basis for the reorganisation of the supply system in the NHS in 1968. Until this, the development of joint contracting had been slow and uneven, but in the period 1969-74 there were substantial increases in contracting for supplies at regional and area level. There were, however, considerable variations between regions. By March 1973 revenue expenditure on supplies in the NHS had increased to £270 million per annum. Some 22 per cent of this was accounted for by central contracts and 31 per cent by regional and area contracting.

At the time of the 1974 NHS reorganisation, the number of area health authorities was by coincidence almost the same as the supply areas created by the 1968 Hunt reorganisation. The areas took on the supplies, purchasing, and distribution responsibilities for the disbanded local health authorities and the medical executive committees.

After 1948 each hospital management committee had its own supplies officer, and in 1978, 86 out of 90 areas had a supplies officer. He is now responsible to the administrator of the area, although at the same time there is a regional supplies officer with overall responsibility for ensuring a satisfactory supplies system. Under the 1974 reorganisation, the regions have duties of surveillance over areas, and some of the supplies responsibilities of areas have been more clearly defined. The regional supplies officer who is responsible for ensuring that the areas are functioning satisfactorily in respect of supplies does not have any power over the area officers. In each region, there is at least one teaching hospital which traditionally has been independent of any other part of the NHS, although that right has disappeared under reorganisation. Nevertheless, it is not surprising to find that the status of the teaching hospital is still such that some of them continue to conduct their affairs as if the 1973 Act had never been passed, at least in respect of some supply functions. Others do participate in national, regional, and area contracts, and co-operate in rationalising NHS supplies.

Within the area authority, there may be some supplies staff in districts; where they do exist, most are responsible to the area supplies officer, who in turn is responsible to the area administrator. Some area health authorities include teaching hospitals and they will usually have at least one supplies officer who is part of the staff of the area supplies officer.

The change from the 1948 supplies system to the 1974 supplies system caused an enormous upheaval for most supplies officers. Each of the new regional and area authorities had to have their establishment for all staff approved and then they advertised for supplies officers among other vacancies. Naturally, experienced supplies officers applied for appropriate posts, apart from a number who took advantage of an early retirement opportunity built into the reorganisation. As a result of the creation of new posts and the formal advertisement for applications and the subsequent selection procedure, many supplies officers appear to have been worried by uncertainty during the changeover period and that seems to have led to a considerable worsening of morale.

Having been appointed to a new administrative structure, many supplies officers found that a great deal of time was needed to understand their new responsibilities and in particular to incorporate into the supplies system the needs of the school health service, and the former local authority public health activities that now draw their supplies from the area authority. As a result of these many disturbances, there is a widespread feeling that further reorganisation should take place, but great reluctance because of the psychological and efficiency problems that would arise from a further change.

Somewhat parochial views seem to have shaped the development of the supplies system within the NHS. On the one hand, history has encouraged independence and, on the other, as a result of the independence, any change in arrangements creates a considerable uncertainty among supplies officers, almost certainly leading to decreasing efficiency and increasing costs. But there is a very great danger in seeing the problem of supplies organisation in terms of the need to satisfy supplies officers because, if the present system is unsatisfactory, they will be the ones to suffer from an attempt to maintain an inherently unsatisfactory organisation.

It became apparent during the 1950s that the independent ordering of supplies by each hospital group was leading to uneconomic purchasing. Slowly a number of experiments were made whereby one supplies officer would purchase such things as milk on a contract that was open to a neighbouring supplies officer to benefit from. At the national level, the Ministry of Health, as it then was, did have a few national 'contracts' and was able to make available to hospital and regional authorities opportunities to buy under contracts negotiated by other government bodies, such as Her Majesty's Stationery Office in respect of paper, typewriters and office equipment.

A committee was set up within the Ministry in 1966 and the Hunt Committee's report in 1968 placed on record the desirability of a regrouping of contracts so that more area authorities would buy on behalf of a number of areas, and that regions similarly would buy on behalf of neighbouring regions. That wider contracting perspective has led to more extensive buying under contracts shared by a number of authorities, but there do not appear to be any published reports dealing with the benefits in terms of prices or deliveries.

One further result of the autonomy of each health authority is the absence of national statistics about hospital purchasing. The existing national contracts lead to the production of annual statistics of purchases made under them but nobody knows even the total number of other contracts in existence, nor the amount spent on each of them, nor whether the prices paid are the best available. There is a great deal of interchange of information, particularly within regions, and between regions through the monthly meetings of all regional supplies officers but it must be emphasised that there is no national system and therefore no national statistics and no national supplies structure in terms of warehousing or product research.

The latest situation about DHSS knowledge of NHS contracts is summarised in the following letter from the Department of 22 November 1977:

> Regional Health Authorities have been asked to send us some basic information about each regional or inter-regional contract they make, viz. period of contract, commodity, estimated value and subjective analysis sub-code (i.e. relating commodity to the Finance Division subhead). We also expect them to monitor area contracts in their own region similarly and at the end of each financial year to send us a summary.
>
> By comparison of what we receive against information received in our Finance Division from Authority Treasurers, we hope over a period to build up a picture of how contracting procedures are developing under certain broad subheads. In view of present staffing difficulties in the NHS and in this Branch, we cannot say yet if all Regions will be able to meet our request or how much time we shall be able to devote to sorting out discrepancies and I am therefore unable to say what information we may be able to release outside the NHS in time.
>
> As regards copies of contract documents sent to us by Authorities, since they include contract prices, I am afraid they are confidential.

Each supplies officer tends to specialise in one or more product groups, where the size of the area or region justifies this. Each supplies officer encourages careful discussion about the products by the final users and efforts are made to inspect products on delivery. Before new contracts are placed, a careful attempt at specification is made through working parties comprising users as well as supplies officers. Again, there is no national system for recording the results of these endeavours and no knowledge exists about the satisfactoriness of deliveries and the quality of products outside of the area or region concerned.

It seems to be widely believed that consultations of this nature are very important and should be extended into a kind of excessive democracy that is not based on expertise. For example, the working parties concerned with the ordering of crockery will include those whose views about the colour of a cup are unlikely to possess any greater authority than that of anyone else, and certainly not more than that of a suitably experienced designer or supplies officer. There is a danger of too much consultation without any evidence of need, perhaps because of the traditional importance of medical and nursing opinion in hospitals in general.

Although this is a trivial aspect of hospital supplies, it illustrates the importance of the social structure of hospitals as it affects supplies as well as most other activities. One result of this sociological characteristic is the difficulty for supplies officers of establishing their authority over other departments and offices of hospitals. One would assume, for example, that the supplies officer could easily become the only officer authorised to issue orders to suppliers and to ensure that, unless he has issued an order, the account from the supplier would not be paid. In practice, there are usually a number of officers within an area having their own order book, and supplies officers have not yet been able to end this system. In the case of pharmacists, the law requires that orders for drugs should be made directly by the pharmacist. But in some areas and hospitals there is a continuing struggle between the supplies officer and the catering manager, for example, about who should order food. However, the conflicts seem to have lessened since 1974.

Clearly the calibre of supplies officers is a major influence on the effectiveness of the NHS supplies system. A survey carried out by the Association of NHS Supplies Officers in 1977 showed that 38 per cent of supplies staff of all levels were under 35 years of age. Eighty-seven per cent had no professional qualification but 7.3 per cent were studying for them. The 13 per cent who were qualified were members of the Institute of Health Service Administrators, the Institute of Purchasing and Public Supplies, or were graduates. Of the 107 regional and area supplies officers, 59 had one qualification, 37 had more than one, 10 had none, and one was studying. DHSS now runs specialist short courses for training supplies staff with regional support.

Many supplies officers have difficulty over the ordering of supplies by medical staff who claim that their clinical judgement has to have unfettered freedom in ordering anything that they want when sometimes it is difficult to see how any important treatment aspect is involved. Some doctors insist on a particular kind of hypodermic needle because it has the name of a manufacturer on it, even when the identical product without the name can be bought by the supplies officer at a lower price. Such anecdotes are not perhaps to be taken too seriously, but it must be remembered that most doctors do lack any engineering knowledge and frequently forget their knowledge of the basic natural sciences and thus impose their views through the authority of their status rather than through the authority of knowledge.

The distribution of supplies within an area and a hospital involves the NHS in all the usual problems of procurement and supplies. Perhaps the problem is greater than normal within hospitals because of inadequate capital investment that has led to the absence of satisfactory storage areas.

In 1975 the DHSS recommended regional and area health authorities throughout the country to create a network of central stores that will enable purchases to be made in larger quantities and to streamline deliveries from manufacturers to hospitals. The advantages of central stores have been documented by the DHSS. In 1977 23 large central stores existed.[1] However, it is not clear whether sufficiently detailed studies were carried out to determine the size and location of central stores and most area health authorities have interpreted the need for central stores as the need for central area stores. There does not appear to have been much discussion with manufacturers as to the geographical distribution of central stores, although at least one major manufacturer was consulted by a region on the general design and use of such large stores.

The Law and the Secretary of State's Role in Supplies

The peculiar position of supplies within the NHS and for other health purposes, as defined by the National Health Service Reorganisation Act 1973, depends to some extent on the legal powers and duties of the Secretary of State. Broadly speaking, it is accepted that the Secretary of State can direct area and regional authorities to purchase supplies in any particular way but for practical purposes he can merely advise them in varying degrees of persistence on how they might set about this. As we do not in fact have a national health service in the sense of a unified service run by DHSS, there is no power given to the Secretary of State to ensure a rational and economic supplies system.

On the other hand, there are certain national contracts originated by DHSS as well as some national contracts originated by other ministeries which NHS authorities may make use of if they so wish. In a few instances, such as X-ray equipment, it is mandatory for an authority to buy equipment through the national contract. Insofar as hospital construction and equipment is concerned, it appears that no health authority can undertake any building work beyond the value of £100,000 without detailed approval from DHSS about the design and content of the building. The only other mandatory contracts are for clinical thermometers (mercury in glass), CSSD paper and bags, and standard disposable plastic administration sets for blood and blood products and injectable solutions[2] (DHSS letter to author of 17 November 1977).

The contrary argument is that in fact there is a unified health service, and that it is sheer timidity or false political sensitivity that prevents the intelligent application of a national supplies policy by the Secretary of State. Clause I of the 1946 Act says:

> it shall be the duty of the Minister of Health to promote the establishment in England and Wales of a comprehensive health service designed to secure improvement in the physical and mental health of the people of England and Wales and the prevention, diagnosis and treatment of illness, and for that purpose to provide or secure the effective provision of services in accordance with the following provisions of this Act.

Clause 10 of the Act says:

> Where, in the exercise of powers to purchase conferred on him by Part 6 of this Act, the Minister requires any hospital (as defined by the last foregoing section), whether or not carried on for profit, he may also acquire, either by agreement or compulsorily in accordance with the provisions of the Second Schedule to this Act, any equipment, furniture or other moveable property used in or in connection with the hospital premises, and the provisions of the said Schedule relating to compensation and certain other matters shall apply.

Clause 12 of the Act says in Section 1(c): 'To acquire on behalf of the Minister and to maintain equipment, furniture and other moveable property required for the purposes of any such hospital'.

Clause 64 says:

> A local health authority may purchase and store and supply to the following authorities, that is to say (a) any other local health authority; (b) any regional hospital board, or board of governors of a teaching hospital, or hospital management committee; or (c) any executive council; any goods or materials required for the discharge of the functions of the authority supplies, on such terms as may be agreed between the two authorities.

In the National Health Service Reorganisation Act 1973 the following relevant clauses appear:

> Clause 2(1)—Without prejudice to his powers apart from this subsection,
>
> the Secretary of State shall have power—
>
> (a) to provide such services as he considers appropriate for the purpose of discharging any duties imposed on him by the Health Service Acts; and
>
> (b) to do any other thing whatsoever which is calculated to facilitate, or is conducive or incidental to, the discharge of such a duty.

The interpretation of Acts of Parliament is a difficult task and sometimes can only be settled by a court of law, and on occasions that may involve appeal to the House of Lords. There does not appear to be any relevant case to settle the issue of the powers of the Secretary of State in this connection. My conclusion is that the Secretary of State does have powers, and indeed responsibilities, to ensure that the NHS operates satisfactorily in the view of the general public, the professions, and the Treasury, and therefore he must ensure that expenditure on goods, services, and buildings are undertaken in the most economic and efficient form. Thus it would appear that he has an obligation to discover whether health service supplies are being properly provided in this sense and, if not, to provide them himself.

It would be unlikely that a supplies function concerned with essentially similar health services could be efficient if divided up between over 100 independent health authorities, supplemented by the national contracts undertaken by the Department of Health and Social Security. It must be remembered that the different authorities do not exist as a result of a carefully designed system with due regard to supply needs, but are accidental to a division based on political and geographical negotiations. That does not mean that every product used anywhere in the NHS should be purchased on a single contract covering the whole country. Each major product has to be assessed individually.

Supplies and the Department of Health and Social Security

The Department is responsible for the implementation of the Secretary of State's legal responsibilities in respect of the NHS and its supplies. The ministry has 87,000 staff, but most of them are concerned with social security.

There are six main sections of DHSS concerned with health service supplies. In the Supply Division there are three branches:

1. *Health Service Supply*: Health Service equipment supplies: organisation, specifications, purchasing.
2. *Disablement Services*: Services and supplies for the disabled: (a) artificial limbs, hearing aids, miscellaneous aids for the severely disabled; (b) invalid transport and surgical appliances, administration of Artificial Limb and Appliance Centres.
3. *Scientific and Technical*: Scientific and technical services: research and development.

In addition, there is the hospital building division and the industry and exports division. About five hundred staff are concerned with this range of services in respect of health service supplies in DHSS but no exact count has been made by the investigators.

It must be stressed that these branches have little direct power on NHS supplies – they do not tell the areas and hospitals what to buy. They influence purchasing by assessing suppliers, testing equipment, and passing on information. DHSS do control hospital building, but only when a region or area has asked for a building and it has been authorised within the national budget for the NHS. They do control X-ray purchases. And there are three exceptions to the freedom to purchase products that have been mentioned earlier in this chapter.

I should perhaps add that the DHSS letter also states:

> the clause making these contracts mandatory is printed on the appropriate pages of the Health Service Supply Purchasing Guide which you will understand we are not able to send you as the information contained is confidential between the Department/NHS and the suppliers. We would not wish to do anything to jeopardise our relations with those suppliers.

The work of the Scientific and Technical Branch is particularly relevant to this project and the following extracts from a note prepared in July 1976 by DHSS for use in training supplies officers will describe some of its major functions:

> Maintaining a high standard of patient care demands continued attention to all aspects of medical equipment, including design, supervision of production methods and quality control in factories, and reliability of performance in use. Moreover, if standards are to be improved, it is important that more advanced instrumentation should become available for existing clinical procedures, and also that new medical procedures are made possible through the development of novel instrumentation.
>
> A major contribution to ensuring the high standard of equipment in Health Service hospitals is made by Supply Division, which assists Industries and Exports Division in its Production Authority role for the medical supplies industry, covering medical, surgical, laboratory and some domestic type equipment, and also pharmaceutical supplies. The responsibility for licensing the production and manufacture of drugs is vested in the Health Ministers who are assisted by the Committee on Safety of Medicines, the Medicines Commission and the Medicines Inspectorate of the Public and Environmental Health Division.
>
> **The Scientific and Technical Branch**
>
> Among the many equipments and materials with which STB deals are surgical instruments, X-ray equipment, pharmaceuticals, sterilisers, patient monitoring equipment, dental materials, invalid transport, artificial limbs and haemodialysis units. Appropriately, its staff are from many disciplines: electrical, electronic, X-ray and mechanical engineers, pharmacists, biochemists, physicists, textile and food technologists and mechanical engineers. STB consists of several groups, designated General Science, Electrical Engineering, Mechanical Engineering, and Physics R & D, whose separate activities are described later. Broadly speaking, however, all groups have responsibility to a greater or lesser extent for the following functions:
>
> *Accidents and Equipment Defects*
>
> Accidents and other incidents involving equipment failure may have a significance extending far beyond the hospitals in which they occur. An imperfect instrument delivered to one hospital, for instance, may be only one of an entire production consignment of similarly defect-

ive goods, other members of which have been delivered elsewhere.

Health Service Authorities have been urged to report hazardous incidents involving equipment or supplies, and any defects in equipment which could give rise to a hazard. Incidents are investigated as necessary and if the circumstances are such that there may be a hazard to other users, Health Service Authorities are notified, normally by a hazard warning circular but in cases where only a few items of equipment are involved and these can be positively located action may be restricted to notification of the appropriate Authority.

Investigations frequently involve visits to hospitals and manufacturers by STB staff and on some occasions the presentation of evidence at inquests and courts of enquiry. Action taken as a consequence of a defect may result in withdrawal of equipment from service and modification or redesign by manufacturers. Hospitals are informed of any necessary further action on their part.

Research and Development

There was formerly little departmental promotion and sponsorship of medical equipment R & D. The rapidly accelerating pace of technology and developments applicable in the medical field, however, has called for an increased involvement on the part of the Department, which is reflected in the rise in expenditure from £100,000 in 1964 to over £2.0 million in 1975.

When in 1964 a committee was set up to promote equipment R & D, the funds available permitted little more than the evaluation of equipment currently available with a view to advising hospitals on a 'best-buy' basis. Although evaluation of British and foreign equipment continues to be an important part of the work of STB, a more formal programme has since evolved to meet the present and future equipment needs of the Health Service. The aim of the R & D programme, expressed in most basic terms, is to identify a need, current or potential, for new equipment, and then to encourage the development of a suitable equipment which will be widely accepted within the NHS. Sometimes a factor influencing a decision to promote R & D will be the absence of a suitable equipment from a UK supplier.

Advisory and Information Services

Professional advice on technical matters is sought by hospitals, industry and other government departments. STB provides names of suppliers of equipment, often indicating 'best-buys'; supplies information on the use of equipment as, for example, in methods of sterilization or on the planning of an X-ray department or a CSSD; and advises Supply Division on technical aspects of import and export policy. Other enquiries to STB might relate for example to safety aspects of electro-medical equipment or possible environmental hazards to cardiac pacemaker users.

Information is also provided via a Supply Division bulletin entitled *Health Equipment Information* which is published several times a year and distributed to all hospitals. The bulletin is mainly devoted to the publication of results of equipment evaluations, to reports of investigations into accidents and equipment failure, and the outcome of R & D projects.

Specialised Services Provided Directly by STB

Several specialised technical services are provided to patients, not, as is usual, through the National Health Service, but directly through STB. Products and services are provided in respect of both artificial limbs and invalid transport (road vehicles and wheelchairs) through 27 Artificial Limb and Appliance Centres (ALACs) throughout the country, and similarly for artificial eyes by way of the Artificial Eye Service.

Electrical Engineering Group

The Electrical Engineering Group provides, within STB, the major source of expertise in electrical and electronic engineering. Its main concerns are radiology, electro-medical equipment, equipment safety and electronic aids for the disabled. The evaluation of equipment and service on standards committees are among important activities of this group.

Radiology

Technical advice is provided by the group on equipment and materials used in X-ray diagnosis and radiotherapy, including cobalt units and linear accelerators. Purchases of this equipment within the National Health Service are made under central contracting arrangements; the scale of this activity is illustrated by the fact that the annual expenditure is about £14 million on equipment and over £11 million on X-ray film. Specialised equipment may cost £100,000 or more (for example, the new body scanner developed by EMI which is expected to cost about £250,000). Services provided by the group include inspection of each installation of new equipment in hospitals, quality assurance, supervision of maintenance and repairs, and the investigation of defects; advice is also provided on selection and layout of equipment for new or replanned X-ray departments.

Electromedical Equipment

The term 'electromedical' is generally understood to cover apparatus of a diagnostic, therapeutic or surgical nature which is applied directly to the patient, as distinct from medical electrical equipment not so applied (for example, automated laboratory apparatus). Typical categories which are the concern of this group are electrocardiographs, electro-encephalographs, defibrillators, surgical diathermy apparatus, electrical stimulators, and patient monitoring equipment. Services provided by this group are mainly those of evaluation and advice to hospitals on choice of equipment; research and development aspects of electro-medical equipment are largely the province of the Physics R & D Group.

Notes

1. Annual Report DHSS 1976, par. 134, p. 32.
2. DHSS letter to author, 17 November 1977.

4 THE MINISTER AND THE INDUSTRY

In 1973, a senior civil servant at DHSS said in a speech that there were nearly 2,000 firms and 17 trade associations in the 'medical supplies industry' in Britain, plus a number of architectural and engineering consortia concerned with health services. A special relationship with the industry was envisaged from the start of the NHS as the government was the industry's main customer. Appropriate sections of DHSS exist for that purpose and continuous advice and help is given to any firm seeking DHSS services.

Total imports in 1972 of X-ray equipment (£3.7m), electromedical equipment (£2.4m), and other medical and dental equipment (£14m) totalled about £20m. Exports of medical equipment and instruments were £42m in 1972. Invisible exports were estimated to be worth £40m annually. About £2m annually was spent by DHSS in research and development grants for new medical equipment. DHSS employs a number of officers who tour the world regularly helping foreign governments with information about NHS experience and finding out about opportunities for British exports.

In 1971 DHSS had convened a conference on medical exports under the independent chairmanship of Lord Hayter. In his report Lord Hayter made a number of recommendations, some of which have slowly been adopted but no radical changes occurred. In July 1972 DHSS wrote to hospital boards about some of his proposals for selecting items of new equipment that would allow 'a fixed quantity contract with a guaranteed take-up' to be placed, thus giving manufacturers the security they need for planned, economic production. The products chosen were the Sonicaid FM2 Foetal Heart Monitor and the Dissonograph NE4102 Ultrasonic B Scope. No such contracts were placed.

As explained in Chapter 3, the Scientific and Technical Branch of DHSS Supplies Division is responsible for assessing the capabilities of potential suppliers and will usually inspect premises and processes before the manufacturer can become an approved supplier although that does not guarantee any sales to the NHS. Where important safety and health factors are involved, the links with firms may be close and frequent. In some cases, suppliers will not be visited at all.

In 1976 DHSS launched a sudden initiative to accelerate the growth of exports and established an internal working party under the chairmanship of A.J. Collier. The recommendations focused on the need to compile a 'limited list' of medical and scientific equipment that would be based on the careful testing and evaluation of available products. Those winning through to the list were likely to become popular overseas in view of the DHSS stamp of approval they would receive.

The new programme for evaluation of electromedical equipment is being carried out in four existing NHS centres which are experienced in the testing of medical equipment, each for a specific category of equipment. These are: Oxford (electrocardiographs), Newcastle (cardioscopes), Sheffield (defibrillators) and Cardiff (surgical diathermy).

The DHSS has provided staff and additional test equipment at each centre. The centres have an ongoing remit so that, after a period of catching up with equipment already on the market, they should arrive at a position which allows new equipment to be evaluated very quickly so providing up-to-date information to the NHS.

Equipment is being tested against the latest international standards (International Electrotechnical Commission) so far as possible, so that the results of the evaluations will also be useful to manufacturers in their efforts to sell overseas, apart from their main function of guiding NHS purchasers. Unfortunately, most of the standards are advanced drafts which, besides having the possibility of changes being introduced, suffer from the disadvantage of being extremely innovatory. However, there is no reasonable alternative. Staff of the DHSS Scientific and Technical Branch have been involved in the development of these standards and they are helping the centres to bring them into practical use and to monitor the standard of the work done.

All the evaluations will include a period of user experience in hospitals and attempts have been made to eliminate the effects of personal bias both by structuring the information that is requested of the user and by involving as many users as is practicable.

The four centres have had staff for this project since early 1977. Some months were spent in gaining understanding of and familiarity with the draft IEC standards for safety and performance and in developing the exact test procedures. This has largely been done and the test programme was well under way at each centre by November 1977.

The centres will produce reports on individual sets of equipment which will be brief and factual. The first of these was due to appear about the end of 1977 and was to be submitted to the equipment manufacturer or agent for comment. The DHSS proposed to publish group summaries in *Health Equipment Information* from time to time and the first of them was to be published early in 1978. *Health Equipment*

Information is a confidential magazine restricted to the NHS.

The Collier report received a mixed reception. Three articles appeared in *Health Equipment & Supplies*, a monthly trade paper. One was by E.O. Doughty, an area supplies officer, who liked it despite its defects and said that the main recommendations for a 'limited list' approach to the purchasing of medical and scientific equipment must command overwhelming support: some reduction in the range of equipment is necessary for more economic production and for more effective use of purchasing power.

The second article was by D.A. Patient, chairman of the Medical Instruments Group of the Scientific Instrument Manufacturers Association. He complained that the manufacturers knew nothing of the report until it had been circulated within the NHS. SIMA's opinion was that the report as it stands cannot achieve the aim of improving the whole operation of procurement 'at least not without disastrous consequences to the industry'.

> It is the firm view of manufacturers that any attempt at a 'limited list' would be destructive to good performance even for those who secured a place in it. For those excluded, export would remain their only outlet, and that without the essential basis of a supportive home market. Further, overseas purchasing authorities would inevitably come to view such a list as a 'buyer's guide', so the unfortunate manufacturer would see his export business in even greater jeopardy.
>
> Another proposal, that the Department should elect which equipment should be evaluated, far from stimulating development would quell any manufacturer's innovative enthusiasm for allocating large forward development funds, particularly when he could have no assurance that, even if his final product was effective, it would secure a place in the 'list'.

The third paper, by B. Smith, Area Administrator, Lincolnshire, noted that the Collier committee's terms of reference were concerned with all NHS supplies, but that they restricted themselves to medical equipment that constituted only about 4 per cent of NHS supplies expenditure:

> From the seemingly endless debates on the consequences of the NHS reorganisation, the Collier Report held the promise of relief in the study of a familiar operational function – buying for the National Health Service. The Hospital Supplies Service suffered its own reorgan-

isation following the Hunt Report of 1968 and, having then adjusted to the 'area' philosophy, managed the 1974 transition more smoothly than most other sections of the service, even if some organisational surgery became necessary in some places for reasons of geography.

The achievements of the supplies organisations in providing continuity of service through reorganisation and quickly assimilating new responsibilities for the needs of the community services have gone unsung due to the very fact of success. The Collier Report, I had hoped, would give the supplies service the boost it needed by underlining the importance of its work and by pointing the way to further advancement.

These hopes have not been realised. 'Progress has been made in recent years in securing the more efficient purchasing of non-medical items and medical consumables. Our report concentrates, therefore, on medical equipment . . . ' Thus the Committee complacently evades its terms of reference and, apart from limited comment on some organisational matters, concentrates almost exclusively on what it describes as 'durable equipment used in medical practice'. As such items represent a very small proportion of NHS supplies (one RSO has quoted a figure of 4 per cent) a more accurate title for the report might have been 'The National Health Service and the British Medical Equipment Industry'.

At a conference of the Health Economists Study Group in June 1977, I introduced a discussion of the Collier Report. Many economists were surprised at the assumption that a multiplicity of similar products were considered undesirable, on the grounds that a free market was more likely to lead to the best use of resources on the best available products than any other process.

On 31 May 1977, the Secretary of State announced in the House of Commons that he was setting up

. . . a joint NHS/Departmental Working Group to examine the present arrangements for NHS supplies, in particular the administrative level at which different items are bought and the degree of uniformity of specifications and standards. I want the Working Group to make a special examination of the case for setting up a Supply Board with members drawn mainly from the NHS, which would devise buying policies to be followed by Authorities, and to do it quickly.

I believe that we can buy better for the NHS and help our exports in health service equipment. Before making up my mind whether this

> is the best way forward I want to see the case for it set out for consideration by Ministers, and by Authorities of the NHS, as well as by the professions and staff who work in it, and by the industries which supply it.
>
> I shall be consulting the professions and the NHS and staff representatives about the composition and terms of reference of the Working Group. I hope that it will start quickly, and that it will take no more than six months to complete its work.

Mr B. Salmon, a retired director of J. Lyons & Company Ltd and chairman of the Camden Area Health Authority, was to be chairman. DHSS sent a copy of the statement to the relevant trade associations with a covering letter that said:

> Your Association may be surprised that another investigation into NHS procurement practice is to be undertaken and my purpose in writing is to provide you with some background information and an assurance that industry's interests will be borne in mind.
>
> The proposal for the investigation stems from a report made by Chairmen of three Regional Health Authorities on relationships between this Department and the NHS. This recommended, inter alia, that consideration be given to the suggestion that the supply services should be managed on an agency basis. As a result of a joint NHS/Departmental Working Group will be set up to examine the arrangements for procuring NHS supplies and to consider, in particular, a case for setting up a Supply Board.
>
> I should emphasise that, the proposal for a supply board does not envisage a central procurement executive as such but rather a body to develop an optimum procurement policy, and whose functions might include determination of such matters as levels at which purchasing is carried out, standardisation of procurement practices, guidance on equipment selection, organisation of stores and training. It is because the establishment of a Supply Board would be a major innovation for the Health Service that further consideration is needed to determine its feasibility, how it would operate and what relationships it would have with other bodies.

Mr Salmon sent his report to the Secretary of State on 17 May 1978 and a DHSS circular HC(78)21 summarised its conclusions and invited comments from all health authorities by 30 October.

Apart from a number of useful improvements in NHS supplies organisation, the report emphasised (1) the need for a national computer-based information system about supplies, (2) a national product evaluation programme that would obviate the need for a 'limited list' as envisaged by the Collier Report, and (3) the establishment of a Supply Council on the following basis:

> The Council should be a Special Health Authority and, subject to approval by the Secretary of State, its policy decisions should be binding on the Department and on Health Authorities. It should have no executive responsibilities.
> The Council's functions should be:
> 1. To formulate policy for the organisation of supplies work, including stores, in the Department, Regions and Areas.
> 2. To arrange for the production and introduction of a comprehensive and universal NHS supplies information system, which would be computer-based.
> 3. To establish policy for the evaluation of equipment and supplies used in the NHS, to co-ordinate evaluation programmes, and to advise the Department's Research Liaison Group as to fields in which medical equipment research and development is required.
> 4. To provide information to enable all users, particularly clinicians, to make the best choice of equipment and supplies.
> 5. To determine for each item of supplies the optimum level of purchasing (i.e. national, regional, area, etc.), the best form of contract and, where appropriate, the right specification.
> 6. To carry out these functions in such ways as to encourage a strong and innovative UK health-care industry, capable of satisfying the needs of the NHS and of building up a successful export market.
> 7. To promulgate its policies within the NHS, and to keep them under review.
>
> It is suggested that the Council should have 19 members in addition to its chairman, drawn mainly from the NHS. There would be four ex-officio members from DHSS, and a representative from the British Health-Care Export Council to safeguard the interests of suppliers. The Council should appoint its own small secretariat.

Conclusion

The record of DHSS/industry relations is a strange mixture of positive practical support and confusing improvisation on a policy level. The delay and varied initiatives seem to reflect political intervention into a situation that at the official level appears to work well. No doubt there are many problems and opportunities that require unusual initiative, but the Collier and Salmon episodes inspire no confidence that the right approach is being used.

The arbitrariness of political attitudes is reflected in the terms of reference of the Salmon Committee: as was stated by the Secretary of State, it was required to study the case for a supplies board – but not the case against it.

Even if a supplies board emerged, it would achieve little if it merely tinkered with, or complicated, the existing policies and conventions. It is unlikely to do more. There seems to be a case for a central procurement system, a case for a genuine independent NHS supplies system, and a case for a free-for-all in which the legal independence of the 127 health authorities is allowed to operate. A continuation of the existing mixture has not been justified, either for the NHS or the suppliers.

5 CONTRACTS AND CONTRACTORS

Purchase of goods and services is undertaken at four levels in the NHS. There are *national contracts* negotiated by the DHSS and a number of other government departments that area and regions are free to draw upon. From a legal point of view these are not in fact contracts as they do not involve any obligation on the NHS to purchase a given quantity of goods in a given period of time at a given price, and they are generally regarded as simply statements of intention to undertake business as and when it suits the NHS to take advantage of the availability of certain goods at specified prices. There are also *regional*, *area*, and *local contracts* and purchasing arrangements, and regions and areas can take part in the contracts made by other NHS authorities where obvious economies are to be made if those authorities are named in the contract. Health authorities are also free to make purchasing arrangements with local government authorities but the ten areas studied had no such arrangements, except one whose area supplies officer has discovered savings to the AHA by participating in the GLC petrol and derv contract.

The medical profession is jealous of its 'clinical freedom' and interprets that to mean that each doctor should decide for himself what medical products he should use and hence those that should be purchased. In principle, all goods are ordered by the relevant supplies officer (except for pharmaceuticals which are ordered directly by the pharmacist). In practice, a number of people, such as catering officers and senior nursing officers and engineers, may have order books and continue to use them despite the effort by supplies officers since 1974 to abolish the old system that allows for a proliferation of people able to place orders, sometimes outside his control. However, there is evidence that the majority of orders placed by other than supplies staff are for goods on contracts convened by the supplies department and approved by the supplies department and for manufacturers who have been approved and vetted by the supplies department.

Orders placed by specialists are likely to be influenced by manufacturers' sales representatives or by anecdote and hearsay rather than by systematic study of all available products conforming to a defined specification or need, made by a competent supplies officer with some knowledge of the relevant products available on the market. In some cases, it appears that medical staff insist on a particular product that bears the name of the manufacturer when an identical product, without the name of the manufacturer, exists at a lower price. Some surgeons, for example, continue to order special implements, sometimes especially made for them, without knowing whether something already exists that might suit their purpose. Supplies officers are reluctant to argue with a consultant about a possible instrument, and manufacturers are also reluctant to extend their product range by making the requested article regularly; one firm of instrument manufacturers has 15,000 items in its product range.

Vetting New Firms

When a new firm wishes to do business with DHSS, someone from the Scientific and Technical Branch is very likely to be sent to look at the firm and its general capacity—staff, and quality control procedures in particular—assuming that suitable staff from the branch are available. On such a visit, they might examine a piece of equipment to see if it conforms to any standards relevant to it.

For disposable items, the manufacturing process and the general structure and hygiene of the factory would be examined. They would be particularly concerned with ensuring that production control was satisfactory.

There are a number of new firms each year. The branch is most active in vetting firms in relation to central contracts, such as rubber gloves and disposable syringes for GPs.

Only some suppliers are visited initially and are on regular surveillance. It is hoped that manufacturers will come to DHSS voluntarily for checking. In some cases such vetting could be mandatory within the terms of the Medicines Act. The Act does not apply to equipment.

No fee is charged by DHSS for inspection except in connection with visits to overseas firms.

Relations with Industry

Relations between the department and industry are generally good. DHSS and the branch in particular are willing to assist as much as possible but it may be short of the relevant personnel. It avoids saying that DHSS approves a product but it does have approved lists of suppliers that is meaningful and valuable to exporters.

The Collier Report

The branch has long had the beginnings of an evaluation system through tests in laboratories and then in clinical situations. It now maintains centres in four hospitals which will evaluate separate categories of equipment. These centres are technologically highly equipped and useful. The aim is to establish standards of performance for equipment such as cardiographs, cardioscopes, and cardiac defibrillators. Manufacturers also test finished products, perhaps because in some cases there may be inadequate testing before manufacturing is undertaken and completed.

The Scientific and Technical Branch would need more staff if full product evaluation were undertaken. The present laboratories have inadequate capacity. So far, additional funds have not been provided to the branch for this purpose.

International Standards

It is extremely important to ensure that standards for equipment are properly devised and used and hence the department co-operates with similar concerns in other countries. There are EEC directives about medical equipment, and the branch collaborates with the Bureau of Medical Devices under the Food and Drugs Administration in the USA.

It also works with a group of the International Electro-Technical Commission which is part of the International Standards Organisation and concerned with standards for electromedical equipment.

Levels of Contracting

One perennial problem for NHS supplies is determining the optimum level of contracting: should certain supplies be purchased by central (DHSS), regional, or area contracts, or by local purchase by each district, or by individual hospitals, clinics, or general practitioners? The 1968 Hunt Committee tried to define rules and some rationalisation has occurred since its report. But problems remain, and in June 1975 the Regional Supplies Officers made an analysis of the situation and submitted proposals.

They supported the DHSS plea for large, central stores in order to 'permit flexibility by the use of a variety of purchasing levels and methods'. DHSS anticipated a minimum saving of about 3 per cent on relevant throughput which was then estimated to be £330 millions. Thus suitable investment was desirable, or appropriate accommodation should be rented.

So far as levels of purchasing are concerned, they said:

> The achievement of an optimum purchasing policy depends in some considerable measure upon watching levels of purchasing with levels of competition and production; RSOs believe that the gap which

has been mentioned can be bridged within the existing organisational structure by inter-regional co-operation on a formal basis.

Certainly, there would seem to be a need for co-operative buying beyond regional level; this does already exist in some small measure, but there is urgent need for a very positive attack to expand such co-operation on a truly objective basis, taking full account of the economic situation not only as it affects the service but having regard also to the problems of industry. The pitching of levels of purchasing should always be determined by the application of established economic criteria, which were very clearly outlined in a document published by the Department in November 1969; there is evidence that these criteria are not applied objectively in instances where a level of purchasing between regional and national would seem to be indicated. Furthermore, there is little doubt that in many cases when investigations are conducted on a Regional, Area or District basis to determine methods and levels of purchasing, the resources employed could often be used much more effectively on an inter-regional basis. Within the present organisational structure this can best be overcome by formalising inter-regional co-operation. Such an approach would be entirely consistent with an attempt to contribute to the achievement of the objectives of Command Paper 3291 'Public Purchasing and Industrial Efficiency'.

Progress in the co-ordination of purchasing arrangements has often foundered on the inability to obtain agreement upon common standards and specifications. No doubt, this difficulty stems from parochialism in supplies matters prior to 1968. However, since a large part of supplies expenditure (certainly more than 80 per cent) relates to 'common-user items' for which common standards are possible, it is immediately apparent that there is here significant scope for economy. While the acceptance of common specifications need not prejudge the adoption of a particular level or method of purchasing, it is obvious that unnecessary proliferation of standards must be detrimental to the achievement of an optimum purchasing policy. This view has been confirmed by the activity of the Department of Trade and Industry's Public Sector Standardisation Team which, by reaching agreement on common specifications, is attempting to capitalise on the benefits of rationalisation throughout the public sector.

Thus, RSOs make proposals in this report which would result in economic benefits not only through lower prices but also by rationalisation and in administration, and they are convinced that full advantage should be taken of them. For instance, the achievement of a 1 per cent saving across the entire field of procurement would release funds in the order of £5,500,000 annually. Within specific areas of expenditure DHSS and RSOs should agree firm targets; however, in so doing the willing help and support of management and of users would be essential, which obviously could be expected, bearing in mind the vital economic help which the achievement of this objective could bring to the entire service.

They go on to recommend:

Inter-regional Groupings

1. Initially and in the short term a structure of Inter-regional Committees be established to evaluate procurement, storage and distribution for various selected commodities and to relate these evaluations to industrial capacities.
2. That Committees be formed each comprising three or four Regional Health Authorities. The constitution of each grouping could be varied according to the commodities under consideration.
3. When these groupings have been agreed, the RSOs concerned should immediately consult with each other in order to establish the membership and objectives of a national plan.
4. It would be important that industry and commerce are fully consulted in the deliberations of the Inter-regional Committees and their Working Groups before they reach conclusions and make recommendations. This might be done at special joint meetings at Inter-regional or national levels.
5. Each RSO member of the Inter-regional Committee would normally be responsible for co-ordinating specific commodity evaluations which would be included in a consolidated report to be submitted regularly from the Inter-regional Committees to the Regional Supplies Officers' Committee.

Evaluation of Commodities

6. The Inter-regional Committees should at their first meetings, prepare their own recommendations on commodities that would be most appropriate for them to evaluate.
7. These recommendations should be considered by the RSOs Committee where a national programme of commodity evaluations would be prepared by December 1975.
8. Initially consideration should be confined to those commodities

which offer the quickest potential resource savings.

9. The RSOs Committee would produce consolidated progress reports on the development of the scheme to Regional Administrators and to the Director of the Health Services Supply Branch of the Department.

Evaluation Reports

10. As a first objective, evaluation reports should be presented to the Regional Supplies Officers' Committee within six months from the date of the commencement of each study.

11. The evaluation reports should include the following:–

i. Total estimated consumption of the commodity by the participating Authorities in the Inter-regional groupings.
ii. Present total expenditure.
iii. Number of delivery points.
iv. Availability of storage.
v. Availability of supply sources.
vi. Estimated savings. (This may have to be based on informal quotation procedures and care will need to be taken to ensure that these are not sought from suppliers at the same time as similar enquiries from other Inter-regional Committees.)
vii. Other matters that may be relevant.

12. Because of the magnitude of the purchasing power involved, all investigations for evaluation purposes must be carried out in such a way as to ensure the avoidance of uncertainty in the particular industries or markets concerned. It is therefore essential that discussions with suppliers be kept confidential and the purpose fully explained.

Long-term Objectives

13. Long-term objectives would be prepared once the immediate evaluation exercises were in sight of achievement.

By the end of 1977, five consortia of regions had been created:

1. The four Thames regions and East Anglia region
2. The North region and the Yorkshire region
3. The North Western region and the Mersey region
4. The Oxford region, the Trent region and the West Midlands region
5. The South Western region, the Wessex region and the Wales region.

The groups were set up largely on geographical criteria and meet possibly twice a year. Each group has a chairman and the five chairmen met once in 1977 to discuss types of commodities under review and the difficulties involved in collecting accurate usage information. Each regional supplies officer is given the responsibility of collecting usage data on various commodities; he does so by asking area supplies officers to collect and submit the figures.

The products chosen for investigation are high value, high volume, or highly standardised items such as foodstuffs, disposables, and bedding and linen textiles. There are difficulties in collecting information on amounts used, total value of the products used and manufacturers supplying the commodity. Many area supplies officers feel that they have enough work to do running their day-to-day supplies system. Accurate information has been obtained about bedding, linen, and some non-perishable foodstuffs. Milk purchasing has also been monitored and improved by these consortia, although other perishable food items are more difficult to rationalise on a large scale.

The biggest consortium contract is for bedding and linen textiles. The North East Thames and East Anglia regions have a contract valued at £440,000 per annum and the five northern regions have a £2 million per annum contract.

Other commodities, like small medical and surgical items, although of high value in total consumption, are not yet ready for larger contracts as standard specifications are difficult to achieve in the NHS.

Manufacturers have been consulted to some extent but not actually involved in consortia discussions. For example, Johnson & Johnson volunteered accurate information on what each region had used of its disposable products and they have been able to help rationalise bulk purchasing and deliveries. They have offered 2½ per cent discount for bulk purchasing and delivery, and in 1978 they were examining the possibility of a higher discount.

These regional consortia seem to have been formed in response to a lack of optimum purchasing information from DHSS. DHSS needs accurate retrospective computerised accounts of supplies received in each region for each commodity, giving the price and the name of the manufacturer. A computerised supplies accounting system is being installed in one area to record and collate all supplies taken into stock.

One-off direct delivery items do not lend themselves to the optimum purchasing policy at this stage.

NHS Supplies in Wales

The situation in Wales is different from England, as in the situation in Scotland. Before reorganisation the Welsh Office acted as the equivalent of a regional health authority. But the Civil Service responsible for hospitals in Wales lacked the technical knowledge, so the Technical Services Organisation was created in 1974. It has a Director of Works, a computer head and a Chief Supplies Officer. In addition, it has assumed the responsibilities of the old pricing committee which was concerned with vetting the prescriptions of GPs. Thus it acts as an agent for the Welsh Office and for area health authorities. But it does not control the health authorities. A central supplies organisation had been set up in Wales after the Hunt Report in 1968 and employed specialist staff and made contracts. It was very successful and represented the kind of central organisation that many people favour. With reorganisation, this system has been demolished and the staff working on supplies in areas has increased from 150 in 1974 to 230 in 1976.

The CSO appears to have a higher status than a regional supplies officer. He is responsible to the board of the Technical Services Organisation. There is an All-Wales NHS Supplies Committee which comprises the eight area health authority supplies officers, plus the CSO. The CSO places contracts and the areas do not, apart from local purchases and local contracts. The CSO is the Welsh official responsible for managing central contracts. He now deals with supplies worth 60 per cent of the value of all contracts, whereas before 1974 the proportion he handled was 70 per cent.

There are also sixteen districts with supplies officers now. The old system may have been more effective than the present one because all the areas supplies officers have to be consulted before contracts can be made.

The National Health Service Supply Vocabulary

The NHS spends £600 million a year on over 100,000 products and services that it requires to carry out its enormous task of caring for millions of patients in over 3,000 hospitals. As each hospital was independent before the NHS was set up in 1948 and each still retains some freedom of action, it has proved impossible to obtain comparable information needed for proper management control. That in turn has made it difficult to practice the best purchasing policies. Considerable progress is now possible under the 1974 reorganisation, with responsibilities more clearly defined and largely concentrated in the fourteen regional health boards. But the opportunities merely emphasise the fundamental weaknesses that stem from the absence of a basic system of definition of stores, and hence proper analysis of consumption is impossible.

On the recommendation of regional supplies officers, the Department of Health and Social Security set up a working party in 1968 to examine the problem of coding hospital equipment and supplies so that computerised control for equipping capital projects and for day-to-day supplies could be carried out. This initiative was prompted by the Hunt Committee's review of hospital supplies organisation after a number of parliamentary criticisms of hospital purchasing claimed that there were too many similar items and too many different prices being paid for the same product.

After a number of pilot studies, the Working Party recommended some principles on which the national hospital supply catalogue should be based:

1. There should be a standard method of description for all items in the catalogue, contributing to the development of a common hospital supply language.
2. Item description should consist of the generic item name, followed by a hierarchy of attributes in the order of use/type, material, and size/other details, recognising that modifications may be necessary for some sections of the catalogue.
3. Items should normally be arranged in alphabetical order and component parts should be listed immediately following the item to which they belong.
4. Attributes of items and other details should be arranged in columns, with attributes in alphabetical order for each item or type of item. Six columns should be provided also to indicate the item code, references to other relevant documents, and to the normal unit of issue.
5. Where several names or descriptions for an item are in common use, the alternatives should be cross-referenced to the preferred item name.
6. The catalogue should be produced in loose-leaf with A4 size pages.
7. The catalogue pages should be printed on one side only, with ample space for insertions of manuscript notes or additions.

Classification problems in such a project are considerable and in the end it was decided to use a two-digit alphabetical code so that a total of 676 units could be allocated amongst the 33 catalogue classifications. Within each classification unit, items would be numbered in sequence from 001 to 999 as and when they were included in the catalogue. Complete item codes would therefore have five digits, two alphabetical and three numerical and the maximum capacity of the system could be 675,324 items, as letters and figures would not be used in the same digits of the code. A permanent central organisation would be needed to undertake the work of cataloguing and subsequent maintenance of the catalogue.

One of the consequences of this neutral catalogue is the designation of one product which would be preferred to others of a similar nature that exist on the market. The Working Party recommended that 'where an item is made by several manufacturers various models should not be included and described as separate items unless they have differences'. The exact procedure for identifying the preferred product has not been proposed and clearly the relevant advisory group will be brought in where necessary. There is no intention of recommending a 'best buy' to hospitals but it seems inevitable that in time the catalogue will represent the products and services that seem to be most satisfactory to the advisory group concerned and that in turn should reflect a concensus of opinion among informed supplies officers.

A distinction was made between coding and codification. Codification was seen to involve identification, classification, and a precise description of unique items, while coding was defined as the use of symbols to identify items in order to handle and process information. The additional work of cataloguing was included in with the task of codification and was expected to be carried out by staff who were experts on categories of items used in the hospital service.

Because of the expected cost of this exercise, it was thought necessary to make the vocabulary as simple as possible and applicable to a wide range of activities. The committee decided that all supply items in current use in the hospital service should be included and that the process of cataloguing should not involve any attempt at the initial stages to specify what items should be used. However, after looking at the range of housekeeping (largely food) items used throughout the hospital service, the committee amended its original recommendations. It suggested that there was a strong case to include only those items considered by regional supplies organisations to be suitable for use in the service. In addition, there should be a local regional vocabulary for items not to be included in the national catalogue but nevertheless necessary for certain regions and areas.

The committee began to examine a number of stores lists and equipment schedules from different hospital authorities. This revealed not only a wide range of supply and stock items but considerable variations in the way in which they were described. The possibility of using or adapting an existing catalogue was dismissed as being too time-consuming and expensive.

The first category of items to be studied by a sub-group of the committee was 'Hardware and Crockery'. The sub-group co-opted hospital service officers with expertise in hardware and crockery and a catalogue was drafted which was subjected to a gradual process of refinement and rationalisation.

By May 1976, ten commodity sections of the catalogue had been completed and published, work was in progress on ten others, and work had not yet started on the remaining six. The Annual Report of DHSS for 1976, published in September 1977, said that 13 sections out of 26 had been issued. It is intended that the entire vocabulary will be completed by 1980/81. It will eventually be used for all national, regional, and local contract items and central stores catalogues. Each regional supplies authority will have a copy of the national vocabulary and will draw up its own local vocabulary based on individual purchasing instructions. Some regions have already made progress on the local vocabulary. Z codes are available to describe supply items used at local level and there are facilities for these Z code items to be recorded at regional level and possibly added to the national vocabulary with a more definitive code.

One of the regions in this project has begun work on a local supplies vocabulary at area level and supplies officers are submitting items to be classified and recorded by the region. One area in that region is particularly advanced and is already using the national vocabulary and will provide most of the groundwork for the local vocabulary.

Another project region is creating a local vocabulary at regional level and informing area supplies organisations of specifications and codes. It is intended that eventually both the national and local vocabularies should provide a common language for all levels of NHS staff in the planning, designing, and equipping of new hospital projects, as well as the day-to-day procurement, storage and distribution of supplies. Finally, it is expected to make possible the retrieval of any of this information if required. However, the changeover to the national vocabulary to describe supply items will mean that hospital staff will have to learn to use precise supply definitions.

Food Supplies

Probably the largest single expenditure in the NHS in the field of supplies is in the purchase of food. One reliable estimate suggests that the total expenditure on catering services in 1977 was £260 million and half of that was spent on the purchase of food. With several thousand hospitals catering for millions of patients and hundreds of thousands of staff, the correct method of purchasing, storage, issue and use of food is clearly of major importance to the NHS. Responsibility is organised through the customary hierarchy, with considerable responsibility resting on district catering officers, many of whom will be in charge of one major hospital or will be responsible for a number of hospitals in one district. Within each hospital there will be a caterer who will be in charge of the preparation and serving of food.

One urgent question is the scale of ordering. It would seem sensible to order for the whole of the NHS in national contracts so that the largest possible quantity can be placed on contract and the best possible prices obtained. But the desirability of national contracts depends to a large extent on the organisation of the relevant food industry and if it is so organised that the firms are too small to cope with national contracting it is clearly more sensible to order in regions and areas. Thus a series of enquiries are made reviewing purchasing arrangements for each of the main food product groups, and these studies are organised through the Food Purchasing Advisory Group that meets regularly at DHSS and comprises experts from all levels of the NHS and of the DHSS.

A number of national contracts do exist, such as for biscuits and potato powder. There is no national contract for meat and that is largely due to the organisation of the suppliers. There are numerous local markets throughout the country, and the major exporting countries have their own distribution arrangements in the United Kingdom. These do not allow for effective national contracting, largely because the exporting countries have no difficulty in disposing of their products and do not wish to commit themselves to long-term contracting in view of the variations in prices that can occur. However, more central contracts for food are likely, and margarine is one of the obvious possibilities.

Arranging a national contract is a complex process. DHSS insists on having several suppliers in order to safeguard deliveries and to avoid the creation of monopolies. The number of suppliers may allow some variation in type of food to be provided by each, as in the case of coffee. The difficulties of guaranteeing that a certain quantity will be purchased is due to the different attitude of caterers and to varieties of preferences in parts of the country. As a result, national food contracts do not guarantee the purchase of any definite quantity in the contracted period. Each contract is based on the reports of expert panels, and they are concerned with taste and quality as well as price. Also important within the contract is the definition of the size of individual orders and the number of delivery points: most suppliers would prefer large quantities delivered to a few points, whereas the NHS has in the past preferred to have many delivery points, preferably one in each hospital. However, with the growth of central stores, the distribution problem will begin to diminish, although it remains to be seen whether economies are effected.

One major problem in food contracting is specifying as precisely as possible the type of food to be bought. This includes, for example, oranges, all of which may appear similar to the layman. In fact, there are many different kinds and clearly a contract must ensure that the type required is supplied and paid for. The problem is even more difficult in respect of meat as a great deal of buying is based on the judgement and experience of the individual although specifications are precise.

Where national contracts are not available, it is important to decide the appropriate level within the NHS at which contracting shall take place. This has been a matter for consideration for many years and on the whole it would appear that many sensible arrangements now exist. Food presents difficulties because of variations in quality and availability in different parts of the country. Most tinned fruit and vegetables are purchased 'on the spot' at district level and also in areas. But most areas do not know whether other areas are buying at more advantageous prices.

One of the oddities of the NHS supplies system is that regions are able to place contracts but have no money to purchase goods. That is done through districts and areas. Catering officers are responsible for obtaining and using food, and the regional catering officer can act only in an advisory capacity. In making contracts at regional level, the district and area catering officers will expect to be consulted.

The economies of the central store rests on the idea that stores staff can be taken away from the individual hospital and many are closed down when the central store begins operations. Thus there would be no expert staff left in the hospitals to ensure the custody and issue of stores within the hospital. There may well be discrepancies between area calculations of the value of food delivered and the hospitals' records of deliveries received. There is a separation between accounts departments and delivery sections and therefore the safe custody and proper issue of food could be difficult.

One other major problem about food in the NHS is the amount wasted. Expert estimates suggest that about one-third of all food purchased is wasted. That may be influenced by too much food being issued to kitchens. Considerable effort is being made to control the use of food, to identify whether the quantity supplied is producing the right quantity of meals and whether the quantity of meals required is leading to the proper intake of food to the hospital. There does not appear to be an effective national control system for provisions and their use, and regional officers are encouraging districts to maintain records and to ensure that everyone is aware of the discrepancies that may exist between the number of patients, the number of meals consumed and the number of meals that should have been provided with the quantity of food delivered. One facet of this problem is the need to separate the purchases of food for staff and for patients, and catering officers may prefer a common menu and hence hope that the food not taken up by patients will be taken up by staff, or vice versa. Clearly, that too is related to the process of finding out patients' choice and can be completed more than twenty-four hours before the meal is brought to the patient, by which time his taste or state of health may have changed and the food is not then eaten. In one study made in a London hospital, there seemed to be a discrepancy of nearly 100 per cent in some cases between the amount of food ordered and the yield that should have been possible from the amount of food issued.

The Supplier

The National Health Service constitutes an important and attractive market for manufacturers and distributors of products and services that are needed for treatment and health preservation. Any firm may apply to supply goods and services to the NHS and they are dealt with as all firms are that seek to do business with any government department or other public sector organisation.

They are first required to apply for registration as an approved supplier, and that usually involves a check on their financial and legal status, and can be very much a formality, dependent on the availability of staff to carry out the necessary inspections. Once on the list of approved suppliers, firms are invited from time to time to submit tenders for undertaking particular tasks or supplying particular quantities of goods. There is a careful method of receiving all bids before they are considered and there is no evidence of dishonest dealings in respect of health service supplies.

When a bid is accepted, the appropriate order will be issued and the supplier will be told when and where to deliver the goods. He will usually know before submitting his bid how many 'drops' are required and clearly the number of different points of delivery will influence the price to be charged. The Scientific and Technical Branch of the Supplies Division of the Department of Health and Social Security is responsible for vetting suppliers in terms of their technical competence. This is especially important in respect of hygiene and reliability of quality, and very detailed inspections are made of factories supplying, for example, pharmaceuticals, rubber gloves, and medical equipment where hygiene is of particular importance. In many instances the factories are specially designed or adapted to conform to the requirements of the Scientific and Technical Branch in order that the appropriate standard can be achieved and maintained. Reliability and continuity of quality control are of vital importance and hence the entire process of manufacture, package, storage, and delivery will be examined where necessary in order to be able to safeguard the interests of patients and staff.

One of the most common grievances among suppliers is the absence of any certainty about the quantity of goods that will be in fact purchased. Although they may have tendered to supply, say, 100,000 units of a particular product in one year, there is no contractual obligation on the buying authority to take up that quantity. As a result, it is impossible for the supplier to have any security in his NHS business, and it would seem that he must make an allowance for such uncertainty in the price he offers. On the other hand, with a vast national service with unavoidable irregularities of demand for the vast majority of its needs, the possible economies of long-term fixed contracts are being missed.

There have been exceptions. In one case, in Scotland, a close link was made with a supplier in the design of a particular kind of dressing and a contract was made whereby the health authority stood to benefit from a share in profits as a result of agreeing to collaborate in specification, design and in testing the product, thus reducing the risks to the manufacturer. There are a few other instances of such collaboration. However, in a different context, there has been co-operation between Johnson & Johnson Ltd and a regional supplies officer in respect of advice about the location and design of a central store, where the very considerable experience of a major manufacturer dealing with large numbers of customers throughout the country has led to an expertise that cannot be matched in the NHS. This voluntary co-operation is seen by the firm as a goodwill gesture.

Meanwhile a number of trade associations have grown up over the years to represent the interest of suppliers in negotiations and discussions with DHSS:

Association of the British Pharmaceutical Industry
Association of British Sterilizer Manufacturers
Association of Sanitary Protection Manufacturers

British Dental Trade Association
British Hospital Export Council
British Insulin Manufacturers Association
British Lampblown Scientific Glassware Manufacturers Association Ltd
British Laboratory Ware Association Ltd
British Surgical Trades Association (Inc.)
Association of X-ray Equipment Manufacturers
Conference of Medical & Surgical Adhesive Plaster Manufacturers
Disposable Hypodermic & Allied Equipment Manufacturers Association
Electromedical Trade Association Ltd
Federation of Manufacturing Opticians
Medical Sterile Products Association
National Association of Pharmaceutical Distributors
Opticians Prescription Organisation
Sterilized Suture Manufacturers Association
Surgical Dressings Manufacturers Association
Scientific Instrument Manufacturers Association of Great Britain (Medical Group)
Surgical Rubber Manufacturers Association
UK Medical Equipment Industries
British Anaesthetic & Respiratory Equipment Manufacturers Association

The Collier Report

An important report on NHS purchasing was published in 1975. The Chairman was A.J. Collier, Deputy Secretary, and now Head of the Health and Personal Social Services regional group in DHSS. Its other members were T.R.V. Bolland, Chairman, Bromley AHA; A.J. Brooking, Regional Administrator, South Western RHA; T. Meyer, Chairman, Ealing, Hammersmith & Hounslow AHA; and Dr R. Wrigley, Consultant Advisor to the Secretary of State. The report runs to ten pages.

The Collier Report is the fourth concerned with NHS supplies that has been issued since 1946. There were no industrial representatives on it and it was not published by HMSO. There were no consultations with suppliers. But it is a very important report and an extensive summary appears unavoidable.

The terms of reference were 'to review the existing policy for NHS procurement and to make recommendations as to the most cost effective policy and its implementation, bearing in mind the need to strengthen the home market as a basis for exports'.

These terms reflect the continuing concern by some MPs and some Committees of the House of Commons about the opportunities for expanding exports in those industries which supply the NHS. It is believed that the report was prepared as a result of Barbara Castle's concern with promoting exports when Secretary of State, and that she wanted proposals within six months.

The report says:

> Progress has been made in recent years in securing the more efficient purchasing of non-medical items and medical consumables . . . Our report concentrates, therefore, on medical equipment, which we define as durable equipment used in medical practice, including laboratory equipment, as well as that used more directly for the care, diagnosis and treatment of patients. We have sought to identify the factors preventing the NHS from establishing a system of procurement which is good for the service and strengthens the home market as a basis for export, and to consider which of these are unavoidable and which might be eliminated, and whether any of the adverse factors can be moderated.

The Medical Equipment Industry

Paragraph 2 of the report attempts to describe the medical equipment industry but gives very little evidence to support such conclusions as 'most British firms are well equipped technically, but weaknesses in organisation and management have left many in a position in which they might be taken over or re-organised by larger groups, able to provide a firmer base for the exploitation of scientific and technical skills'.

They go on to say that about 300 of the 2,000 firms supplying health products in the UK are seriously engaged in international trade.

> They show a good credit balance of trade and have a clear growth potential. Medical equipment exports in 1975 were worth £126.5m; imports were worth £70m. Progressively there are many complaints about delivery times and inadequate servicing follow-up is reported by officers visiting overseas markets. But there is general agreement (DHSS, Treasury, Department of Trade & Industry, British Overseas Trade Board) that these industries have considerable export potential and should be helped. *They need government support and a good home base.*

The report says that DHSS represents a major consumer and 'it has a specific responsibility for furthering the economic wellbeing of the industries and firms with interests in medical equipment and products'. The department sends staff overseas to make general market reconnaissances, to exchange information on development and to assess purchasing methods and to make professional and commercial contacts.

Paragraph 6 says that the NHS does not use its buying constructively 'to get value for money and to assist its suppliers'. The 90 area health authorities are largely autonomous and 'the way in which its financial resources have been controlled has discouraged orderly forecast programming; it does not tell its suppliers what it expects to buy; and it operates on a system in which the multiplicity of decisions on what to buy are in the hands of people who are not in a position to know the economic effects of what they decide'.

NHS Organisation and Medical Equipment Buying

The report examines the problems that reorganisation has maintained in relation to competence of the buyer. It points out that the major influence on what particular items of equipment are purchased is 'the end user'.

> He or she acts individually requesting a particular item of equipment and through representation on area medical committees and/or regional equipment advisory groups. At what level the final decision is taken to buy a piece of equipment from a particular supplier, and at what level it is actually purchased depends on its value, on the degree of delegation practised in the region, and on whether there are any central, inter-regional or regional contracting arrangements for the item involved; there is no regular pattern.

Finance

The report endorses 'a common criticism that much equipment is bought in a rush at the end of the financial year', and goes on to say, 'some of the difficulties which overseas buyers find in getting deliveries from the UK can be laid at the door of this end-year buying habit. British suppliers have to keep spare capacity or unnecessarily large stocks; or they have to switch supplies to the home market (which most British firms regard as their first priority) to the detriment of their export performance'.

It goes on to say that regional authorities tended to keep funds back until the end of the year as a hedge against uncertainty over supplementary allocations by DHSS to meet pay and price changes. 'Medical equipment is an element in total expenditure which can be postponed or brought forward in a way which would not be possible for staff costs, nor for medical consumables and disposables, nor for the greater part of medical supplies purchasing.'

The report says the committee considered whether to recommend special financial arrangements which would enable forward commitments an individual authority could not meet to be taken over by the region or DHSS and held for allocation in subsequent years.

> We have decided *against* doing so. A simple way out of a commitment may encourage management irresponsibility; and in the last resort, it is only by responsibility and self-disciplined management that the application of the planning system to the procurement system will be made to work. There may be special situations in which an authority or the department may think it advantageous to make a long-term contract over a number of years, in which the take-up would be unevenly spread between one year and the next; but for the great majority of purchases, authorities must be given firm resource assumptions, and then left to plan and buy within their own resources.

Information

Paragraph 13 says:

> Most of the basic information, moreover, necessary for the determination of optimum levels of procurement and for the programming of purchasing is not readily available. Basic and easily available information such as costs and quantities of purchase of different items of medical equipment throughout the health service are not at the disposal of RHAs or the department. Purchasing records are scattered throughout the different levels of the service. An important consequence is that, without special investigation, it is often not possible for authorities to forecast the take-up of certain products.

Paragraph 16 says, 'we understand that the department is considering proposals for identifying systematically the NHS take-up of equipment (as well as of consumables and drugs). We welcome this. They may become the basis for nationwide systems of information gathering. It may be sufficient however for the information to be gathered regionally and disseminated nationally.'

Implications for Policy

The report points out that the present situation 'with decisions taken by a wide range of interested groups, on inadequate information, and at various levels in the hierarchy of authorities, does nothing to reduce variety and the results can be seen today; for example ECG monitors–53+ models; defibrillators–26+ models; single channel ECG recorders–25+ models; blood pressure transducers–32+ models; surgical diathermy –40+ models'.

> The users in the NHS as a group are likely to get better equipment and a better back-up service if the number of suppliers with whom they deal is limited, but insofar as normal market forces are not at work in this field there needs to be some system of identifying what are in fact the best products to which the purchasing system should be limited. We believe that the professions would be ready to accept some sacrifice in price for the sake of getting really good and reliable equipment. The manufacturer also wants better information and the opportunity to plan his production line more effectively.
>
> This leads us to the conclusion that some kind of 'limited list' approach is needed. If a number of types and manufacturers of a particular piece of equipment are cut down the remaining manufacturers should be able to produce more reliable equipment and better servicing. Indeed development of a limited list approach to medical equipment buying moreover should make it easier to help industry in its export promotion and to assist in the development of new and better types of equipment. But none of this will be possible unless the user is satisfied in principle that the limited list approach should be followed and in practice, with the way in which the limited list is devised and operated.

The committee say that at the root of the problem is the need for evaluation of equipment. They propose that DHSS should run a system that requires the evaluation of medical equipment from five main points of view–safety, technical performance, performance in clinical use, reliability and cost. They see the professions very much involved and that they should be invited to choose which of their number should be advisers on clinical testing and use and the overall acceptability of different types of equipment. There is, they say, a shortage of technical staff within DHSS capable of managing a total evaluation system and

> . . . although most of the work will be done outside the department,

> some additional effort within the department must be diverted to it. This will take time – to recruit and train appropriate staff. Hospital and academic departments throughout the country should be invited to help in the evaluation process.
>
> An evaluation system of this kind will not be cheap. We have not ourselves done an analysis of the costs and benefits of a total evaluation policy but recommend that this should be done on a selective basis, for a particular group of equipment chosen for our evaluation, identifying what level of improvements and servicing would justify the setting up of an evaluation system and then following up the results to see whether the advantages are achieved.
>
> We believe that the limited list approach should be completed by arranging centrally for the purchase of items on the list on the basis of the planned requirements of the individual authorities, who would be required to buy from the list unless they could justify two essential points for any intention to buy outside the central arrangements. We emphasise that there should be no use of mandatory powers as that would show that a system based on agreement and persuasion had failed. It is essential to show everyone concerned that the evaluation process is worthwhile in general and has been applied effectively in particular circumstances.

This apparently does not mean central contracting and purchasing with allocation to health authorities without repayment because that 'carries the risk of distorting priorities, encouraging them to take equipment simply because they do not have to pay for it. This is, no doubt, the best way of helping exports since it would give industry a single customer with the power of decision. But the obverse of these advantages to industry is that such a system would not be sufficiently responsive to the health service and professional needs.'

They also raise the possibility of a central procurement executive 'responsible for all NHS purchasing'. They say that would require a very considerable disruption of staff 'and we doubt whether it is necessary. It would however be right to complete the limited list system by arranging centrally for the purchase of items on the list'.

Exports

Evaluation should lead to compatibility with overseas requirements because standards in equipment are increasingly based on international agreements. No-one can guarantee though that a limited list will be all British; indeed that would be an unlikely outcome. Equally though it would be an unlikely outcome for there to be no British equipment on a limited list. 'The activity involved in evaluation would improve links between the professions and the industry and would thus be of particular benefit to firms operating in this country.' But the main thrust of advantage to the British manufacturer if his equipment is on a limited list which has been drawn up with the help of the UK health care professions will be the great support which such an endorsement will give to that equipment in overseas markets.

NHS Structure and Procurement Policy

'We may say that there is little to be gained and indeed something to be lost by suggesting further changes in NHS organisation. If those responsible for re-organising the NHS had given a top priority to creating the best possible procurement system, they would certainly not have placed the supply function into its existing structure within the service.' The priority was different: 'to give authorities at each level the maximum overall responsibility and therefore the specific responsibility for all the functions of NHS management'. Any change in structure now 'would continue and indeed increase the uncertainties of individual officers who would for the third time in eight years have to apply for a new job in a new structure'.

The report says that the present system can work effectively if the supplies officer has his authority maintained and that there is no delegation to districts. 'However, although we are not suggesting a radical change in budgetary control or structure, we see it as essential that all authorities should formally adopt a policy aimed at achieving effective purchasing policy with rationalisation of types of goods and equipment whenever such a policy can be justified on the grounds of value for money.'

Conclusion

This is not a treatise of best procurement practice. If it had been we would have urged the absolute priority of working through a separate procurement agency, developing its own expertise and with its own relationships and career development; we would have discussed the importance of sound policies on warehousing and transport costs, inventory and variety control; argued the need to forge good links with suppliers, and the shortsightedness of driving the hardest possible bargains with them. Our main concern has been with medical equipment. We believe however that the supplies staff in the NHS are doing much to raise the professional quality of their work and we hope that authorities will recognise the importance of the advice of their supplies officers and the advantage which they can provide, and that authorities will take particular care to ensure the best procurement policy at the right levels in the NHS.

For medical equipment we recommend the development of an organised system of evaluation, leading to the drawing up of limited lists of the main types of equipment, which would then normally be purchased simply to meet the prime needs of NHS authorities.

In an annex, the report reviews current practice and recent achievements in relation to the purchasing of consumables, both medical and non-medical, and also makes the case for area stores. The report concludes with a reproduction of a DHSS circular of August 1974.

6 TEN AREAS AND THEIR SUPPLIERS

Research reports tend to exclude an account of how co-operation was obtained from individuals and organisations being studied. But some indication of difficulties, achievements, and failures is essential to a proper evaluation of the information obtained and interpreted.

The first step in this study was a letter to the Under-Secretary concerned with supply matters at the Department of Health and Social Security in January 1975. Before the Social Science Research Council grant was obtained, I was planning to set up a permanent research unit concerned with hospital supplies and suppliers. Various meetings followed and a beginning had been made when I wrote again to the DHSS in January 1976 to tell them I had received the SSRC grant. Following earlier advice from them, I had written to the regional supplies officers of the four Thames regions to seek their help.

So far as the North East and North West Thames Regional Health Authorities were concerned, a letter to the RSO, followed by a telephone call, led to a visit with the regional supplies officer and his deputy. After this initial interview we dealt mainly with the assistant RSO in one region who offered to let the research assistant attend a meeting of area supplies officers at regional headquarters. At this meeting most of the ASOs agreed to being contacted. The research assistant sent letters to four area supplies officers and then followed this up by a telephone call asking for a visit. After these first visits other visits continued on a regular basis.

One RSO agreed that the project could be carried out in his region provided that he approved of what was being done and that he had the right to stop the project in his region at any stage if he did not approve of what was happening.

After sending a letter to the RSO of the South East Thames Regional Health Authority we had not received a reply after some weeks. We sent another letter and followed this up by a telephone call and the RSO agreed to an interview. He was reluctant to agree to contact being made with his ASOs, but eventually agreed to a contact with one of them. The ASO was sent a letter, this was followed by a telephone call, at which he reluctantly agreed to a visit. After this further visits were arranged as information was required from the area. We did not succeed in getting any more areas in this region involved in the project.

After sending three letters to the RSO of the South West Thames Regional Health Authority and telephoning several times, we discovered that the RSO had been ill for some time, and his deputies were coping with a heavy workload and, although not totally reluctant, felt unable to produce information for the project. After the project was more than half way through, we sent another letter to the RSO and followed this with a telephone call from which an interview resulted with the supplies officers at regional headquarters, although not with the RSO. They provided background information on regional supplies, but were not able to allow the project to work in the areas in their region. However, it was agreed that the project should be introduced to the areas at an ASOs' meeting at regional headquarters and the ASOs were to be asked if they would participate. But we heard no more from them and by this time we were coming to the end of the project.

Thus most information for the project has been gained from the North East and the North West regions with marginal information from the South East Thames region and only basic information from the South West Thames region. The North West and North East RSOs have been extremely helpful and have provided a great deal of extra information and contacts with other officers in the regions, i.e. finance officers, administrators, and nursing officers. In addition, the ASOs in these two regions have also been very helpful, going out of their way to provide extra information, produce copies of order forms, copies of reports and other material. In the South East Thames region, one ASO did agree to interviews and gave much useful information. The South West Thames region has not provided detailed information of use to the project.

This description of our experience in obtaining information and co-operation is not in any way intended to criticise any supplies officer. It is perfectly understandable that opinions should differ about co-operating in research projects and supplies officers are likely to have more difficult burdens than others so that they do not believe it to be correct to give scarce time to such projects. The reader needs to be aware of the facts and to form his own judgement on the significance of the degree of co-operation to the validity of the study.

When we asked for co-operation from regions, areas and firms we promised to publish nothing about them that would identify them without their permission. I sent each informant a draft of the proposed brief factual summary and asked them to correct any error and then to agree to publication under their name. The results are incorporated in the individual reports that follow.

It is relevant to comment that a small number of supplies officers were most unhappy with our drafts and believed that our statements even when factually correct, might cause 'political' unpleasantness in the context of their relations with regions or trade unions. In one case, the officer used his right to anonymity and declined to give us a corrected draft; we have altered it in line with a telephone conversation. Two others chose anonymity without any stated reason. One or two were surprised at the brevity of the agreed factual report; I explained that we were using the rest of the knowledge in appropriate chapters but would not make use of named areas elsewhere.

While such comments and reservations are reasonable these give some grounds for concern at the anxiety generated by this modest enquiry, however slight and varied. It does indicate an intangible factor in the supplies situation—a degree of uncertainty and insecurity that is not entirely a reflection of individual personality differences and which would appear to be avoidable in a different structure and work environment.

The following review of the regions and areas is based on the first quarter of 1978: it is a summary of information obtained in a series of interviews, grouped into a number of common areas.

The North East Thames Regional Health Authority is split into the areas shown in Table 6.1:

Table 6.1: North East Thames Regional Health Authority

Area Health Authority	Population (approx)	Bed Spaces (approx)	Revenue Budget 1975/76 (approx) £m
Essex	1,411,000	10,137	70
Barking & Havering	391,000	3,630	23
Anonymous	613,000	4,859	58
City & East London	594,000	5,348	66
Enfield & Haringey	964,000	2,673	23
Redbridge & Waltham Forest	460,000	5,597	33
	4,433,000	32,244	£273m

The inner London areas of this region are densely populated, with a surplus of acute bed provision, while the Essex area has a current deficiency of acute services and a growing population. Mentally handicapped services are provided mainly in the Essex area, which is inappropriate for the present population distribution. The region is working towards a batter balance of all services in each area in order to create area self-sufficiency. The only exception will be mental illness secure accommodation which will be retained in one part of the region, probably in Essex.

The region is divided into six areas with six ASOs. There are four teaching hospitals in the region which are now under the authority of two inner London areas. There are three capital equipment purchasing teams in the North East Thames region, all under the authority of the regional supplies department. Equipment purchasing for major capital schemes are managed and supervised at regional level, while purchasing for minor schemes is delegated to ASOs. These include health centres and ward upgradings. However, all capital equipment purchasing staff are regional staff and are transferred between areas by the RSO as projects are completed.

The RSO favours a devolution of purchasing authority while retaining all the power necessary to achieve cohesiveness between his ASOs and himself.

Three areas in the region have two districts each but no district supplies organisation. Two other areas have three districts each, and one has five districts, each district with a supplies organisation. In some districts, district supplies staff are formally responsible to the district administration, not to the area supplies organisation.

Regional and area contracting in this region is carried out at area level by ASOs with district supplies staff carrying out the day-to-day storage and distribution of supplies and arranging local service agreements. There is a standard regional tender form used throughout the region. Internal requisition forms vary between areas, and some areas have their own standard quotation and order forms for manufacturers.

The region intends that work on the adaptation of the National Supplies Vocabulary should begin at area level, with areas supplies officers submitting items to be classified into a local vocabulary. This confirmation will then be recorded and co-ordinated for general use in the region. One area in the region is particularly advanced in this field and is already using the National Vocabulary and so will provide the basis for the local vocabulary.

In at least one area in the region, catering and engineering staff are still purchasing outside supplies on convened contracts and without supplies department authority. But this process has been declining since the 1974 reorganisation.

Area 1: Anonymous

This area has three districts two of which are teaching districts. The ASO has a staff of 18, and there are 130 purchasing, administration and stores staff in area and districts.

There are no central stores in the area but a management services team has completed a report suggesting that one central area store should be placed strategically in the area. The problems of achieving central storage for this area are (a) the lack of available facilities in Central London and (b) the different kinds of storage and distribution systems used at present in the districts. For example, one district is operating a 'top-up' system for wards and departments, while another is using the traditional storage methods in available buildings. The National Supplies Vocabulary is not yet being used in this area.

Each district in the area has a similar but independent financial accounting system. There are no finance staff attached to supplies departments, and all goods received notes and invoices are checked by the finance department who receive copies of orders from the supplies department. The area is using the standard regional tender form for contracting and its own quotation and order forms, except in the south district where the catering officer has to use up his own order forms before he can go on to the standard order forms.

The area is in the process of cutting down the variety of internal requisition forms which is a gradual process, related to the two main systems of internal ordering at present operating in the area. At one hospital a 'topping-up' system is employed and at another hospital, supplies are requisitioned from stores.

The largest capital scheme being carried out in the area is in its second phase and the work of equipping it is being carried out by a capital equipment team from the regional authority. Two health centres have recently been completed in the area, and one hospital has had major capital developments.

Catering staff in the area carry out some of their own purchasing directly from manufacturers and without the supervision of the supplies department. However, the area supplies officer is gradually breaking down the autonomy of the catering staff by introducing supplies-convened contracts for food items. Engineers and work staff vary in their purchasing autonomy throughout the area. In one district, supplies staff do all the engineering purchasing from manufacturers but in two other districts the purchasing of engineering consumables is under the authority of the works officer.

The teaching hospitals in the area are advanced in user participation groups for supplies. Medical and nursing staff use these channels to communicate their needs to supplies staff, rather than to receive guidance from them. The ASO does not organise his own supply users' groups.

Approximately fifty representatives call at area headquarters each week, and about the same number at each district supplies organisation. Working to a fairly decentralised supplies policy, the area supplies officer is concerned with acquiring central area stores in order to bring together the districts, particularly the teaching districts, into a central, rational area system.

Area 2: City and East London Area Health Authority

The area has three districts, two of which are teaching districts. There are approximately 50 purchasing and stores staff at area supplies division headquarters unit and 108 stores and supporting staff based in the three districts. Each district has an outposted supplies unit which is administered by a District Supplies Co-ordinator who is accountable to the ASO. Each co-ordinator has a small supporting staff. They do not supervise unit stores. The responsibility for equipping minor capital schemes is undertaken by a section of the Supplies Division Headquarters Unit. The number of capital schemes being dealt with will fluctuate from time to time between 20-25. These stores are expected to disappear gradually, according to a management services report. The district supplies co-ordinators do not convene any regional or area contracts, but administer the day-to-day distribution of supplies, and arrange local service agreements. The district supplies staff are not under district administrative authority.

The ASO supervises the equipment purchasing of all minor capital schemes being carried out in the area. The staff are area supplies staff and are dealing with twenty minor schemes. The supplies organisation is not involved with the checking and passing of invoices. Orders for goods are pre-priced by the supplies department and copies are forwarded to the appropriate treasurer's department. Most invoices go through the system without query: those with queries amount to about 5 per cent and are returned to the supplies department by the finance section.

A standardised group of internal requisition forms are used in the area for stores purposes. Some of these forms are pre-printed for particular commodity groupings. All requisitions for stores purposes are processed through computing systems for purposes of stock control, stores accounting, and costing. The National Supplies Vocabulary is not yet being used in the area.

All catering and engineering purchasing in the area are processed by the Supplies Division Headquarters Unit, including most service and maintenance arrangements. A few are dealt with at district level. The orders sent to manufacturers have to be authorised by the area supplies department. There are two instrument curators in the area; one does some purchasing and is a member of the District Supplies Co-ordinators supporting staff. Printing and stationery for the area is purchased largely through the local district; some printing is done at two in-house printing units.

Users of supplies meet formally to discuss all aspects of availability and quality of goods purchased for hospital use. Supplies staff are either co-opted or members of these user groups. Manufacturers' representatives who call at area supplies headquarters to see the ASO require an appointment. The ASO is concerned with making NHS purchasing more commercial and favours good relations with manufacturers. He maintains that contracting for supplies should be carried out at a level where it produces the maximum commercial advantage for both buyer and seller and that the form of most national contracts, as conceived in the 1950s, put the NHS supplies officer at a commercial disadvantage. He is presently negotiating area contracts for some supply items in preference to larger available regional contracts which do not show the same level of financial saving for the area.

Area 3: Enfield and Haringey Area Health Authority

This is a compact geographical area divided into two districts. There is a centralised area supplies organisation with 23 staff for purchasing, stores, and administration. There is no district supplies activity and central area store, storage being spread throughout the area. It is intended to build a central area store in the same location as the area supplies office but there is some delay because of restricted finance. In the meanwhile only 10 of the 31 staff employed in the area are supplies staff, the remaining 21 being controlled by sector administration.

Major capital schemes in the area are equipped by one of the three regional teams supervised by the regional supplies officer. The capital equipping team presently working in the area very often purchase items in consultation with the area supplies department. Many smaller schemes are delegated to the Area for equipment purposes.

Invoices are checked and passed in the area supplies department by supplies staff, not finance staff, so that invoice queries can be settled immediately and therefore payments made more efficiently and promptly by the finance department. The standard regional tender form is used in the area by the supplies department for all contracts convened. There is a standard area quotation form and order form sent to manufacturers and three standard forms in use for internal requisitioning from the area supplies department. However, there are a number of different forms used for requisitioning supplies from the stores dispersed throughout the area. It is hoped that a higher level of standardisation will be achieved when the central area store has been established.

There is little purchasing carried out in the area that is not under the supervision of the area supplies department. The only non-supplies staff with external ordering books are the area pharmacist, catering officers and two instrument curators. This purchasing is from contracts arranged by the ASO or from manufacturers approved by him, with the exception of pharmaceuticals. The works organisation do not place orders directly for works, labour, or materials. The ASO involves nursing staff in supply committees set up to discuss quality control and other supply matters.

The ASO noted a change in the last few years in his area to a more formal user involvement in supplies matters: telephone calls between medical, nursing and supplies staff giving way to committees and working parties to discuss hospital supplies. Manufacturers' representatives call any time to the area supplies department without needing an appointment. However, it is generally the purchasing officers who see them, not the supplies officer. About thirty firms' representatives call each week at the area supplies department.

Contracting for supplies is kept flexible in the area so that the best possible advantages are gained for both the NHS and the supplies. The area is alert to the possibility of reassessing contracting levels and, in addition to regional and area contracting, scope has been found to purchase on an inter-regional and inter-area basis. Criticism has been made concerning the rather laborious nature of national contracts and of the lengthy time scale between letting a contract and notifying ordering authorities. There were instances where lower prices had been agreed by the area whilst awaiting formal notification of the nationally agreed prices for equipment.

Area 4: Redbridge and Waltham Forest Area Health Authority

The area has two districts with a central area supplies department and no district supplies departments. At present, there are approximately 17 stores of varying sizes in the area, with the 3 largest stores and their staff under area supplies control. There are 30 purchasing and administration staff working at the area supplies headquarters and the majority of the stores staff work under the control of the ASO. It is envisaged by the ASO that the three largest stores in the area will be commodity stores serving both districts and one store is already providing a centralised textile store for the area.

All capital schemes in the area are being equipped by area supplies staff with management delegated from the region to the ASO. Invoices are passed and checked by finance staff separate from the supplies staff although the ASO would like to see a closer physical proximity between finance invoice staff and supplies staff in order to speed up the checking of queries and the payment of manufacturers. The standard regional tender form is used by the area for contracting and there is a standard area order form sent to manufacturers. However, internal stores and non-stores requisition forms vary throughout the area and range from pre-printed forms to handwritten notes. A standardisation of internal requisition forms will be established with the commodity stores. All engineering and catering supplies are purchased by supplies staff. Food is purchased within a system of regular frequent joint supplies and catering consultations.

The ASO runs consumer advisory groups consisting of medical, nursing and administrative staff who discuss all aspects of purchasing and supplies. In addition, the catering/supplies working party meets most months to discuss food purchasing. Users supply experiences are also discussed at medical and nursing committees and the ASO is kept informed of these by senior nursing staff.

Approximately 30-40 manufacturers' representatives call each week to the area supplies department, but are seen mainly by purchasing staff. The ASO himself sees very few. The idea of large-scale contracting based on estimated requirements, in the manner of the 1950s and 1960s, is beginning to change according to the ASO. Contracting is becoming a more realistic procedure for both the NHS and suppliers, based on fixed quantity contracts, to limited distribution centres. NHS supplies officers, particularly at area level, want to make purchasing more businesslike and negotiate with manufacturers from positions of strength, offering realistic quantities and deliveries in exchange for the right commodity at the right price.

The North West Thames Regional Health Authority is split into the areas shown in Table 6.2.

Table 6.2: North West Thames Regional Health Authority

Area Health Authority	Population (approx)	Bed Spaces (approx)	Revenue Budget 1975/76 (approx) £m
Bedford	490,000	3,268	23
Hertford	839,000	8,033	51
Barnet	411,000	3,178	25
Brent & Harrow	413,000	3,588	33
Ealing, Hammersmith & Hounslow	674,000	5,037	56
Hillingdon	232,000	1,696	19
Kensington, Chelsea & Westminster	401,000	6,614	69
	3,460,000	31,414	£276m

This region has a declining and ageing population. The decrease is uneven but is the sum of an increase of population in the Hertfordshire and Bedfordshire areas and a decrease in the inner London areas. Compared with national norms, the Hertfordshire and Bedfordshire areas have a deficit of acute and geriatric services, with the inner London areas having a surplus of acute services. There are four undergraduate teaching hospitals, one post-graduate teaching hospital, one hospital associated with a clinical research centre in the region, and several post-graduate hospitals administered by boards of governors. There are seven areas with seven supplies officers and no common pattern of supplies organisation. The types of organisation range from fully centralised areas through partially centralised areas with outpost staff at district level to a decentralised district-based structure. The Regional Health Authority's policy is to encourage centralised area supplies organisation, and it supports the recommendation of the Collier Report. Regional contracting has been removed from area level to regional level, and contracts are convened by the Regional Supplies Officer only.

Capital schemes are equipped by regional supplies staff outposted to areas and recalled to the regional pool after schemes are completed.

The NHS Supplies Vocabulary is presently being used in the one area which has a central supplies and stores organisation and is being introduced in two other areas. The regional supplies catalogue, adapted from National Vocabulary, has been created for use in the areas and is maintained by the RSO.

Area 5: Barnet Area Health Authority

The area is divided into two health districts and has a centralised area supplies organisation with a central area store. There are 57 purchasing, administrative and stores staff in the organisation including 13 storemen/storekeepers outposted to the districts for the purpose of receiving and distributing supplies delivered to the major hospitals.

The National Supplies Vocabulary has been adopted for all items held in stock, related documents and area catalogues. The latter are co-ordinated on a regional basis by the regional supplies division. The standard regional contract and tender forms and the standard regional six-part order forms are used. Pre-printed requisition forms have been designed for obtaining commonly used items from the area stores. For items which are not on the pre-printed requisitions, blank stock requisitions are used which are completed by users from information contained in the area catalogues.

Regional staff are outposted to the area for the purpose of dealing with the supplies aspects of major capital schemes. Their performance is monitored by the Area Supplies Officer. There are ten major capital works schemes of over £50,000 on hand in the area. Some area treasurer's staff work in the area supplies division monitoring expenditure and control accounts and checking and passing invoices for stock items so that queries can be dealt with immediately by both finance and supplies staff. The input from the finance staff to the computer is weekly and the supplies department receive a print-out of balances in respect of stock that has been issued in the previous week.

The purchase of certain chemicals and cultures is carried out by agreement by Pathology Laboratory staff while, under authority delegated by the ASO, catering managers order fresh provisions from nominated suppliers off contracts negotiated by the area supplies division. The district works departments place orders for building works and labour, but all building and engineering stock and non-stock items are purchased by the area supplies division. Building and engineering sub-stores are operated by supplies staff at each of the three major hospitals.

During the planning and implementation of the centralisation of the supplies function, area working groups were formed comprising representatives of supplies and users to consider the implications of a change to a centralised system and to help in the preparation of procedures, preprinted requisitions and area catalogues. These groups were of great value and continue in being as a forum for the discussion of the service being provided, the rationalisation and standardisation of products, the introduction of new items and consultation on the contents of pre-printed requisitions, etc. There are several groups made up, as necessary, of medical, nursing, and administrative staff, each group dealing with different ranges of commodities. The chairman in each case is a member of the Supplies Division staff.

Approximately 30 manufacturers' representatives call at the area supplies division each week. Many call by appointment but some call on the off chance. All are seen if at all possible. Some stock items held in the area stores are purchased off national, regional, or area contracts and the rest are purchased from suppliers by the area supplies division. The centralisation of the supplies function is now complete and, although there were inevitably some problems associated with the changeover, these have now largely been overcome and the new organisation has settled down into a working routine.

Area 6: Brent and Harrow Area Health Authority

The area has two districts and a large mental illness hospital. There are 34 purchasing and administrative and clerical staff and 28 stores staff working in the area managed by the area supplies officer. At area supplies headquarters, the supplies officer works with two purchasing and two secretarial staff, and the remaining staff work in the two districts and the mental illness hospital.

There is no area central store but each district and the mental illness hospital have separate central stores. At the moment the three stores serve each of the two districts and the mental illness hospital exclusively and all classes of stores are held in each store. Consideration is being given to the development of three commodity stores and eventually an area store subject to feasibility studies.

The National Supplies Vocabulary is not yet being used in the area, although some stores are computerised and the introduction of a complete computerisation of stores is under consideration using the National Vocabulary.

There are 20 capital schemes in the area at present, of varying size up to £500,000 in cost, the equipment for which is scheduled and purchased by outposted regional purchasing staff.

The system of checking and passing invoices varies between districts in the area. One district has finance staff attached to the supplies department where the invoices are checked, whilst in the other units invoices are dealt with in the finance departments.

The standard six-part regional order form sent to manufacturers is used throughout the area. Even non-supplies staff who place orders directly, i.e. catering officers, are using this form. The standard regional quotation and contract forms are also used throughout the area. A standard area internal requisition form is used for non-stock items. The forms used for stock items vary according to the accounting and finance systems used at district and hospital level. Most stock requisition forms are pre-printed with commodities.

There are two appliance officers in the area; one is on the supplies staff and one comes under district administration authority. The area supplies department organises formal user consultation meetings and medical, nursing and other working parties relay their supply problems and suggestions back to the area supplies.

Manufacturers' representatives visit the area supplies headquarters, particularly in connection with capital projects. Many of them visit the district supplies officers at the rate of approximately 50 per week per district.

Six regional contracts, previously convened by the ASO, have been taken to regional headquarters where they are negotiated by the RSO. However, the ASO participates at the adjudication stage and makes his expertise available by serving on contract working parties.

Area 7: Anonymous

The area has four districts and two teaching hospitals. There are three central supplies staff and the remaining 74 purchasing and administrative staff work in the districts. There are approximately 90 other stores staff also attached to the districts. Each of the four districts has its own supplies organisation under the authority of an assistant ASO. The ASO does not expect his staff to work in physical proximity to area headquarters and approves of the district supplies structure. However, he is concerned that the district supplies staff are still accountable mainly to district administration and not to himself. There are no central area stores but a feasibility study is being carried out with the possibility of establishing commodity stores.

The National Supplies Vocabulary is not being used at present in the area.

One capital works scheme is being carried out in the area at present and this is being equipped by an outposted regional team. Minor schemes include health centres, and they are being equipped by outposted regional staff but under the general supervision of area supplies departments, to whom the region delegates a management responsibility.

The checking and passing of invoices in the area is done by two methods. In two districts, the invoices are dealt with by supplies staff; in the other two districts they are checked and passed by finance staff within a centralised financial accounting department. The standard regional tender, contract and quotation forms are in use throughout the area, and the standard six-part order form is also being used in the area.

The system of internal requisition forms is at present under review and it is hoped that eventually there will be only two forms in circulation, one pre-printed for stock items using the National Supplies Vocabulary, and the other for non-stock items. The different forms now being used are being collected and a report will be written outlining both the old system and the proposed new one.

Catering staff in the area place their own orders for supplies directly with manufacturers but only under 'supplies-convened' contracts and arrangements. Engineering staff negotiate their own labour and works contracts but do not buy equipment and supplies. Pathology laboratory staff purchase chemicals and solutions without any supplies department supervision. However, all pathology laboratory purchasing in the region is being reviewed by the regional scientific officer who will eventually make regional contracts for chemicals and solutions required for laboratory work.

District supplies organisations have meetings with heads of departments in order to discuss consumers' opinions and suggestions on supplies. All manufacturers' representatives who visit area and district supplies organisations are asked to make appointments. One representative per day is allowed an interview.

The ASO advocates careful appraisal when deciding on the best level at which to make NHS contracts. The main considerations are the type of commodity, the state of the economy, and the storage and distribution facilities available in any one area. The most viable level for a contract for hospital supply items is where there are maximum advantages advantages for both parties involved in the contract.

Area 8: Anonymous

The area is divided into three sectors; in each sector there is a district general hospital and a number of health centres and clinics. There is a total of twelve purchasing staff, including the ASO, plus four clerical staff, all of whom are located centrally. There are stores in two hospitals, where eighteen people are employed. Textiles, stationery and printing stores are organised on an area stores basis. At the largest district general hospital a supplies co-ordinator and an assistant are established. As soon as more accommodation becomes available further centralisation of stores will take place. The National Supplies Vocabulary is not being used at present in the area.

Capital scheme equipment purchasing in the area is supervised by the regional supplies department who delegate staff. There is a continuing problem of receiving and storing equipment and supplies for capital schemes in the area, which has very inadequate storage facilities generally.

The area finance system is centralised at two locations, but there still exists a few traditional variations in each sector left over from the pre-1974 reorganisation. Recently finance staff took over the checking and passing of invoices from supplies staff. The standard regional tender and contract forms and the six-part order form sent to manufacturers are used throughout the area. Internal requisition forms vary throughout the area but eventually it is hoped to standardise on two forms, one for non-stock and one for stock items, when a more centralised system of store is introduced.

All catering, engineering and pathology laboratory supplies are ordered under the supervision of the area supplies division and contracts for these items are convened by supplies staff.

The area supplies division does not organise formal consumer meetings but senior supplies staff attend regular hospital and area meetings at which supplies matters are discussed. The ASO favours an informal continuous dialogue between the supplies division and medical, nursing and administration staff, in the course of which questions of quality and availability of supplies can emerge.

Approximately 40-50 manufacturers' representatives call at the area supplies division each month, most without appointments although a few are asked to call by purchasing staff.

The RSO has removed all regional contracting away from areas to regional headquarters and regional staff although the area officers are still expected to contribute their expertise. The ASO suggests that there is a general trend towards a reappraisal of contracting levels in the NHS, according to the type of commodity, the economic situation and the market position of the manufacturer. The contracting carried out in the NHS after the Hunt Report assumed that it was more economical to make large contracts covering as many areas and regions as possible and that national contracts must be the most economical. Now supplies officers are examining commodities more carefully and in the last three years the suppliers have become significant in decisions of levels of contracting. Supplies officers are now advised by manufacturers, backed up by facts and figures, on the level at which a contract for a commodity will be acceptable and economical for both buyer and seller.

Area 9: Kensington, Chelsea and Westminster Area Health Authority

The area has three districts and three teaching hospitals. The area supplies department has a small staff of 5 purchasing and administration and 5 stores staff. The remaining 58 purchasing and 75 stores staff work in the district supplies organisations.

There are no central area stores at present although a recent management services study has suggested that an area stores be established. The National Supplies Vocabulary is not yet being used in the area.

Two health centres and a geriatric day hospital are being built in the area and the capital equipment is being purchased by regional supplies staff outposted to the area.

The system of checking and passing invoices varies between the districts. In one district, supplies staff receive, check and pass all their own invoices before the finance department makes payment to manufacturers. In the other two districts, the finance departments check and pass invoices separately from the supplies department. The standard regional, tender and contract forms are used throughout the area and the standard regional six-part order form is used by all but two of the hospitals in the area. The district treasurer has said that the order forms are inappropriate to the accounting system used in the two hospitals and a changeover would mean an intolerable increase in the workload for his finance staff.

There is a variety of internal requisition forms at present in circulation in the area. The ASO is beginning a survey of the forms with a view to some standardisation, although without a uniform storage and distribution system the standardisation will be limited.

The system of non-supplies staff purchasing in the area varies between districts. In one district, the pathology laboratory, the clinical measurement department and patients appliance officer are purchasing without supplies convened contracts or supervision. In another district, instrument curators are placing orders with manufacturers without supplies department supervision. Over the whole area the greatest part of catering supplies are purchased without supplies department authority and may or may not be using supplies convened contracts for food items. However, the catering managers now refer more frequently to the district supplies staff for purchasing advice. Works departments carry out their own purchasing except in two hospitals where the supplies department is in control of engineering supplies. Appliance officers in all districts are not supplies staff and are doing their own purchasing.

User consultation is mainly carried out at district level where supplies staff organise consumer groups to discuss quality, availability and other supply matters. The ASO holds monthly co-ordinating meetings with district staff who relay this information. He also meets monthly with catering officers with the intention of increasing supplies purchasing control.

Only one manufacturers' representative is seen each day at area supplies headquarters. However, approximately ten call each week at the district supplies office and are seen mainly by appointment.

This area has comparatively few area contracts, using mainly regional contracts which have now been moved to regional supplies supervision.

The South East Thames Regional Health Authority is split into the areas shown in Table 6.3.

Table 6.3: South East Thames Regional Health Authority

Area Health Authority	Population (approx)	Bed Spaces (approx)	Revenue Budget 1975/76 (approx) £m
East Sussex	647,000	6,212	39
Kent	1,437,000	14,614	89
Greenwich & Bexley	434,000	4,212	37
Bromley	304,000	3,391	20
Lambeth, Southwark & Lewisham	830,000	5,970	88
	3,652,000	34,399	£273m

In this region there is an over-provision of acute hospital services, together with a shortage of mental illness services and with an almost total absence of mentally handicapped facilities in Central London. Elsewhere in the region, the local population growth has resulted in a severe shortage of health care facilities, in particular in the Medway towns and among the elderly on the south coast. It is hoped that the 1974 NHS reorganisation will eventually achieve a better balance between the areas in the region of institutional, community, and personal social services. The aim of the region is to divert resources to upgrade neglected services in each area, in particular those for the mentally ill, the handicapped, and the elderly, and to provide an appropriate level of acute services in each area.

Before the 1974 reorganisation the region was divided into seven supply areas, with six ASOs. The area without a supplies officer was the teaching hospitals group in inner London. They decided not to have an ASO and were able to do this as the separate boards of governors of these hospitals were directly answerable to DHSS and not the regional authority.

After the 1974 reorganisation, the region was divided into five areas and five supplies officers were appointed. In theory, the teaching hospitals had become subject to regional authority and their supplies system was absorbed by the local area authority into which they had been placed.

The regional supplies organisation is managed on a decentralised basis by the RSO and his staff of four. The day-to-day work of purchasing, storage, and distribution is carried out at area and district level. In addition, capital equipping supplies staff in the region are based and managed in areas. The five ASOs also convene all regional, inter-regional, and area contracts. The regional and inter-regional contracts are apportioned in a rational workload basis and according to the particular expertise of the area officers. The bulk of all contracts in the region are regional contracts (over 60 per cent) and the remainder are inter-area, area, or district contracts. There are approximately ten inter-regional contracts operating at present.

Area 10: Anonymous

There are four districts in this area, with three teaching hospitals and two dental schools. The ASO works with a small area staff, delegating most of the day-to-day management of supplies done to local district level. District supplies staff make local service arrangements although they do not convene national, regional, inter-regional or area contracts as these are convened by the ASOs in this region. The supplies staffing level in the area is under review by the ASO who intends to restructure the stores and supplies organisation provided the staff union consent.

The area is without a central area store for supplies but a proposal to rationalise the two largest stores servicing each of two districts is presently the subject of a management study. As well as reducing stock holdings on a variety of goods the changes proposed are meant to simplify the paperwork by reducing the number of internal order forms in circulation. Because of the present decentralised storage system, the checking of goods received is not under the systematic control of the ASO. The National Supplies Vocabulary format is not yet in use in the area.

There have been no major capital work schemes started in the area since the 1974 reorganisation. In two teaching hospitals, major capital works are ending and the capital equipping supplies staff, although in theory part of the area supplies staff, are working under the authority of the district administration. Several minor capital schemes have been completed in the region since 1974.

Catering and engineering works supplies purchasing in the area are still not under the complete authority of the supplies department, but progress has been made in the last three years. All pathology laboratories supplies in the area are purchased by the supplies department. User committees in the area provide information on the quality and suitability of items purchased by the supplies department. Although the district supplies staff do not organise any of these committees, they attend some and keep in touch with user attitudes and opinions.

A standard regional order form for supplies from manufacturers is presently being introduced into the area. The standard regional contract and quotation form are already in use in the area. Internal requisition forms vary throughout the area, and many of the variations are related to the type of finance system operated in a particular district. The relationship between finance and supplies varies between districts, with supplies staff checking and passing invoices for goods received in one district, while in the other district finance staff are carrying out this task separately from the supplies department.

On average, three or four firms' representatives call at the area supplies headquarters every week, and approximately thirty call at each district office. The ASO has ruled that these representatives may be received on only two mornings.

The ASO has a flexible and pragmatic approach to standardisation of supplies and contracts, taking into account real costs to both the NHS and the manufacturer. It is thought to be sensible to standardise on supply items where it ensures a consistent quality and durability and where the savings accrued justify the costs. By the same token, contracting should be carried at the level at which both the NHS supplies officer and the manufacturer have confidence and control, and then expanded into a larger contract if advantages can be shown for both buyer and seller. Bigger contracts might be better but not necessarily so, depending on the supply item and the storage and distribution available in the area.

The South West Thames Regional Health Authority is split up into the areas shown in Table 6.4.

Table 6.4: South West Thames Regional Health Authority

Area Health Authority	Population (approx)	Bed Spaces (approx)	Revenue Budget 1975/76 (approx) £m
Surrey	1,000,000	8,196	75
West Sussex	623,000	4,490	33
Croydon	325,000	4,092	21
Merton, Sutton and Wandsworth	663,000	9,793	67
Kingston & Richmond	244,000	3,158	18
	2,855,000	29,729	£214m

Although the regional supplies department follows a general philosophy of centralised organisation, it has not yet been possible since the 1974 reorganisation to put this into practice, except in the two single district areas of Croydon and Kingston and Richmond. The remaining three areas, particularly West Sussex, are geographically large, with large populations to service, so the supplies system is still being managed at district level as in the days before the 1974 reorganisation.

District supplies staff are largely under the authority of district administration. There is also a general policy at regional level to work towards area stores wherever possible but so far the only feasibility study being carried out is for the Croydon area where it is hoped to create a central area store. It is hoped that the National Supplies Vocabulary will be used in this area after the stores have been created.

Given that the RSO is committed to a policy of a centralised supplies organisation, the extent of centralisation varies according to the geography, history and population of each area. For example, it is not expected that a centralised system in the Surrey area would mean all supplies staff working in one place but they will be under the authority and management of the ASO. As with the three other Thames regions, whether they regard themselves as centralised or not, there exists similar contracting and purchasing activity, with district supplies staff purchasing supplies off national, regional, inter-regional and area contracts. The district staff deal with day-to-day distribution matters and make arrangements for local domestic services.

After the 1974 Health Service reorganisation, the DHSS recommended that area health authorities should be similar in population, size, number of beds or geographical extent and that a viable supply area should generally contain not less than 5,000 hospital beds. Although it was suggested that ASOs should be appointed for viable supply areas only, the variations in areas is considerable and the only region which did not appoint a supplies officer for each of their areas was Birmingham Health Authority.

The project areas also vary in size with number of beds per area ranging from less than 2,000 beds to between 13,000 and 14,000 beds. Population sizes also vary between approximately 200,000 in an area and 1,500,000 in another area. However, the number of bed spaces available is not evenly distributed according to the population of an area. For example, an area with one of the smallest number of bed spaces has one of the most dense populations. The Hunt reorganisation of NHS supplies in 1968 produced a fairly well-balanced supplies organisation. The superimposition of the 1974 reorganisation on to the supplies system upset the balance and created an uneven distribution.

The workload of area and regional supplies organisations varies considerably, effectively influencing the extent to which area supplies organisations are able to centralise and rationalise their purchasing, storage and distribution systems. The unevenness of supply areas is not only confined to population, bed spaces and geographical extent, but also to the extra workload imposed by the addition of community health services and family practitioner services purchasing and distribution of supplies. One area which has a small number of bed spaces and a large population has one of the largest numbers of health centres and clinics among the project areas. The number of clinics and health centres ranges between less than ten in some areas to over fifty in others.

The extent of centralisation of the supplies organisation varies between regions as well as between areas within a region. One region in the project operates a deliberate policy of decentralisation. This method of organising purchasing with considerable delegation of responsibility to areas and districts suits the geography of the region as well as the historical management of areas and districts, particularly those with teaching hospitals. The other two regions are both working towards a more centralised supplies organisation, encouraging their areas to control purchasing with the minimum of district activity. However, in spite of the regional policies, the degrees of centralisation in each area varies considerably, ranging from totally centralised purchasing, storage and distribution to area supplies organisations working with a skeleton staff and a minimal knowledge of the purchasing, storage, and distribution systems within their districts. The smallest area had staff of five including the area supplies officer, compared with an area with forty-four staff working in the most centralised system.

The number of district supplies staff also varies considerably from fourteen stores staff basically receiving and distributing requisition orders from a central area store to approximately 150 staff carrying out purchasing, storage and distribution at district level. The largest district staff levels occur in uncentralised stores with teaching hospitals. In some areas a percentage of stores staff and stores in the districts are not yet under the authority of the area supplies organisation. This means that rationalisation of supplies, stores and staff cannot be carried out by the supplies organisation.

Two of the areas in the project operate a central area store. The rest are the subject of feasibility studies by management services, who take into account the size and nature of the area and available finance. In most cases, the management services study is expected to show financial savings from a changeover to central area stores. Although this is important, the other factors (such as a greater degree of control and standardisation and better service to the user) are seen as equally, if not more, important to the supplies officers themselves. The studies are not recommending one central store in all cases but sometimes a series of commodity stores or general stores serving the districts. No regional or inter-area stores is being established at the present time in the project areas.

The National Supplies Vocabulary, so far as it has been published, is being applied to two area stores, and others are intending to use it when central stores are established.

Capital Scheme Supplies and Equipment Purchasing

In the most decentralised region capital scheme equipment purchasing is being done under the supervision of the district administration. In one other region the supervision of minor capital scheme purchasing is delegated to area supplies staff, while major schemes are supervised by regional supplies staff. A third region has capital equipment purchasing teams who move around the areas. There is also some monitoring by area supplies staff where the schemes are small. The area staff also liaise closely with regional staff on the minor schemes.

Tender, Quotation and Other External Order Forms

All the project areas use standard regional tender and contract forms. Most areas are also using standard regional quotation forms or are in the process of introducing them. The six-part order form sent to manufacturers for goods to be supplied are standardised within each area, based on a regional form. The main differences are that individual area headings are used but the layout of all is similar. One or two areas have odd hospitals still using their own order forms but on the whole there is a high degree of standardisation.

Internal Requisition Forms for Stock and Non-stock Items

Only two areas in the project have standard internal requisition forms. Some are in the process of standardising their forms but the majority use a great variety. The type and number of forms seems to vary, according to either the amount of control the supplies organisation has over storage and distribution of supplies, or on the financial accounting system in operation in the area. In one area, the treasurer insists on two hospitals using a different internal requisition form to facilitate his accounting system, while in other areas forms vary where a computerised accounting system is used. In one instance, internal requisition forms have been designed by the hospital administration which controls its own stores and distribution.

Authorised Buyers

In three of our areas, all purchasing is supervised by the supplies officer, but in the other areas the catering and engineering staff continue some independent purchasing as before 1974 reorganisation. The level of independent purchasing varies from one instrument curator in an area who is still under local administrative authority, to an area where catering staff and works staff undertake most of their purchasing without reference to any supplies authority. However, the majority of all revenue purchasing in the project area is now done from contracts and arrangements convened by supplies officers or under supplies department supervision. At present, pathology laboratory chemicals and solutions, traditionally purchased by pathology laboratory staff without any contractual agreements with manufacturers, are being scrutinised by supplies officers, and one regional scientific officer was planning to place a regional contract with manufacturers and possibly making bulk purchase savings.

National, Regional and Area

Whether level of centralisation of supplies organisation is present in the areas in the project, there is a similar system of contracting. Only one instance of contracting by district supplies staff was recorded, and that was due to the use of the expertise of district staff to negotiate the contract, after which it was drawn up by the ASO. District supplies staff confine themselves to the day-to-day distribution of supplies and the negotiation of local domestic services, such as window cleaning, waste disposal, and the repair and maintenance of typewriters. Area supplies officers convene all area contracts and, in some regions, the regional and inter-regional contracts also.

One region has taken all regional contracting to regional supplies headquarters where they are convened by regional staff, although area staff are expected to contribute their expertise at the negotiating and adjudication stages. Each project region was operating between 40 and 50 regional and inter-regional contracts for supplies in 1978, with a range between areas of less than six in one area to over twenty in another. The number of contracts per area does not appear to be related to the degree of centralisation of the area supplies department. For example, the most centralised area supplies organisation has approximately six area contracts, while one of the most decentralised areas had 21 area contracts. Some of the project areas gave specific instances of the inadequacies of national and regional contracts, sometimes as a justification for having abandoned the use of them or for convening their own.

The national soup contract was mentioned by one area supplies officer as being unsuitable for his area needs and he has changed, therefore, to an area contract which affords a higher level of quality and variety of soup as well as lower prices.

Several areas mentioned the regional and inter-regional bedding and linen textiles and clothing contracts as having reached the stage where quality control at the call-off stage is unsatisfactory. Much work has gone into specifications and the selection of manufacturers but supplies are arriving at areas and hospitals which are not of the original specification. Sometimes the material used is wrong or the making up of the clothing is inadequate. One RSO suggested that the NHS bedding, linen and textiles contracts have reached a size where quality control should be handled in the factory by DHSS or regional representatives. Recent spot checks on deliveries of patient clothing at one hospital revealed that where the specification said that the clothing should be made of inflammable materials, the actual materials used have proved to be non-flame resistant.

Several instances were mentioned of polythene bags purchased from regional contracts not being of the original specification agreed with the manufacturer. In some cases, the problem had been discovered at the time of delivery by storesmen, while another area had learned in a more practical way at the stage at which the bags were being filled with kitchen refuse and had torn in the process.

Some areas mentioned that national contracts for furniture are unsatisfactory because of the length of time taken for deliveries. One area mentioned a recent wait of six months for national contract desks.

The national contract for fluorescent tubes was also said to be unsatisfactory: not only were deliveries taking up to six months, but the tubes are more expensive than those negotiated on a regional contract and spot checks on tubes found they did not comply with original specifications.

One area supplies officer eventually had to buy some vacuum cleaners from a local store after those ordered from a national contract did not appear after six months. The added bonus to his transaction was that the vacuum cleaners were cheaper at the local co-operative society than those due to be purchased on a national contract.

One area supplies organisation was able to negotiate better prices at area level for CSSD bags but was obliged to carry on using the mandatory national contract. The same area had also just stopped using a regional tea contract as an area contract with a different supplier afforded a cheaper, better quality product.

These examples tend to support the NHS supplies officers' approval of a more flexible system in which contracts can be convened and disbanded so that the NHS may gain maximum benefit from their supplies system. They also point to the weaknesses of large NHS contracting in maintaining quality control throughout the duration of a contract.

User Participation in the Supply System

Most of the NHS supplies officers taking part in this project believe that the consumer or user has a useful contribution to make to purchasing and contracting for supplies. Supplies officers have also found user participation can be a useful contribution to bringing about higher levels of standardisation in supplies. Nursing staff in particular are more aware of the financial implications of cutting down on the variety of goods and sometimes help to educate medical staff in this direction. In a few instances, supplies officers complained that consumer groups had a negative effect on increased standardisation when they were used for one-way communication, conveying user needs to the supplies organisation only.

At least four of the project areas have organised groups at which medical, nursing, and administrative staff participate in an exchange of ideas on supply problems. Nursing staff from one area had been invited to participate in supplies work at regional level and were contributing to the contracting for a wide range of medical and surgical items. The remaining project areas are involved to a lesser degree in consumer consultation, usually through supplies officers attending specialist committees at the invitation of medical and nursing staff.

On the whole, the level of user involvement with supplies has become more formal since the 1974 reorganisation.

Accounting Systems and Supplies

Some barriers to increased efficiency in the NHS supplies organisation come from financial accounting systems used in the NHS at national, area, and district levels. For many years, supplies officers have advocated a rolling three-year revenue budget instead of the annual budget which has to be spent or forfeited inside a twelve months' period. Last minute ordering of medical equipment and other supplies has placed an administrative strain on the supplies organisation and has prevented rational decision-making on certain supply items and also long term planning of purchasing.

In April 1977, the situation changed slightly in at least one region: one per cent of a revenue budget could be carried over into the following financial year. However, the underspending penalty has been exchanged for an overspending penalty of up to 20 per cent which can be deducted from the following year's budget.

In 1977, the financial limit on revenue purchasing was raised from £2,000 to £5,000 per item and for selected items of machinery and equipment up to £10,000 on a discretionary basis.

Within areas and districts, the different types of accounting systems present barriers to a more rational internal requisitioning system, and in some instances, the variety of internal requisition forms is due to the financial accounting system in operation.

There are still variations between areas and districts on the checking and passing of invoices. In some project areas, the supplies staff have little influence on payments made to manufacturers where there are discounts available for prompt payment. In three of the project areas, finance staff check all invoices separately from the supplies department, and in another, finance staff check and pass invoices but within the supplies department. In one area, supplies staff check and pass all invoices for payment to manufacturers and suppliers. The rest of the project areas are involved in a variety of systems with both finance and supplies staff checking invoices according to the district and its accounting system.

In most areas, area supplies staff have no way of guaranteeing that all prompt payment discounts are taken up by the finance department. As each region and area is responsible for keeping its own financial house in order, according to their own financial instructions, there is no central information on individual accounting methods and policies. Variations arise between areas using computers and those that do not. The greatest pressure on finance departments to take up quick payment discounts comes from internal and external auditors and not from the supplies department.

Manufacturers and Suppliers

The number of manufacturers' representatives calling at supplies departments varied between areas. Where the area supplies department is small and isolated from the hospitals, the number calling tends to be smaller. On average, the project areas have up to fifty calling each week at either area or district offices. Although supplies departments discourage hospital departments from seeing representatives, most of them do not know how many representatives visit catering, engineering, medical and nursing staff in the area. Some supplies departments insist on representatives calling by appointment only but the majority see as many as they have time for.

Supplies officers tend to rely on their own supplies journals for detailed technical information about products and use manufacturers' representatives as a source of general market information or call them in if demonstrations are required. The supplies officers' own information system has expanded with the increase of inter-regional and regional activity and the publication of a supplies handbook. Individual region and area supplies departments carry out product testing on manufacturers' goods and publish the results in supplies journals.

Some project areas reported interactions with manufacturers which have made their purchasing more effective. For example, in one region a new method of contracting for drugs has been introduced to reduce the overall workload of the supplies department. Approximately ninety drug companies were invited to a meeting to talk about the problems involved for them in selling to the NHS. It was discovered at this meeting that most of them adjust their contract prices to take account of inaccurate quantity estimates produced by the NHS. In many cases they were using their own computerised records on the uptake of drugs during a contract in order to negotiate. In effect, the NHS supplies staff involved in the drugs contracts were wasting a great deal of time collecting information within their own areas. Now the regional contract is convened without estimated quantities. The workload on drugs contracts in this region has been halved for the supplies staff, and manufacturers were delighted to be asked to collaborate in this exercise.

In the same region, a large manufacturer of disposable paper products is helping supplies staff to benefit from the reduction in costs afforded by decreasing the number of deliveries made within an area. If a supplies department can take 'one drop' bulk deliveries at times when the manufacturer has transport available in the area, the supplies department receives an additional discount. Some supplies departments in the region do not have adequate storage facilities to take these large deliveries.

In some of the project areas, the supplies department had begun to ask manufacturers to submit a cost breakdown of their products before a contract is made. This system has been fairly well established for the supply of labour-intensive services where an increase in price during a contract had to be justified by the supplier. Little progress has been made in this area where the cost breakdown of products is involved, as manufacturers are less willing to discuss factory production costs. A group of manufacturers of medical and surgical dressings appealed to the DHSS via their trade association after being asked to submit cost breakdowns for a regional contract. They were not prepared to submit their cost breakdowns for inclusion in a contract. The DHSS upheld the manufacturers' appeal against supplies officers.

Another example of manufacturers' reluctance to help the NHS purchase more effectively has been the sales drive of a particular supplier who has tried to expand the market for disposable patients clothing and theatre drapes. One or two areas reported that the company produced dubious cost effective analyses of the use of disposable, as compared with traditional, items. Much of this type of selling has become more difficult for manufacturers since 1974 and their own cost effective studies now have to be measured against official DHSS studies.

Apart from these negative experiences, all supplies officers in the project expect to have good working relationships with manufacturers to the satisfaction of both parties. Secrecy is no longer expected about the quality and reliability of a product and the supplier, nor about consumption of the product by hospitals. Supplies officers appear to be working hard at obtaining enough information on the use of supplies to negotiate sensibly.

Part Two

THE SUPPLIERS

7 THE PRODUCT AND THE USER

The use of manufactured products is an important part of modern medicine, but the relationship between the product and the patient is by no means simple. Some means is needed to decide which products should be made, by whom and to what degree of quality. The determination and maintenance of the last is important when the product will usually influence directly the patient's health.

The market model does not help the NHS because the providers of money are not those who decide purchases. The orders are placed for the most part by supplies officers, but they act on the wishes of many professions and experts of all kinds working within the NHS. In many instances, the experts will not know the price of the product they request or will be indifferent because of the importance (to them) of other health considerations.

The user of the product has considerable influence on purchasing. The user is the employee using the product, not the patient on whom it is used. One user may be subject to the wishes of another user. In one teaching hospital, the domestic manager responsible for cleaning is unable to use one disinfectant throughout his district because one consultant insists on a particular mixture of disinfectants in his operating theatres.

Considerable efforts are made by supplies officers to involve medical and nursing staff in choosing products that can become standard in their area or region and numerous committees exist for this purpose. One senior nursing officer responsible for operating theatres in one district told us of her involvement with two working parties. In one, concerned with the standardisation of disposables, she found that her colleagues were reluctant to choose standard items unless they happened to coincide with personal preference. However, the considerable endeavour to involve users aims to take account of their knowledge of products and manufacturers.

This nursing officer is often interviewed by sales representatives: they are unable to visit staff on wards, but nurses' offices are open to them. Most of those who came to see her were from manufacturers of disposable products. She mentioned the campaign by Johnson and Johnson to convert theatre sisters to the use of disposable theatre gowns and drapes. Apart from using some as emergency stocks, she felt that they would be economical only if disposables were used exclusively and hospital laundries abandoned.

We interviewed five users from different areas as follows:

1. District domestic manager,
2. Senior nursing officer,
3. Consultant anaesthetist,
4. Head of a medical physics department,
5. Chief technician of a pathology laboratory.

We discussed certain common matters with all of them, although each interviewed raised special issues as well:

1. Methods used to acquire products,
2. Their contacts with suppliers,
3. Channels for complaints about products,
4. Sources of information about new products,
5. Servicing of equipment.

The analyses of their views produced the matrix shown in Table 7.1.

In all project areas and regions, the financial restrictions on purchasing equipment are very similar as are the management procedures by which decisions on equipment are made. Equipment needs are divided (according to cost) as either revenue items or capital items.

In 1978, equipment costing up to £5,000 per item was classified as revenue expenditure and over £5,000 as capital expenditure. Heads of departments requiring new equipment costing less than £5,000 make bids within their department and a list of priorities is produced. Subsequently, departmental bids are submitted to a medical executive committee which looks at all departmental priority lists and draws up another priority list which is then submitted to the district management team in the area. At this point, the district management team is authorised to request the equipment with the greatest priority. All capital items of equipment costing over £5,000 go through the same priority sieve as for revenue items, but the chain of scrutiny is extended to the area management team who submit lists to regional level scrutiny; they go either to the regional scientific committee or to the regional medical committee.

Since 1974, the main changes that have occurred in this system of selecting priorities is the replacement of the local board of governors, who used to make final decisions on revenue items, by a district management team. The financial limits of revenue expenditure have been changed from less than £1,000 per item to items costing £5,000 and over. At present, capital expenditure equipment items, apart from those to be used within a capital building scheme, are reviewed in the light of the overall needs of the region, with RSOs acting in an advisory capacity. However, it is not possible to purchase all types of equipment with the aim of rationalising overall regional needs. For example, patient connected equipment is difficult to operate on a central regional basis, but with laboratory equipment it is possible to close down small units and concentrate blood, urine and other testing in fewer locations within a region. Even this rationalisation depends on the size and geography of the region and on internal transport and communication systems. Decisions on equipment purchasing at each stage from hospital to regional level are usually formal committee decisions, with the RSO acting at each level in an advisory capacity.

Decision-making on the Type and Manufacturer of Equipment

Heads of medical and scientific departments in the NHS decide on equipment needed within their departments before the processes of establishing priorities and eliminating bids takes place. At this stage they have already fairly clear ideas of the type of equipment they need related to the tasks it is expected to perform and the workload and staff levels in the department. At this stage also, a department head will have a particular manufacturer in mind. Sometimes, pieces of fairly specific equipment are made by only one or two manufacturers and in some cases only one. If the equipment selected is made by a range of manufacturers, the department head will know the range of prices, the quality and reliability of the equipment and the supplier. This knowledge is obtained from colleagues in the area or region and in other hospitals throughout the country.

Manufacturers have their equipment tested 'in use' in many hospitals and the medical and scientific staff write up results which are published in professional journals. Although supplies department staff are sometimes asked to collect details of prices from manufacturers, this is infrequent. Technical leaflets and catalogues are received by heads of medical and scientific departments and manufacturers' representatives call directly at the department where their equipment is used.

Ordering Equipment for Departmental Use

When the purchase of a piece of revenue equipment has been approved, the department head either orders it directly from the manufacturer or sends his request to the supplies department for the item to be ordered. Only two of the heads of department interviewed ordered equipment directly from manufacturers and this was for revenue items only. The others had their orders for revenue and capital equipment processed by the area supplies department.

Looking at the decision-making process as a whole, this would appear to be the only stage at which supplies staff are involved and one where the majority of decisions on type, cost and manufacturer have already been made. It was suggested by one head of department that medical and surgical purchasing staff lack adequate education and training (general and specific) to deal with medical staff and clinical preference.

Contact between Users of Equipment and Manufacturers

All the users interviewed received technical and advertising literature through the post and manufacturers' representatives called to see them directly. These representatives bring equipment to the department to be tested 'in use' and are also a source of information on 'in use' testing in other hospitals and regions and on the equipment market generally. Some of them know about equipment industries, which is important in laboratory equipment because it cannot be used without the necessary chemicals and solutions.

New Products and Developments in Equipment

Most of the users interviewed suggested that basic inventions in equipment come from manufacturers' research laboratories or independent research centres. Hospital 'in house' contributions are usually modifications or improvements to existing equipment. Sometimes the modifications are specific to a department, while others lend themselves to a more general NHS application. Where there is scope for widespread use of hospital 'in house' developments, manufacturers are sometimes involved in making prototypes and marketing the equipment. In other instances, a hospital department will produce the prototype and involve a manufacturer in the marketing and selling only. The degree of financial or other benefits afforded to the NHS by these 'in house' developments varies considerably. A department usually expects to make a discreet exchange between itself and the manufacturer, excluding other departments, the area health authority and other bodies. If the hospital inventions are sold for cash or royalties, very often the financial benefit is lost to the department and absorbed into the area health authority budget.

One head of medical physics interviewed, whose own department has developed some useful accessories for electronic equipment which has since been manufactured and marketed, does not bother either with cash payments or royalties. Instead, he exchanges the invention for free equipment or payment in kind. Apparently, manufacturers are happy to do this because it involves tax concessions for them and a minimum of bureaucratic dealing with bodies such as the National Research Development Corporation and the regional and area health authorities. An economic value of development or invention is arrived at by the hospital department and the manufacturer and is not usually worked out with any mathematical precision.

Another head of department interviewed chooses either a capital sum or a system of royalties for his department's inventions. On the whole, he prefers a capital sum which is worked out on the basis of the man-hours involved in the development and the expected profit of the manufacturer. If he chooses royalties in exchange, they are usually between 5 and 10 per cent on each item of equipment sold, but he can remember one instance of receiving a 12 per cent royalty from a manufacturer. Overall, the department head tries to see that as much of the financial gain as possible comes back directly to his department, although this sometimes involves fighting area health authorities who try to use the money as a general boost to their revenue budgets. Sometimes the department wins by the strength of the head's personality.

Medical schools which invent or develop equipment usually bargain against research funds provided by the manufacturer. One chief technician interviewed said that on the whole manufacturers get the best of the deal, whatever method of payment is used.

Quality Control of Equipment

All users interviewed said that complaints about inferior or faulty equipment are made by them directly to manufacturers. However, hazardous equipment has to be reported to area and regional health authorities and to the DHSS Laboratory Equipment Advisory Group who issue hazard warnings to all hospitals. All interviewees said that there are few formal channels within the NHS through which to complain about the quality and reliability of equipment and manufacturers if the problem is not one of hazard. However, there exists a very effective informal grapevine which circulates information about manufacturers and their equipment. This covers a range of complaints from bad deliveries, service and maintenance to shoddy workmanship. Most of this information comes from 'in use' equipment and supplies within hospital departments.

Servicing and Maintenance

The amount of service and maintenance carried out by hospitals varies from region to region, and depends on the size of the medical physics departments and the electro-bio-medical engineering departments in the areas. On the whole, since 1974, medical physics departments have expanded in the NHS but the expansion has not been even throughout the country. It seems to be influenced largely by history rather than need. Traditionally, areas which do a large part of their own service and maintenance confine themselves to servicing patient-connected equipment, such as patient monitors, ventilators, and incubators, because this type of equipment is given priority over laboratory equipment in terms of patient care. The pathology laboratory chief technician interviewed said that his scientific staff carry out all first-line maintenance on their own equipment, as well as some of the more complex maintenance. They allocate other maintenance to the medical physics department, whose priorities are patient-connected equipment, and the last resort is to the manufacturer.

Works department staff do no service and maintenance except perhaps for changing plugs. A head of a medical physics department said that the main reason for carrying out 'in house' service and maintenance is to avoid manufacturers' costs, but felt that works staff should not extend their servicing role beyond electrical plug changing and other minor repairs.

When medical physics departments have time over from patient-connected service and maintenance, they expect to extend themselves into pathology laboratory equipment.

It was suggested that service and maintenance contracts with manufacturers on purchase are unnecessary as there is no such thing as preventive maintenance in complex electronic equipment. Only some electrical and mechanical equipment lends itself to preventive maintenance and most medical physics departments are already coping adequately with such breakdowns.

When manufacturers are called in to maintain equipment, the service varies considerably. Some are good, and others are inefficient, unreliable and expensive. One head of medical physics suggested that in his experience standards dropped sharply when large companies made their service and maintenance into a separate company division. The separate division is expected to function like the manufacturing divisions and to make a profit or at least to break even. The separation of manufacture and service also brings problems in co-ordination and continuity after the equipment has been installed. Good service is usually found in those companies which have their maintenance incorporated into the goodwill and efficiency of the company as a whole. Their engineers are better qualified and more readily available and have usually been involved in the installation of the equipment. On the whole, it is the large American companies who excel at combining quality and efficiency of equipment with good service and maintenance, although this means a higher initial outlay for the NHS on the price of the equipment.

Where hospitals are expanding their own service and maintenance, there appears to be some demarcation problems between different departments and the roles they expect to play. At least two areas in the project are currently drafting lists of all equipment used in the area and the service and maintenance arrangements in operation for each piece of equipment. Some alarming omissions and overlappings are coming to light where works staff, medical physics staff, manufacturers, and other hospital staff are all involved with repairing and maintaining equipment. In extreme cases, some equipment is being completely overlooked and is never serviced. In one of these areas, a working party has been set up to look at equipment servicing in its entirety and will decide on potential savings to be made, safety standards and the level of responsibility of each department involved. The working party is made up of supplies staff who make service and maintenance agreements with manufacturers, medical physics staff and works department staff. The situation is also being discussed at DHSS level where there is some concern about the costs as well as patient safety where there are so many service and maintenance variations.

The Regional Scientific Officer

As early as 1968, the Zuckerman Report led to the appointment of regional scientific officers to advise and be responsible for scientific equipment purchased by the NHS for use in hospitals. Not all regions appointed scientific officers at this time but there has been a large number of appointments since 1974. The Zuckerman Report also made a distinction between medical and scientific equipment, mainly for NHS administrative purposes. Scientific equipment was to include all radio-therapy, radiology, pathology and physiological measuring equipment (EEG, ECG and EMG) and monitoring equipment; medical equipment was to include patient treatment equipment such as ventilators, incubators and anaesthetic equipment. At present, some of the equipment manufactured can be used for either diagnosis or treatment and consequently the distinctions between medical and scientific equipment are somewhat blurred.

The regional scientific officer is expected to advise at all levels within the NHS structure on the selection of priorities in equipment, but he controls to a greater extent the equipment items that reach regional committee level for selection. At the same time that he is looking at local district and area needs he is expected to take a long-term view of the region's needs and advise the DHSS on his region's activities in the scientific equipment field. The regional scientific officer is required to be secretary of regional scientific committees where capital equipment priorities are assessed. There are usually seven standing committees at regional level, each one concerned with equipment relating to a particular discipline. Where equipment crosses boundaries and involves more than one discipline, multi-disciplinary working parties consider the lists and assess priorities. At the level of both standing committee and working party, decisions are made with reference to overall regional, as well as local district and area, policy.

Since 1974 it has become a priority of the regional scientific officers to cut out waste and reduce costs with a replacement and redeployment plan within the region. The equipment replacement programme is quite complex and is being worked out by most regional scientific officers. Some regions are working on a gradual replacement plan whereby equipment is replaced before it is redundant and redeployed in a part of the region where it will receive a smaller workload.

The problem in some regions is that the total annual replacement budget for equipment is not enough to carry out the programme. This has meant that the regional scientific officer has to rationalise the total amount of equipment in the region, reducing the number of X-ray units, for example, in areas that are over-equipped, and concentrating some laboratory equipment in one or two areas instead of having it in each area of the region. In 1977, it was ruled that in certain regions all hospital departments had to surrender their old equipment on receiving replacements.

The concern for the state of British firms manufacturing scientific equipment is justified, according to some regional scientific officers. In 1978, it seemed that 90 per cent of all X-ray equipment used in the NHS was imported, mostly from Germany and Holland. Approximately 95 per cent of pathology laboratory equipment is also imported, mainly from the USA, although the use of Swedish equipment is increasing steadily. Haematology equipment is mainly imported from the USA; ECG and EEG equipment used in the NHS is largely German, Japanese or Swedish. The only equipment for which British manufacturers are still predominant is ultrasound equipment, scanners and some X-ray equipment accessories. Most British companies manufacturing scientific equipment do not appear to have the research, development and testing

Table 7.1: Users' Views

	Ordering Procedure				Contact with Suppliers		Sources New Product Information							Channels of Complaint/Suggestions re Products						Types of Complaints		Equipment Servicing		
	Direct ordering (to £500)	Through ASO	Through District Administrator	Through Area Medical Committee	Through representatives	Mail advertising	Exhibition	Journals	Representatives	King's Fund	Own research & development	Hospital Supplies Bulletin (DHSS)	Other colleagues	ASO	Direct to manufacturers (& ASO)	Medical staff: modify instruments	Manufacturers' research	Regional Scientific Officer	DHSS 'Hazard' procedure	Late delivery	Bad servicing from suppliers	Within hospital	By manufacturers	Independent servicing engineer
																						%	%	
District Domestic Manager		X	X		X				X	X		X	X	X	X				X	X	X	90	10	
Senior Nursing Officer			X		X				X							X	X		X			10	90	
Consultant Anaesthetist				X	X		X	X					X	X				X	X			50	50	
Medical Physicist	X				X	X		X	X		X		X					X	X					
Chief Technician of Pathology Laboratory	X			X	X	X	X		X							X		X	X			X	X	X

Comments:

District Domestic Manager

Few delivery problems but have not had to rely on area stores to maintain topping-up system. Good contacts between domestic managers, cleaners and supplies staff; problems on deliveries, quality control, and testing new products dealt with routinely. Medical staff refuse to try out new disinfectants in theatres in case they endanger patients.

Senior Nursing Officer

Ordering procedures cause delay; would prefer direct to ASO. Favours 1974 changes; has enhanced nurses, lowered doctors, mainly through committees and through increased regional influence in place of doctor-dominated autonomous hospitals.

Medical Physicist

Budget items: 1977/78 £54,000 salaries
14,500 radio-active isotopes
8,000 general repairs
3,000 computer maintenance
4,000 other

£83,500 plus £49,000 on capital items

Has developed some useful accessories for electronic equipment which have been manufactured and marketed. Does not seek payment or royalties but manufacturers give free equipment to department.

facilities of foreign competitors. British firms have a poor reputation for quality control, sometimes because of the poor quality of production engineers.

About eight years ago, the DHSS did some research into the potential use of a piece of blood and urine analysing equipment. They were advised on the probable use of this equipment by a panel of teaching hospitals and official DHSS scientific advisers. The department then asked a large British company to manufacture these machines at the rate at which the advisers had suggested they would be used in the NHS. The company agreed to manufacture the equipment and began to carry out research and development. Eventually, the department's estimated requirements proved to be inaccurate, and after having made twenty machines, the company found that there was no demand. The DHSS agreed to purchase the twenty machines, although the majority of them were never used by any NHS hospitals. After this episode, the company virtually left the market for this type of equipment having decided that it was unwise to research, develop and manufacture equipment in isolation from the commercial market.

8 THE HEALTH CARE SUPPLY INDUSTRIES

It would be reasonable to expect that a study of this nature would supply a clear definition of health care industries. But it is extremely difficult to formulate such a definition and some of the reasons may be apparent from earlier chapters. Logically, 'health care supply industries' should cover all industries supplying goods and services to promote the care of health and the cure of illness. Such a definition would leave very little of a modern economy uninvolved in health care or cure. A vast range of resources goes into the construction, equipment and operation of a major modern hospital; it calls upon all modern technological production as well as innumerable personal and professional services. Much hospital management is concerned with the equivalent of hotel management, a fact that links the hospital with the many industries that supply goods, equipment, furnishings and building materials used in accommodation services.

A more selective and useful range of relevant goods (and hence industries) emerges from a consideration of Table 8.1, which is based on the *Health and Personal Social Services Statistics for England 1975* (HMSO) and refers to the financing of the NHS for 1973-4. It indicates that the total expenditure of the regional hospital boards was about £1,500 million. Approximately one-third of that went to the purchasing of goods and services used in hospitals for both patients and staff. There are numerous limitations to such figures and in particular it should be noticed that they refer only to England, and exclude Wales, Scotland, and Northern Ireland. However, in a letter from the DHSS dated 3 August 1977 it is stated that 'the total expenditure on NHS supplies, equipment, goods and services for the past years' including both capital and revenue expenditure is estimated to have been:

1971-72	£260m
1972-73	£298m
1973-74	£351m
1974-75	£430m
1975-76	£593m

The table in the statistics for 1975 that identifies particular supplies was not compiled for the 1976 statistics in view of the changeover 'to

Table 8.1: NHS Finance 1973-74

			£m
Table 2.1, p. 18	Total costs: National Health GB and welfare services		3,603
	Hospitals: Current		1,778
	Capital		260
Table 2.7, p. 22	RHBs: England and Wales		1,500
	Salaries and Wages		1,033
Table 2.9, p. 24	Supplies: England	£m 1973/4	
	Provisions	66	
	Uniforms and clothing	11	
	Drugs	43	
	Dressing	9	
	Medical and surgical appliances and equipment	72	
	General services	57	
	Maintenance	43	
	Domestic repairs, etc.	23	
	Other	68	
	Blood transfusion, mass X-ray	23	
	Central administration	52	467
Table 13.1, p. 169	Goods and services under central contracts		127
	DHSS contracts		67
	of which: artificial limbs	7	
	dental equipment	0.2	
	drugs and dressings	5	
	dialysis equipment	0.4	
	path. and blood	4	
	radiological equipment	10	

Source: Health and Personal Social Services Statistics for England 1975, HMSO, 1976.

presenting statistics on a functional rather than a subjective basis'. That means, for example, that no figure is any longer quoted for total salaries paid to NHS staff; they are incorporated in the total cost of supplying particular services such as blood transfusion. Therefore, the only tentative conclusion one can draw is that the DHSS estimate the cost of NHS supplies to have increased by about two-thirds from 1973-74 to 1975-76. On a similar reckoning, the total figure for supplies in Table 8.1 of £467 million for 1973-74 would have been £767 million for 1975-76.

However, it must be stressed that figures can be calculated in different ways for different purposes and the autonomy of NHS authorities means that no complete statistics for NHS supplies expenditure exist.

It will be seen from Table 8.1 that only a few items of supplies appear to be peculiar to the NHS and are different from products that might be bought by any other organisation. These products are:

Drugs	£43m
Dressings	£9m
Medical and surgical appliances and equipment	£72m
Blood transfusion and mass X-ray	£23m
Relevant goods supplied under DHSS contracts	£27m
	£174m

Arguably, a proportion of all other NHS expenses should be charged to these items. In addition, there is the capital expenditure on hospitals of £260 million. Assuming all that capital was classifiable as distinctively medical, the total current and capital expenditure of the NHS on distinctively medicinal needs would have amounted to £434 million in the financial year from 1 April 1973 to 31 March 1974. It must be stressed that no such calculations can be made for any subsequent year because of the change in the methods of statistical calculation.

In view of the very limited resources available to this project, it seemed sensible to concentrate our attention on supplies and services that were peculiar to the NHS and to exclude all other supplies expenditure from any detailed consideration. We had to restrict our area of attention even more for many reasons of research practice and we ended up by making a detailed study of ten area health authorities and ten manufacturers of electromedical equipment, all situated within Greater London. The firms were selected as randomly as possible and there was no attempt to pick firms that were in some way unusual, apart from their willingness to co-operate. Further details are given in Chapter 9.

There is at least one other major area of NHS supplies that is characteristic: disposable medical products. If those are defined as products that are not used more than once, it would be interesting to know the quantity of disposables bought and how their use has increased in recent years. Needless to say, no such statistics exist and one can only make reasonable estimates based on a few clues. It would seem that total sales in the United Kingdom now amount to over £10 million and may be

£15 million.[1] There is, however, an authoritative directory of disposable products and producers published by the King's Fund Centre. The first (1962) edition listed 100 firms and 170 product groups. The use of disposables in hospitals appears to have started about 1960. That may well have been linked with the introduction of central sterile supply departments, the first of which in Britain was set up in 1958. Those departments have encouraged the proper preparation of packs for operations, bandages and a host of other medical aids that are dangerous to patients if unsterile.

The problems of using sterile supplies and re-using them, with considerable capital expenditure and large numbers of staff, prompted a concern with new products that would avoid all the burdens of conventional products.

The eighth edition, published in 1977, lists 183 firms but the number of product groups cannot readily be compared in view of the increase in their variety but probably something like 200 distinctive groups are listed. The catalogue is not comprehensive and includes only firms that were known by the compilers to exist and who, having been invited, agreed to submit some of the basic information requested. However, for most practical purposes, the directory lists the suppliers of disposable medical products. Nevertheless, much of the materials and machinery used in producing them could be diverted to non-medical use and some of the largest firms also operate in non-medical markets.

Thus in seeking the truly specialised medical product, the only proper category appears to be electromedical equipment.

There are many problems in identifying manufacturers of electromedical equipment in the UK. 'Electromedical equipment' has to be defined before all manufacturers of it can be listed, but the nature of the equipment and the continuous expansion of supply makes it impossible to identify in advance what this range of specialised manufacturers might comprise. Therefore, it seemed sensible to begin by trying to find out the names and addresses of firms who said that they manufactured such equipment. There appear to be three major sources of such information. The first is a list of suppliers compiled on a commercial basis by publishers. The best known of such lists is *The Hospitals and Health Services Yearbook and Directory of Hospital Suppliers*, published by the Institute of Health Service Administrators. The 1977 edition divides all supplies into 58 groups. Group 36 is entitled 'Electromedical Equipment' and comprises 90 firms. *The Health Services Yearbook* is compiled only every two years, and it suffers from the inevitable failure of all firms to supply information that will enable an entry to be made. It is also impossible to be sure that every firm that manufactures the equipment received an invitation to supply information.

In order to obtain the best possible coverage, a second source of information was sought. The Division of Bio-engineering at the Clinical Research Centre, Northwick Park Hospital, Middlesex, was approached. The centre is maintained by the Medical Research Council and carries out advanced medical research. One of the functions of the Division of Bio-engineering is to provide two information services. The first is called the Bio-medical Instrumentation Advisory Service (BIAS). That gives advice 'on commercially available instrumentation, equipment and materials'. To be able to do that, the catalogues of over 4,000 suppliers are available and are regularly updated. An analysis of the suppliers is made under 2,500 product groups, and is backed up by a library of buyers' guides, year books, exhibition catalogues, survey articles and data on other information and services.

The field covered by the service is continually growing in response to enquiries, particularly from people working in the Clinical Research Centre. Information on bio-medical instrumentation, and the materials and components for constructing these instruments, is essential to the work of the Bio-engineering Division. This covers electronics, analytical and general laboratory apparatus, chemical suppliers, aids for the disabled, hospital equipment, computers, calculators and many other associated forms of equipment.

The suppliers index lists the names and addresses of all the manufacturers and suppliers in the system, using 'visible indexing' cards filed in alphabetical order of company names. White cards are used for UK companies. The product index is compiled and presented in the same way. Cards are made out with a title for each product heading and are cross-referenced where appropriate.

The service is free to any member of the Medical Research Council staff and to grant holders. A small charge is made to others.

The other service available is known as the Fast Access Information Retrieval (FAIR). It is a computerised system indexing all relevant articles concerned with bio-engineering subjects. It extends to certain general matters, such as economic and industrial studies, but there are very few of them and they are mainly superficial papers that sometimes appear in technical journals concerned with other subjects.

The BIAS system would appear to be valuable to NHS supplies officers in order to ensure that they have the latest available information before undertaking any important specialised purchase. However, very few area or regional authorities are subscribers, although there are occasional enquiries from some of them. The service was used in the purchasing of equipment for the new Charing Cross Hospital. The director of the Division of Bio-engineering, H. Wolff, was able to obtain the agreement to rational purchasing of the 90 consultants concerned, as opposed to each consultant simply asking for what he knew about. That exercise was in about 1972 and there have not been any complaints with the results. No other hospital has made similar use of the system on such a scale.

This study used BIAS and *The Hospitals Yearbook* when a survey of electromedical manufacturers was undertaken.

The Hospitals Yearbook subdivides its groups and the three entitled Heart, Kidney and Lung Equipment, X-ray Apparatus and Accessories, and Mechanical and Electrical Measuring Instruments and Other Electromedical Equipment were used. From the firms listed there and similar firms listed at the Clinical Research Centre, 119 firms were chosen (excluding the ten firms in our experimental group).

A questionnaire was compiled and was sent out to an initial 25 firms on 25 July 1977. Reminders were sent on 8 September to 18 firms who had not answered. Questionnaires and letters were sent out to the remaining 94 during the next two weeks in September, and reminders to those who had not answered on 21 October 1977.

During December, ten of the firms who had not answered and who were situated around London were telephoned in an endeavour to encourage them to fill in the questionnaire, but all declined, saying they considered the information wanted to be confidential.

By the end of 1977, 13 firms had completed and returned the questionnaire and 36 replied in some other way. No reply was received from the remainder. (See Table 8.2.) An analysis of replies is given in Tables 8.3 and 8.4.

Table 8.2: Survey Response

Firms completing questionnaire	13
Firms refusing to give information	13
Firms saying not manufacturers of electromedical equipment	11
Firms returning questionnaire unanswered	9
Firms giving superficial information	3
	49
Firms not replying	70
Total	119

Table 8.3: Hospital Supplies Project, Survey of Electromedical Manufacturers 1977, Finance

Annual Accounts 1976 or nearest available year

Mfr	Total Home Sales £'000	Export Sales £'000	Total Annual Sales £'000	% to NHS	Research & Development	Net Profit £	Balance Sheet Assets £'000	No. of staff employed
1	254	152	406	Unknown	£10,000	8,966	144.5	24
2	1,700	–	1,700	95	Not Applic.	N/A	N/A	43
3	87	12	99	58	D 6,000	2,000 loss	?	17
4	6	2	8	80	–	–	–	30
5	10,600	112,900	123,500	2 (Medical sales)	R £12m D £8m	N/A	£30m	2,420
6	–	–	–	–	–	–	–	4
7	250	750	1,000	10	£40,000	80,000	450	72
8	20	5	25	60	D £500	5,000	?	3
9	703	326	1,029	65.7	D 45,785	38,784	2,094	39
10	See Table 4							
11	935	5	940	80	D 18,000	45,156	72,555	86
12	300	650	950	30	–	–	–	–
13	1,310	367	1,677	26	£20,000	86,000	697,000	292

N/A Not available, R Research, D Development.

Table 8.4: Hospital Supplies Project, Survey of Electromedical Manufacturers 1977, NHS Business

Mfr.	No. of Qualified Scientists etc.	No. of AHAs supplied	Satisfactory aspects	Unsatisfactory aspects	Comments
1	0	Most prob. all	Better payers than firms	Absolute absence of forward planning	All paperwork, orders, invoices different for each AHA
2	10	90%	Payment of accounts	Retention of 5% of invoices pending inspection by DHSS (can take 2 years)	X-ray unique. All orders placed by DHSS
3	2	43	1 Prompt payment 2 Large market for a particular product	1 Too many administrators 2 Useless competition between areas —sim. development in different areas	Large increases in tech/eng. staff in areas but much eqpt still being sent back to mfrs thus defeating purpose of extra staff
4	0	Many	All	None	
5	540	All	Pay when due	Inability to measure & be concerned with cost effectiveness of eqpt on their charge	
6	2	–	–	–	
7	12	7	Enthusiasm to improve org. and service	Communication between groups	A former President Inst. of Hospital Engineering—answers based on more than own business
8	0	?	There seems to be lack of communication between ord. agency & end user		1 director and 2 employees—all part-time
9	6	All	Payment within 3 months	Certain teaching hospitals with inefficient accounts depts. Slow payments.	Service accounts difficult with NHS. Great reluctance to pay realistic prices. Loss-making activity.
10	–	Prob. all	–	–	

Mfr.	No. of Qualified Scientists etc.	No. of AHAs supplied	Satisfactory aspects	Unsatisfactory aspects	Comments
11	10	?		No credit risks	Contractors (often our customers) may be in liquidation between us selling to to them and receiving cash. Sometimes dicey contractors are appointed.
12	–	–	–	–	
13	2	80%	No views	No views	

The third source of information was the *Business Monitor* published by the Business Statistics Office, which is part of the government statistical service. This publishes many quarterly statistical reports for different industries.

Several of them appear to be relevant to this study, but I decided to ask the Business Statistics Office to provide such information as it could about the particular range of products with which we were concerned. The office is unable to supply information if there is any risk of any particular firm being identified and because only a small number of firms were concerned, it was difficult for the office to assist as much as it would have wished. The information provided is given in Table 8.5. It will be seen that on this reckoning there were 41 available manufacturers with total sales of approximately £37 million, of which £13 million was obtained from export markets. Only 6 firms employed more than 400 people.

Table 8.5: Business Statistics Office, Sales of UK Manufacturers Production 1976, Readings Taken from Business Monitor PQ 364

			employment	
1	Heading 32		0-399	400+
	Electromedical apparatus:	enterprises	9	6
	Diagnostic equipment	total sales	£3,150 th	£24,603 th

(exports: 7 enterprises total sales £8,916 th)

			employment	
2	Heading 33		0-499	500+
	Electromedical apparatus:	enterprises	11	nil
	Therapeutic equipment	total sales	£6,154 th	
	(exports: 7 enterprises total sales £2,198 th)			
3	Heading 35		0-99	100+
	Electromedical apparatus:	enterprises	7	8
	Other	total sales	£2,118 th	£2,256 th
	(exports: 8 enterprises total sales £2,222 th)			

Source: Business Statistics Office, May 1977.

Conclusions

It is clear that there is a lack of published data about the health care supply industries, particularly for electromedical equipment. There are major difficulties in obtaining such data as many manufacturers are reluctant to disclose information which they regard as important and hence confidential or firms are reluctant to become involved in answering any more surveys. We have also approached all the relevant trade associations, but again it appears that either they do not have relevant data, or will not disclose it.

It would be wrong to assume that such information is essential. Firms are not in business to answer questionnaires and it is understandable that they are worried about competition or the possibility of competition, or the possibility of unhelpful government action if facts and figures are disclosed. On the other hand, it does appear to be a particularly British, or perhaps European, convention that businesses can only survive if they operate in the maximum possible secrecy. The American situation is very different and such openness does not appear to have damaged the American economy.

More immediately, one would have thought that the continued intervention of the Secretary of State for Health into the affairs of the health care industries in recent years would have alerted firms and trade associations to the need for the greatest amount of disclosure in order to ensure that any government policies are based on knowledge of the relevant facts and a proper appreciation of the consequences of policy decisions. The Collier Report, in particular, should have been a warning to the industries of the dangers of silence: it was prepared in great haste, it makes many assumptions about the range of products available and the significance of that range and it was not discussed with the industry in the course of preparation. As a result, there were many shortcomings in the report, it created considerable anxiety, it took up a great deal of the time of busy managers and, finally, was buried in effect by DHSS. It may have led to the creation of the working party to examine the case for a NHS supplies board; that would appear to be operating on a different basis, but again with inadequate consultation during preparation with the industries concerned.

There is in fact a very strong case for the fullest possible survey of the industries concerned with the NHS, embracing the role of imports, the number of similar products on the market, effective competition, and the extent of research and development work carried out in the industry. The financing of such a project might be done jointly between DHSS and the trade associations, but if not, the industries should consider undertaking the work themselves.

So far as the survey we carried out is concerned, the approach to 119 firms resulted in only 13 responses and not all of those produced completed questionnaires. It is not easy to assess the significance of such a survey. From one point of view it would appear that we have a response rate of about 10 per cent and that is likely to be statistically insignificant. On the other hand, we cannot be certain that all 119 firms received the questionnaire. If the 13 responses are seen as a proportion out of the 49 from whom some response was obtained, then the situation would appear to be something like a 26 per cent response. Neither basis of calculation produces an entirely satisfactory survey, to say the least, but it would be a mistake to dismiss the findings altogether.

On the basis of the 13 questionnaires returned with most sections completed, it would appear that most firms dealt with most area health authorities and thus would appear to have considerable experience of doing business with the NHS. Many of them were pleased with the prompt payment procedures of the NHS as compared with private industry's reluctance to pay, particularly in the last two or three years of recession, but most firms criticised the NHS for bureaucracy in many of its worst forms, a lack of planning of purchasing and a lack of financial and supplies control, and unsatisfactory servicing arrangements and payment for servicing in respect of electromedical equipment. Many authorities have complained of high servicing costs asked for by manufacturers and have begun a process of training their own staff to look after equipment. But having recruited additional staff for this purpose, there is evidence that they are still using manufacturers for the most difficult and expensive work. It would be difficult to evaluate the existing situation, but it is perhaps to be doubted whether the most economical form of servicing has yet been achieved.

The overall impression, however, of relations between suppliers and the health service in the light of this survey is one of relative contentment. It might also be complacency and one would like to see evidence of greater initiative from manufacturers in overcoming the defects of the NHS or helping the NHS to overcome some of its defects, but it must be remembered that we have not attempted a comparative survey of relations between firms in the private sector of the economy and it may well be that some of the faults identified are common to all forms of business activity.

Electromedical Equipment

This report does not aim to deal with the scientific and technological aspects of electromedical equipment, but it is clearly essential to grasp some of the basic characteristics and problems associated with such equipment.

There is an obvious difference between basic scientific research and the development of medical equipment. There is also an important distinction between research and production that needs to be as clear as possible if the difficulties in this sphere of the economy are to be appreciated. Research decisions are often made by colleges and research institutes divorced from any concern with practical application and, on the other hand, by manufacturers who are greatly concerned with the application of the knowledge discovered with the least necessary cost and in the shortest possible time. Sometimes the two approaches to research coincide and manufacturers sponsor 'pure' research, or a researcher working in a college makes a discovery that he communicates speedily to industry. But for most purposes the divorce is absolute and industry is solely concerned with investigations that are necessary in order to design products that can be manufactured and sold so as to cover all their costs, including a provision for the future, usually called 'profit'.

The chief difficulty for the manufacturer is to decide where to start. If he has an investment in an existing business, he tends to seek further opportunities within spheres of work that he has already tapped, and would usually prefer to adapt and improve an existing product than go into an entirely new product field, even if it is related to the equipment and expertise the firm already possesses. There is no obvious way of developing even on that basis. The firm will receive a wide number of comments on its products from many sources, particularly from customers and from its sales representatives and neither of those sources is necessarily objective. Sales representatives have a prejudice in favour of developing products that are easy to sell, and particularly, perhaps, wish the firm to complete a product range so that customers are encouraged to deal with a single manufacturer for a group of related requirements. For example, a manufacturer of X-ray machines is likely to build up a range so that he can equip a complete X-ray department in hospitals of all sizes. He cannot be sure that such a product range will be bought and he is faced with competition, often from abroad, and does not know whether a competitor somewhere is developing a similar product or service.

We found no evidence of manufacturers scanning the market carefully and trying to identify needs within the NHS that they could usefully transform into solutions by means of electromedical equipment. That could mean that everything it needs is already being produced. On the other hand, there are rumours of inventions, from both doctors and scientists within the NHS and some of them do lead to new products, or modifications of existing ones.

There are other sources of innovation that we have not investigated. But what does appear to be missing is any kind of planned review of medical practices that lend themselves sensibly, economically, aesthetically and ethically to mechanisation in some form or another, interpreting that word to cover electrical and electronic devices. There would be many problems in initiating and guiding such a continuous surveillance of need, but there are no obvious reasons against its being attempted and developed, however slowly. Presumably this would need a combination of effort by the NHS, probably through the DHSS, and some or all of the relevant manufacturers, at least those operating in the United Kingdom.

In some cases, new products do develop as a result of a problem revealed in the course of treatment. The example that was reported to us arose from a particular kind of surgical operation and the happy accident of one member of the surgical team knowing an engineer with particular interests and abilities, who could help to devise the particular mechanism that seems to have solved the problem. The process of solution involved many hours of discussion, observation of a number of operations and numerous tests and experiments both within the laboratory and the hospital. That effort has left open a number of problems that still have to be solved. Moreover, the mechanism devised is only used by one surgeon and the same kind of operation can be performed by other surgeons using different techniques, possibly because one surgeon does not know what other surgeons are using.

Some of the problems facing manufacturers can be gauged from the following extract from the 1976 Annual Report of the American Health Industry Manufacturers Association:

> *Medical and Scientific Section*
>
> The projects completed by the Medical and Scientific Section during the past year covered a wide range of technical and scientific subjects. Under the chairmanship of Robert L. Valentine, PhD (Sherwood Medical), were projects related to product development, pre-market testing, postmarket testing, postmarket surveillance and biomedical liaison. In addition, special activities were carried out by the Medical and Scientific Section's various committee's for both devices and diagnostics.
>
> In keeping with the section's heavy emphasis on education, both divisions of the section worked to sponsor an educational seminar on 'The "How To" on Premarket Clearance for Medical Devices and Diagnostics.'
>
> The section's diagnostics division was involved in a variety of activities designed to interpret and comment on the regulatory developments of the Federal government and to educate members accordingly. The Biomedical Liaison Committee compiled and published three directories of diagnostic product manufacturers in the United States, Japan and Europe. A report on techniques for the handling of hazardous materials in the laboratory was developed by the Special Activities Committee. The Premarket Testing Committee formulated a proposed plan for supplying pedigreed serum samples to member companies. Meanwhile, an educational project in the area of postmarket field corrective action was undertaken by the diagnostics and devices Postmarket Surveillance Committees.
>
> In the area of premarket testing of devices, two task forces conducted significant projects on trace metals in medical materials and on resources for premarket testing. A third task force completed a bibliography on preclinical testing, and its equally important document on clinical visits was near completion at year's end.
>
> The Devices Special Activities Committee provided oversight for two significant activities. First, the Blood Oxygenator Task Force, after many hours of work, produced a draft document relating to blood oxygenator standards. Second, a study of the incidence of particular matter in various intravenous devices was conducted. Three lengthy research reports resulting from the efforts of the Particulate Matter Subcommittee have been forwarded to the FDA [Food and

Drugs Administration] in furtherance of HIMA's work with the Agency on this subject. This research, the results of which have now been widely circulated, will form the basis of a HIMA program to be presented at the 1977 Annual Meeting of the Association for the Advancement of Medical Instrumentation.

In addition to the above activities, the Section in 1976 contributed in a significant manner to HIMA's work on FDA's proposed Good Laboratory Practices regulations and to communicating with the Environmental Protection Agency concerning the evaluation of toxicological reports on the sterilizing agent ethylene oxide.

International Trade in Health Care Supplies

It is beyond the scope of this study to attempt to review health care industries throughout the world, but international trade in health care supplies is a dimension of the British problem that must receive some consideration. Perhaps the main question to ask is: what international factors influence the NHS and its suppliers? Is there competition between the NHS and overseas customers of British manufacturers? Are many supplies obtained from overseas manufacturers by the NHS? What barriers exist to international trade in health care supplies?

There is no evidence that the NHS suffers from the interest of British manufacturers in exporting. There is no doubt that very great efforts to expand exports in recent years have been made by many manufacturers with very considerable pressure being exerted by DHSS to promote exports.

In 1964, the British Hospitals Export Council was established by the industry and in 1976 it changed its name to the British Health Care Export Council. It now has 250 members representing all aspects of health care activity, from the early stages of planning, equipping, staffing and maintenance.

In 1975, the DHSS published a report on NHS purchasing prepared by a working party under the chairmanship of A.J. Collier, Deputy Secretary of the department. It has been discussed earlier, but it is appropriate to note here that it was concerned with reviewing NHS procurement and to make recommendations about it 'bearing in mind the need to strengthen the home market as a basis for exports'. Unfortunately, there was no consultation with the industry about the report and in fact they did not know of its existence until it had begun to be circulated. The report was not well received by the industry which is well aware of the importance of exporting. The chairman of the Medical Instruments Group of the Scientific Instrument Manufacturers Association, D.A. Patient, said that 'most of our companies do far more than 50 per cent of their business overseas and export is the real life blood of business which has available only a relatively small home market'.

One of the major recommendations of the report was for a 'limited list' of approved manufacturers and there was associated with that a suggestion that all equipment should be passed through a rigorous evaluation scheme. Such a list, it was thought, would bring benefits by reducing the number of suppliers and in turn give great support to assist development of new equipment. Mr Patient comments: 'all this raises the spectre of what happened to the UK X-ray industry thirty years ago as a result of similar policies to those outlined in this current report'.

Many manufacturers believe that the 'limited list' approach would be destructive of good performance even for those who secured a place in it. For those excluded, export would remain their only outlet, and that without the essential basis of a supporting home market. Overseas purchasing authorities would inevitably come to view such a list as a 'buyers' guide', so the unfortunate manufacturer would see his export business in even greater jeopardy.

So far as the evaluation proposal is concerned, Mr Patient believed that it would discourage manufacturers from allocating funds for development, particularly as there could be no assurance that 'even if the final product was effective, it would secure a place in the list'.

Whilst favouring the evaluation system, the Scientific Instrument Manufacturers Association believe that health authorities should give attention to the question of defining minimum performance standards for equipment required for a given purpose. Manufacturers could then design to meet this, plus whatever additional features they might choose to offer, knowing that at least their equipment would be evaluated, and thereafter be accepted, provided it met the requirements.

In 1975, the British export of medical equipment was valued at £127 million which showed an increase of 55 per cent over 1974. In 1976, there was only a small increase in value over the preceding year. Thus Britain has not done well in seizing opportunities for expansion. It has been estimated that in the OPEC countries there will be an investment in health care of £3,000 million over the next five years. There is particular interest in turnkey projects and package contracts, whereby either complete hospitals are planned, designed, built and equipped or whole departments of hospitals are provided by a single supplier.

Foreign Companies in the UK

No comprehensive study exists of the number of foreign companies operating in the medical supplies industry in the UK but there is no doubt that there are a great number, largely subsidiaries of American companies. This is especially true in respect of pharmaceuticals, but Swiss and other foreign companies are also significant. Johnson and Johnson is a well-known American firm operating extensively in the UK and the American Hospital Supply Corporation now has interests here.

It is therefore important to obtain some view of the American industry and fortunately a considerable amount of information is available in that country. In an article in *Fortune* in January 1970 entitled 'The Medical Industrial Complex' by H.B. Meyers, it was reported that expenditure for health care in the United States in 1969 amounted to 63 billion dollars. The market was growing at that time at an annual rate of between 10 and 15 per cent. There were about 500 important firms in the industry. In a specialised journal, *Surgical Business* (January 1976), the total medical care expenditure in 1976 was put at over 130 billion dollars. That, of course, was an estimate for the year and represents about double the expenditure of 1969. In a publication entitled *United States Industrial Outlook 1977*, it was reported that the total expenditure on X-ray and electromedical equipment in 1976 had amounted to 890 million dollars, which represented a 30 per cent increase over the previous year. Ten years earlier the total expenditure was 233 million dollars. The estimate for 1977 was 1,110 million dollars.

Note

1. S. Hyman, *The Hospital Supplies Market–Disposable/Expendable Products: Britain, France, West Germany*, Frost and Sullivan Inc., 1976.

9 TEN SUPPLIERS OF ELECTROMEDICAL EQUIPMENT

Ten firms agreed to take part in the project. They were recruited, on the advice of the King's Fund Hospital Centre, by using the *Hospitals' Yearbook* as the best way of finding the names and addresses of firms dealing with relevant supplies to the NHS.

A long list of firms was drawn up. As it was decided that it would be necessary to deal with firms in and around the London area, that list was first reduced by eliminating eligible firms based elsewhere.

A letter was written to all of these firms asking for a meeting. Some of the firms on the list were eliminated after they had replied saying that they were not manufacturers but wholesalers or distributors of medical and surgical equipment. We then telephoned the managing directors of the remaining manufacturing firms and personal contact helped to persuade them to co-operate with the project where they had indicated some hesitation in meeting us.

In this way, ten firms out of the 19 firms we first approached were found who agreed to co-operate with the project.

We promised to treat any information obtained as confidential and proposed to seek their approval to any report that mentioned their name. If for any reason they did not wish their name to appear, the report would be about an anonymous firm and their identity would be disguised. Given the geographical constraints, the firms were chosen with an acceptable degree of randomness and this would appear to be representative of manufacturers of electromedical equipment in the United Kingdom. The following individual reports were based on a series of quarterly visits, and the information obtained has been summarised under the same categories for each firm in order to facilitate comparison. A summary is given at the end, but the reader is able to form his own conclusions from the separate reports.

Firm A: Cardiac Recorders Ltd, 34 Scarborough Road, London N4

A small British company formed nineteen years ago to manufacture coronary and intensive care monitoring equipment, defibrillators, pacemakers, electro-cardiac life support systems and incontinence aids. The company has expanded steadily over the last five years with a turnover of £434,000 in 1972 to £1,200,000 in 1976. There are a total of 120 staff employed, including research and development staff, plant workers, sales, service and administration staff. There are three production sites, one in Sheffield making incontinence aids, one in Fife, Scotland, and the main factory in North London. Although the company is small by general industrial standards, it is large in terms of British electromedical manufacturers. The company's sales are divided into approximately 50 per cent home market and 50 per cent export, with the export market increasing steadily. Sales to the NHS hospitals are approximately 90 per cent of all home sales.

New Products and Developments

The company has just developed a portable monitor and defibrillator which is now on sale to the NHS. The Scientific and Technical Branch of DHSS took about a year to complete their evaluation, but the company had begun to sell to the NHS before the evaluation was complete.

There have been no recent developments in equipment apart from this portable monitor and defibrillator but the company is constantly redesigning, modifying, and improving their equipment.

Manufacturing and Selling for the NHS

There are six salesmen/engineers working in the UK field, mostly calling on NHS hospitals. They have contact with most hospitals and demonstrate their equipment to medical and engineering staff; they have little direct contact with supplies officers. All supplies staff interviewed in the project described the company as a manufacturer of high quality equipment with reliable service and maintenance; generally, a good firm to do business with.

Although there are no compulsions attached to dealing with the DHSS, the company maintains a good working relationship with the Scientific and Technical Branch and submits its equipment for quality checks and evaluation, mainly as a gesture of goodwill and in order to maintain its high standards and reputation. However, the company is aware that the Scientific and Technical Branch sometimes takes a long time to carry out evaluations. In a highly competitive market this has obvious drawbacks for manufacturers. The company is usually asked by the DHSS to participate in any NHS/manufacturer enquiries carried out. For example, the managing director is participating in discussions on both the Collier Report and the survey of service and maintenance of medical and scientific equipment being carried out by the DHSS.

NHS Paperwork and System of Payments to Manufacturers

The company has noticed a gradual increase in paperwork in the last three or four years attached to selling equipment to the NHS. However, there has also been a marked improvement in payments made by hospitals for goods received. By and large, payments are made promptly, although a small percentage of NHS hospitals still take up to three months to settle accounts.

Most quotation forms sent from different areas and regions in the NHS have become standard and present no administrative problems for the company. However, these forms are usually sent singly and the company have to make photocopies for their own use. Order forms too have become more standardised and straightforward and it is usually clear where the invoices should be sent and the equipment delivered.

A salesman for the company has noticed an increase in the number of NHS staff sitting in on pre-tender negotiations in hospitals. He cited an example of a meeting where he was demonstrating his company's equipment at which there were three administrative, two medical and two nursing staff in attendance.

Orders for equipment come from hospitals, districts, areas and sometimes regions for revenue equipment, although by and large the orders from the region are for capital purchasing.

The NHS still tends to order revenue equipment in bulk at the end of the financial year. However, the company does not mind this because after nineteen years they are fairly well prepared. It is also good for a company to have this type of rush as it keeps the organisation on its toes.

The company has had very few dealings with regional scientific officers and the managing director does not see the point of increasing them when he has direct access to the DHSS.

Service and Maintenance

In the last two or three years the NHS has become more demanding about manufacturers' service and maintenance agreements. This obviously presents no problems for the company as there was unanimous praise amongst NHS staff interviewed for the service and maintenance provided by this company. At the same time, there has been an increase in the amount of maintenance to equipment carried out by hospitals themselves. The company has been involved with the DHSS in the launching of a circular to districts, areas and regions saying that only manufacturers and other approved bodies should maintain and modify electromedical equipment. This circular has been drawn up with the help of some manufacturers who are concerned about the numbers of hospital engineers and odd-job men who take equipment to pieces, either to adapt it or repair it. Obviously safety standards are in jeopardy when this happens and lives could be lost if the equipment is not maintained by experts.

Deliveries of Equipment to Hospitals

The company has its own delivery service. One delivery van servies the south of England and salesmen deliver over other parts of the country. The Scotland and Sheffield branches also make deliveries via their sales staff. The company sometimes uses British Rail, but never road transport. The company does not at present charge for deliveries to hospitals.

Competition from Other Manufacturers

In the past few years competition has increased and there are more manufacturers, both British and foreign, attempting to sell electronic medical equipment to the NHS. Most of the competition is from abroad, mainly the USA, Germany and Holland. Most of the English manufacturers, we were told, went out of business in 1962-3 after they had underestimated the difficulties in dealing with the NHS. Firms gave up completely on monitoring equipment after some inaccurate forecasting of NHS needs by the DHSS. At present, there are only four British firms specialising in the manufacture of cardiac monitoring equipment. The profit margin on this type of equipment is small compared with other industries so the company survives on its long-standing goodwill with the NHS, good equipment, constant modification and development of products to suit customers' needs and a steady low profit. The company was the first to develop the defibrillator in England and the second in the world.

Wholesalers and Distributors

Almost all home market sales are distributed by the company itself. The exceptions are one-off requests from wholesalers who have been asked by a hospital to obtain a piece of equipment made specifically by this company. These cases are few. Agents and distributors are used mainly for export sales to the USA and most European countries. The company has been approached by distribution agents who sell in the Middle East and African markets on a package deal basis, but so far has not become involved.

Advertising and Publicity

The company's sales representatives distribute catalogues and sales literature to medical and engineering staff in the NHS hospitals they visit. Little advertising is done by direct mail, but the company advertises in trade and professional journals. Its advertising is to a specific market and as such excludes most NHS supplies staff, although it has advertised in the handbook of the Association of National Health Service Supplies Officers.

Sales representatives do not take orders for equipment, but are still considered by the company as being directly responsible for sales to the NHS. They are considered to be a source of advertising and market research for the company as well as having a service and maintenance function. They feed back information on equipment being used in NHS hospitals and on the company's own 'in use' testing of equipment. Occasionally, a salesman makes a direct sale to a consultant who wants a piece of equipment, but this means that the consultant has already persuaded the supplies department to accept his order.

Trade Associations

The company belongs to a trade association and is closely involved with the British Institute of Safety. This brings it into much closer working contact with DHSS, as the managing director represents his association to the DHSS. The advantages of belonging to a trade association are difficult to quantify in terms of sales and turnover. It is rather a prestige benefit plus a more direct access to DHSS.

Firm B: GEC Medical Equipment Ltd, PO Box No 2, East Lane, Wembley, Middx HA9 7PR

A principal subsidiary of a large British electrical and electronics organisation, it manufactures and supplies a comprehensive range of diagnostic X-ray and ultrasonic imaging equipment. Its annual turnover is approximately £18 million, the X-ray side of production accounting at present for about 75 per cent of business.

Sales are divided almost equally between export and home markets. In the latter case, the company gained during the financial year 1976-7, an approximate 24 per cent share of the DHSS £17 million spent on X-ray equipment; main competition coming from West Germany, Holland, France and the United States.

Staff employed total 1,100 comprising production at the company's factories in Wembley and Croydon; administration mainly from head office in Wembley; sales and service at the twenty branch offices in the UK and in centres abroad.

The company operates overseas through its own independent sales and service centres, from corporate centres and also through overseas agents. Equipment is exported to 82 countries, notably in the Middle East, Africa, the Far East and Australasia; there is a planned commitment to increase their presence in Europe and the USA. Its publicity department ensures attendance at an increasing number of overseas exhibitions.

Product Planning and Development

A wide range of equipment of varying complexity is manufactured, suiting the requirements of all medical centres from local clinics to the largest teaching hospitals. In the X-ray field, major equipment may be broadly divided into three categories:

1. Generator systems as a power source for an extensive range of X-ray tubes. This involves both static installations and mobile units.
2. Support systems for both tubes and patients. These vary widely in design according to the nature of the examination and the ability of the patient to adapt to it.
3. Fluoroscopic image intensifier systems for dynamic viewing of the image.

Every effort is made to ensure individual units easily connect to form totally co-ordinated systems and as far as is technically possible, policy is to make new products compatible with existing ones. Development of new products is based upon a complete understanding of market requirements through continuing dialogue with the medical disciplines the company serves and the latest technology from the massive research facilities of the holding company and from Medical Physics Departments of the NHS.

General policy is to design for international acceptance, influential factors being reliability, value for money and the ability to maintain and service new units in the field. Once a design has been accepted, prototypes are launched and environmentally tested in the company's laboratory before proving themselves in hospital field trials. The developmental procedure can thus take from three to five years and so the original concept needs to be ahead of its time. Recent developments include a capacitor discharge mobile generator, which it is believed is the best on the market.

Service and Maintenance

Included in the purchase price of an item of equipment are delivery and installation costs. In addition, a warranty is given for the first year, during which a predetermined number of free service visits are made; their frequency depends on the complexity of the equipment installed.

After this initial year, company service engineers will undertake preventive maintenance on a contract basis if requested and will periodically visit the hospital by appointment, charging on an hourly basis. In addition engineers provide a twenty-four hour emergency service to all users in the event of a breakdown.

The company runs a training scheme for hospital engineers to enable them to carry out first-line repair and maintenance, but is resisting the trend towards hospitals' gaining entire control over maintenance of its equipment. Some areas and regions have been trying to break existing service contracts and avoid preventive maintenance contracts at the time of purchase. This has forced the company to reappraise its maintenance system, especially as there have been occasional claims by the DHSS that a visit has been made unnecessarily or a charge is excessive. The company claims that its apparently high charges arise from the DHSS demands for stringent safety standards and also from the need to maintain in each area sufficient engineers to enable an efficient programme of immediate as well as preventive maintenance. By and large, the DHSS allocates insufficient funds for capital and replacement expenditure and the company finds itself maintaining items of equipment which should be replaced.

Business Dealings with the DHSS

The company is anxious to maintain good relations with DHSS personnel at all levels because the DHSS is its major single customer in the UK.

Money channelled through the NHS is classified basically into two funding arrangements, i.e. 'capital' or 'revenue' schemes, and the company uses two distinct methods according to the type of scheme. Revenue money in the main covers ongoing costs of replacement items and these are dealt with by the area health authorities through their respective regional health authorities. Individual orders from the AHA and RHA are placed directly with the company and invoiced to the authority concerned on the company's own standard invoice document. By contrast, capital funds can only be allocated to the regional health authorities by the DHSS because they often involve complete re-equipping of existing X-ray rooms and the equipping of new departments.

Orders received from the DHSS are invoiced on a DHSS designed form and are paid direct to the company against an 'annual contract' which is the single most important document relating to UK sales. At the beginning of the DHSS financial year the company is required to submit quotations covering the range of items offered, adding or deleting new or obsolete units. As is the case with other government-controlled contracts, the DHSS have the right to petition for a price reduction where they feel an extreme profit is likely to be made. In this way equipment purchase costs are established for the year although the company is allowed to make representations, requesting an increase in contract prices due to exceptional, unforeseen circumstances arising during the year. The contract is however, more than a price-regulating document because its acceptance implies, in addition, an acceptance of the technical specifications of each equipment item. These specifications are investigated by the DHSS Scientific and Technical Branch. Ultimately, the assessment of equipment performance and safety is determined by the specification laid down, great attention being paid to radiological protection as well as the usual electrical and mechanical requirements.

The DHSS are also concerned with equipment prototypes on field evaluation trials and interested parties monitor the unit's performance. The Scientific and Technical Branch are invited to suggest modifications and when all parties are satisfied, the evaluation ends and specifications can be drawn up, enabling the new equipment to be added to the current DHSS contract. The company bears the cost of such trials, no charges are levied on the hospitals concerned. With this close co-operation during design and development, both the company and the NHS benefit in the ultimate production of new and better equipment.

The relationship is not without its problems. Any company would wish production to be in line with demand. The DHSS is a singularly difficult customer in that the inability of NHS departments to carry over revenue allocations from one year to another can lead to rush ordering of equipment with consequent, occasional inability of the company to supply at the close of the financial year or alternatively excess stocks being held in readiness for anticipated orders which do not arrive due to funds being allocated elsewhere.

Firm C: Charles Harmer & Sons Ltd, 29-31 Danbury Street, Islington, London N1

A small British company occupying two four-storey shops in north London, it has been selling X-ray accessories since 1886. It was the first company to manufacture metal X-ray film cassettes. Their main products are X-ray cassettes, illuminators and wheeled stands. The cassettes are made to take any type of film made by a variety of manufacturers. Twenty-three staff are employed; twenty-one are engaged in production, one is a typist, the other is the managing director and grandson of the founder.

The annual turnover of the company is small and we have been asked not to disclose it. Of the equipment manufactured 80 per cent is sold to the NHS, 15 per cent is exported and 5 per cent is sold to industry and private medicine. At present export sales are expanding, particularly to the Middle East and Africa. The company is selling its products to agents who are building and equipping new hospitals in these areas. Although the exact extent is not known, their NHS business has contracted in the last two or three years because of the financial restrictions on capital building and plant.

New Products and Developments

During the past few years the company has been concerned with modifying the design of X-ray accessories to fit in with the needs of the NHS. For example, some accessories are tailor-made to suit specific requirements of different radiology departments. They have designed a hinged X-ray viewer that, where space is limited, can be swung back out of the way when not in use. Prototypes of new designs are 'in use' tested in hospitals where they will be given maximum testing for quality and durability, e.g. busy accident units where the equipment receives harsh treatment.

The company was asked by the DHSS to design a nurse-proof battery-operated X-ray viewer so that it is impossible for nursing staff to use anything except batteries. This demand arose after a nurse wired up a battery-operated viewer to the mains after the battery had become exhausted, although it was marked 'DC current only' and the viewer blew up. A battery-operated model was then produced by the company that cannot be adapted for mains operation. The DHSS will incorporate the company's prototype into a standard specification with safety instructions issued to hospitals.

Other modifications to equipment are mainly simplifications of manufacture which cut out waste at the production level.

Business with the NHS

The company is selling X-ray cassettes under a national contract and so the Scientific and Technical Branch of the DHSS carry out periodic quality checks on the equipment. The Scientific and Technical Branch has been using this company's expertise to design a prototype X-ray viewer in order to produce standard specifications for the NHS. However, the branch worked on the prototype for several months before asking for the company's advice, and the X-ray viewer the branch produced was made of a metal of too heavy a gauge with badly designed illumination and which would cost three times as much as the company's own illuminator. It is now expected that the DHSS will produce a standard specification for X-ray viewers based on this company's model.

The managing director has also been asked by the DHSS to participate in discussions on the National Supplies Vocabulary. The DHSS are holding a series of meetings to discuss all sections of the vocabulary with the appropriate manufacturers. At this meeting, DHSS representatives explain the system of coding used on the twenty-six volumes of the Vocabulary within the section on diagnostic equipment.

The company does not have much contact with supplies staff except at the ordering stage. It deals mainly with engineers, radiologists and radiographers and does not consider that supplies staff are technically able to make purchasing decisions on X-ray equipment. The managing director mentioned an example of a NHS supplies officer who rang him to ask for a price quotation on an X-ray viewer and asked if he could explain what an X-ray viewer is.

NHS Paperwork, Administration and Payment System

Most orders received from the NHS are standard documents and present no problems for the company. However, it would help if two or possibly three quotation forms were sent instead of one so that the company had a file and working copy to keep. Although it is an isolated case, the firm was asked to quote 1973 prices as well as 1977 prices for a new hospital development last year which has been delayed for four years and where the region is trying to update its price schedules. This involved the company in time-consuming activity, going through old price records.

Quick payment discounts are given to NHS customers at the rate of 5 per cent for a payment made on the fourteenth of the month following the date of the invoice. Most NHS purchasers take advantage of this. Bulk delivery discounts are given to the NHS by giving free carriage on large orders.

Service and Maintenance

The NHS sends back X-ray accessories directly to the company for repair so there are no service engineers employed in the field. Some minor repairs, such as tubes and lamps in illuminators, can be tackled by hospital staff themselves but since the company guarantees its equipment for six months, the hospitals usually send equipment back for repair.

Competition from Other Manufacturers

The company is one of only two British manufacturers of X-ray cassettes. 60 per cent of cassettes used by the NHS are imported from the USA, Germany, Holland, Austria and Sweden. However, 99 per cent of X-ray illuminators purchased by the NHS are made in Britain.

Wholesalers and Distributors

At present the company sells 50 per cent of their equipment directly and 50 per cent is handled by distributors and wholesalers: four years ago 80 per cent of their sales were made through wholesalers. The wholesalers employ sales representatives and provide advertising and delivery services. Since the company has no sales staff and only one van, the wholesaler fulfils a useful function. The wholesalers' field staff is able to monitor 'in use' testing of equipment. The company uses approximately eight wholesalers: over 50 per cent of their non-direct sales is handled by one firm. The NHS does not pay more for the company's equipment if they buy it through a distributor, as the distributor is given a 20-25 per cent discount from the manufacturer. Sometimes both the company and the wholesaler are asked to quote prices for the same equipment. There is no arrangement made between them although quite often each knows that the other is also tendering. Either could gain the business, depending on deliveries as well as prices. Wholesalers are known to undercut manufacturers and lose money in order to gain NHS business. However, in most cases the manufacturer and the wholesaler will know that they have both been approached by the NHS and will agree on who should quote the most advantageous offer. Sometimes the company will agree to forego the business because the deliveries are inconvenient.

Advertising and Publicity

The company relies a great deal on wholesalers' representatives to carry out their advertising and distribute their catalogues. In addition, they send out catalogues to regional supplies officers, radiologists and X-ray departments generally. They advertise in the *Hospitals' Yearbook* and the handbook of the Association of National Health Service Supplies Officers. Advertisements are also placed in a monthly radiography magazine.

Almost all the NHS supplies staff interviewed had never heard of this company. The one who did know of it and purchased from it did so through wholesalers because they said the equipment is cheaper and deliveries are more efficient.

Trade Associations

The company does not belong to any trade associations because there are few manufacturers in Britain making this type of equipment.

Firm D: Hewlett Packard Ltd, King Street Lane, Winnersh, Wokingham, Berks RG11 5AR

Part of a large American owned multi-national company with six main divisions, one of which is the worldwide medical division with its headquarters in Boston, Mass. The UK medical division has a total of forty staff including administrative, technical, service and sales engineers, and its medical equipment is manufactured mainly in Germany, the remainder in the USA. The range of equipment made by the medical division is large and includes patient monitoring equipment for intensive care, cardiac and coronary care, patient management computing systems, defibrillators, long function equipment, peri-natal monitoring equipment, X-ray products and consumable products for use with equipment. In total about 50 per cent of the UK medical division business is in patient monitoring equipment. The worldwide turnover of the medical electronics division is approximately £60 million, which represents 10 per cent of the whole company worldwide.

New Products and Developments

The company's medical equipment is manufactured outside the UK and the impetus for new products comes from all over the world. Most ideas for equipment or modifications comes from medical staff in hospitals, although the company has a 9 per cent research and development budget allocated from the annual profits. 'In house' research carried out by the company is mainly concerned with making equipment more reliable and increasing the number of functions, although in the past a large part of the research and development budget was spent on very large computerised patient management equipment designed to analyse patient monitoring information for a whole region.

In the last eighteen months the company has developed a new oxymeter, a lung testing machine, and a portable four-channel ECG machine which is the same size as the previous single channel machine. They have also just marketed the first battery/mains-operated defibrillator which is safer than the other defibrillators on the market and has been approved by the DHSS. In the consumable category, the company is selling pre-gelled electrodes for use with ECG equipment.

Generally in the field of medical electronic equipment, developments have been towards micro-equipment and all large manufacturers are working towards decreasing the size of equipment while increasing its functions.

Business Dealings with the NHS

The company deals with all levels of the NHS but mainly with medical and technical staff. The eight medical engineers/salesmen have only limited contact with NHS supplies staff, usually at the stage where a piece of equipment is being ordered. In spite of this limited contact, all the supplies staff interviewed had heard of the company, most said their equipment was used in the area and all of them said the equipment was very good but expensive. The most common comments were that the company's equipment represents the Rolls Royce end of the medical electronics equipment market.

Recently the company has extended its contact with regional supplies staff in some regions by arranging meetings to discuss the problem of NHS money being wasted by medical and nursing staff using their budgets to order small quantities of consumables, such as electrodes for ECG machines and disposable patient attachments. The company has been suggesting at these meetings that an area contract for these items would be cheaper for both the company and the NHS. However, the reorganised health service allows budget holders to spend a limited amount without reference to a higher authority, so it is up to supplies officers to persuade them to use regional or area contracts.

The company was asked to sell equipment to the DHSS so that it could be evaluated at the new testing centres set up throughout the country in response to the Collier report. Their patient monitoring equipment has been sent to three testing centres and the electro-bio-medical engineering departments of the regional health authorities supervising the tests. The company has told the DHSS that it does not approve of the idea of an eventual limited list of manufacturers emerging from these tests although it is quite sure it should be included in the list.

The company has a good working relationship with the Scientific and Technical Branch and usually arranges for all new products and developments to be submitted to the Branch for checking and testing. Perhaps because the DHSS is dealing with a prestige company, the checking of equipment is usually quick and efficient. For example, a new defibrillator was completed early in 1977 and was tested in July 1977 while the company's medical manager waited so that he was able to return to his company the same day with the equipment accepted by DHSS.

NHS Paperwork, Administration and Ordering Systems

On the whole, the company finds NHS quotation and order forms are similar throughout the country and present no administrative problems. However, standard quotation forms do not have enough space for the company to give sufficient details of equipment and it prints its own quotation forms which are designed to meet the company's needs. This is a company that can afford to do this, whereas some of the smaller organisations who make medical equipment would not print quotation forms when the NHS ones are inadequate.

The company finds that NHS customers usually pay invoices of equipment within thirty days of delivery. They offer a quick payment discount of 3½ per cent for payment within fifteen days and 4 per cent if cash is sent with the order. Usually the 4 per cent discounts are taken on very large capital scheme orders but the fifteen day 3½ per cent discount is not taken frequently by NHS customers and sometimes the system is abused when an area or a region, asking for discount prices, fails to pay within the fifteen-day period.

The company never charges for carriage or delivery in addition to quoted prices as the equipment costs to the NHS includes an overall percentage for delivery. It uses its own transport system of thirty vehicles which it shares with the other five UK divisions.

Service and Maintenance

All equipment purchased by the NHS from the company is serviced free for the first year. These service costs are included in the selling price of the equipment. In 1977, the company employed nine service engineers, one service supervisor, a service manager, and a technical support man at headquarters. The service staff operate from four branches in the UK. The company is aware of an increase in NHS 'in house' servicing of equipment in regions where medical physics and electro-bio-medical departments are flourishing. The company's response to this is to offer to provide formal instruction for NHS engineers which they call a support programme. In this way they cut down on the risk to patients and the good name of the company which sometimes arise from unskilled interference in electromedical equipment. The company has a library of a thousand video-cassette tapes available to hospitals in the UK to train medical, nursing and engineering staff in the use of their equipment. All the company's equipment has a seven-year guarantee of spare part replacement after the life of the equipment is officially over. They make as many new products as possible compatible with old ones to cut out waste and to make NHS purchasing more economic. All the supplies staff interviewed remarked upon the high standards of the company's service and maintenance.

Competition from Other Manufacturers

The company's biggest rivals in the field of patient monitoring equipment are a large Swiss-owned multinational company and a large Danish-owned company.

Wholesalers and Distributors

The company does not use wholesalers and distributors but does have a distributor in Ireland who markets and maintains their equipment in hospitals. The exception is for a new type of stethoscope which the company is manufacturing and which they feel would be better marketed by a distributor.

Advertising and Publicity

The company has an annual budget of 2 per cent of its turnover to spend on advertising, a large proportion of which is spent on a regular mailing list to NHS staff who are sent catalogues and technical leaflets. Their advertising is aimed largely at specialist medical staff in the NHS and they do not deal with supplies officers to any great extent. However, regional supplies officers have recently been added to their regular mailing list along with regional scientific officers, regional medical officers, and regional electro-bio-medical engineers.

The company employs eight medical engineers as salesmen, who contact medical staff, electro-bio-medical engineers and medical physics departments in hospitals. Sales representatives take technical literature around to hospitals with them, arrange demonstrations, and monitor 'in use' testing of equipment and communicate the need for products to their company. These salesmen/engineers are chosen for their high calibre as technicians and representatives of the company. Selling is an important part of the philosophy of the company and staff are expected to sell a good reputation as well as excellent equipment. Exhibitions are less favoured by the company as a source of advertising in the last three years, and of fifty held every year, the company takes part in approximately sixteen.

Trade Associations

The company belongs to two large trade associations which they believe has the advantage of keeping them in close contact with other manufacturers and gives them additional representation with the DHSS. However, the company prides itself on its direct, informal and efficient working relationships with the DHSS.

Firm E: Kontron Instruments Ltd, PO Box 188, Watford, WD2 4YX

Part of the Swiss Hoffmann-La Roche worldwide organisation. The UK company specialises in the marketing and selling of medical and analytical equipment manufactured within and for the organisation. The medical equipment consists of patient monitors and patient monitoring systems, which are manufactured in the UK by an associated company, respiratory equipment, cardiology equipment, ultrasonic equipment for obstetrics and cardiology accessories. The analytical equipment, which includes gamma and beta counters, centrifuges, amino-acid analysers and blood grouping equipment is manufactured within the organisation in France, Germany and Switzerland. The equipment sold by the company is divided into approximately 70 per cent medical and 30 per cent analytical, although there is a movement towards an increase in the amount of analytical equipment sold. The turnover of the Kontron organisation worldwide is in the order of £80 million, with the UK company's turnover approaching £3 million.

The company started selling to the NHS in 1973 and at present 99 per cent of their medical equipment sales and 80 per cent of their analytical equipment sales are to the NHS; the remaining 20 per cent of the analytical sales are to industry. The company has a staff of about thirty, which includes sales and service, whilst its associated United Kingdom company has over 100.

New Products and Developments

In mid-1977 the UK company launched an ultrasonic real-time scanner for use in foetal monitoring at a symposium at Birmingham University. This is the company's first real-time scanner to be launched on the British market and it is now selling them to the NHS. The company has also recently begun to manufacture ventilation and respiratory equipment which is now being used in NHS hospitals. Ideas for new equipment come from worldwide sources and are discussed at monthly meetings of the international divisions of the company. Sales representatives feed back information on equipment needs in the NHS hospitals to product specialists in the company who are themselves in touch with leading hospital specialists in the field.

The most significant development factor has been the rapid growth of technological knowledge in both medical and analytical equipment. At the present time, equipment is much cheaper in relative terms compared with fifteen years ago. Analytical equipment has become more complex and its information output has kept pace with the increased workload of the NHS hospitals.

Business Dealings with the NHS

The UK company employs twelve sales representatives who visit medical and technical staff at all authority levels of the NHS but do not see supplies staff as a general rule.

Recently the company was asked to sell equipment to the DHSS to be tested at two hospitals as a result of the Collier Report recommendations to the NHS to work on a limited list of medical equipment and manufacturers. The company does not approve of a limited list even if it is included as it could inhibit the continuous development of electromedical equipment.

On the whole the company does not have its equipment tested and approved by the DHSS before it is marketed, but would not object to this. However, it feels that its equipment is tested thoroughly during production by experts and then again by 'in use' testing in hospitals. The company feels also that although the Scientific and Technical Branch of the DHSS employs technically competent staff, they are working within a bureaucratic straitjacket and not at the same pace as manufacturing companies. This means that their evaluations of equipment are not fast enough to suit the competitive market situation. The company has, since 1976, established a good working relationship with several regional supplies officers which is proving to be an important source of NHS communications. This is reflected in the comments of some of the supplies staff interviewed who said that the company and its equipment are now being recommended by the regional scientific officer in their region.

NHS Paperwork, Administration and Ordering Systems

Order forms are fairly standard throughout the NHS and there are no administrative problems for the company. Quotation forms are also fairly standard but on the whole the company prints its own as the space provided for details of equipment on NHS forms is inadequate.

The company does not offer quick payment discounts as it is assumed that the NHS customers would not take advantage of them. Most NHS authorities purchasing from the company pay within sixty days of receiving equipment. There are no fixed quantity discounts offered by the company. Sometimes a NHS customer will get a single item of equipment with a discount from the list price if a good case is presented. For example, an area health authority recently purchased some equipment costing £7,000 for £6,800 as this was all they had left in their equipment allocation.

Service and Maintenance

The UK company employs five service engineers and the servicing side of the company is expected to expand rapidly over the next few years. The company has noted the expansion of medical physics departments in the NHS with the growth of 'in house' maintenance and approves of this. However, they would not expect hospitals to service some of the company's equipment, particularly analytical equipment. Where equipment is expensive and complex, possibly serving a whole region, the company makes a service engineer available to train users and bring the equipment into operation. The company has set up additional training courses for NHS technical staff to enable them to maintain medical equipment. This scheme has the approval of the regional scientific officers in the regions where the courses are being held. Service and maintenance problems for both the NHS and manufacturers have brought the company into closer contact with the regional scientific officers, most of whom are trying to rationalise all service and maintenance in their regions. In many NHS regions, service contracts are being established which will reduce all costs including administrative and paperwork as well as maintain high standards of safety for both staff and patients.

Competition from Other Manufacturers

It is acknowledged as selling high quality equipment and is one of the leading manufacturers in the field. The two other large manufacturers supplying to the NHS are an American and a Danish company, with two small British companies providing a small percentage of monitoring equipment. However, the company has entered the field of ventilation and respiration equipment and is hoping to rival the two large British manufacturers who sell to the NHS, although the biggest supplier to the NHS is an American company that holds 90 per cent of the world market as well as 90 per cent of the NHS market.

Wholesalers and Distributors

The UK company does not use wholesalers and distributors but has agents in Ireland and Scotland who market, sell and service their medical and analytical equipment.

Advertising and Publicity

The company has implemented a new sales system whereby each of the twelve sales representatives will specialise in a product as well as being assigned an area of the NHS market. These representatives visit medical and technical staff at all levels of the NHS authority with only occasional visits to supplies staff. They distribute technical information and arrange 'in use' testing of equipment.

In the last year, the company has been following a policy of direct mail advertising as it proved successful in the launching of the ultrasonic real-time foetal monitor. The company received two hundred enquiries from NHS hospitals for demonstrations as a direct result of the mail advertising.

The company also has a high regard for journal advertising. It feels that showing equipment at exhibitions has limited value. There is a tendency to be more selective and the majority of equipment exhibitions are not attended. The symposium at Birmingham University was different inasmuch as it was self-financing and exhibitions are not.

Trade Associations

The company has links with one trade association.

Firm F: Anonymous

A small British company started in 1970 since which time it has been selling equipment to the NHS. It employs approximately sixteen staff and its products are mainly cardiac and intensive care monitoring equipment. There are no sales staff employed and the bulk of sales and services of equipment is carried out by the company's distributors. The company sells 60 per cent of its equipment; 40 per cent is handled by appointed distributors throughout the UK. Approximately 84 per cent of the company's sales are to the NHS, while the remaining 16 per cent is export sales, but this 16 per cent is increasing steadily. Eighty per cent of the equipment made is for portable bedside use and 20 per cent is larger computer-linked patient management equipment. The turnover of the company in 1976 was approximately £110,000.

New Products and Developments

In the monitoring equipment industry generally, the main developments in the last few years have been to make portable equipment and to make it safer for patient and user, together with an increase in computerised patient management.

The company's own developments have been in the field of monitoring equipment which is under production and they have also made an electrical safety device for testing monitoring equipment in hospitals in response to the increase in NHS 'in house' servicing and maintenance of equipment. Most of the company's development ideas have come from contacts with NHS hospitals who sometimes ask them to develop prototypes.

Business Dealings with the NHS

The company has had very little contact with the DHSS and the Scientific and Technical Branch has been carrying out its own research and development of equipment as well as its own evaluations. In 1971/72 the company was asked to sell some monitoring equipment to the DHSS to be evaluated. The equipment was purchased and despatched, but the company did not receive the results of the evaluation from the DHSS. Since then the company has sold equipment to the DHSS to be evaluated in one of the testing centres set up as a direct result of the Collier Report. The managing director is expecting to hear the results of these evaluations in the near future.

NHS Paperwork, Administration and Ordering Systems

The company has no complaints with NHS quotation and ordering forms as they are fairly standardised and safety requirements are clearly stated. Order forms do vary slightly in format between regions, but not to an extent that produces problems for the organisation.

The company's experience with NHS payment for equipment is good, as the NHS usually pay within sixty days of delivery of equipment. The company offers a 2½ per cent discount for payment within thirty days, but only few of the NHS customers take advantage of this.

The bulk of equipment purchased by the NHS is delivered by British Rail or National Carriers and in the last few years it has had to transfer all carriage and delivery charges to the NHS. Hospitals are charged as near as possible the exact delivery cost whether it is road, rail or the company's own transport.

The company is concerned about the flood of end-of-financial-year orders from the NHS and would prefer not to have flat out production for the first three months of the calendar year, the summer months being relatively idle.

Service and Maintenance

The company employs only one service engineer so that the bulk of all its servicing is carried out by distributors. The company has noted with approval an expansion of medical physics and medical electronics departments in the last three years in hospitals and a consequent growth of 'in house' service and maintenance.

Competition from Other Manufacturers

When the company started in 1970, it was the only British organisation supplying earth free patient monitoring equipment. At that time, the only other manufacturers were large multi-national companies. At this stage it held about 20 per cent of the NHS market for all monitoring equipment but today its market share is unknown. At present there are approximately six British-based firms still supplying patient monitoring equipment to the NHS, but only two are significant, while the bulk of the market is held by the large multi-national companies.

Wholesalers and Distributors

Forty per cent of the company's equipment is distributed by wholesalers and agents who carry out the advertising, sales and maintenance. Agents are used in the North of England, Scotland and for export sales. One agent alone handles 20 per cent of the company's equipment. So far the company has resisted involvement with agents who sell package deals to developing countries although they have been approached to do so. It would be difficult for such a small firm to take the financial consequences if a package deal fell through because of its tight production budget and cash-flow problems. It cannot afford to tie up cash in goods produced for speculative ventures.

Advertising and Publicity

Since the company employs only one sales representative, it relies on the managing director's contacts with medical and technical staff in various hospitals throughout the country. He is mainly responsible for the company's advertising and sales to the NHS. The company does not have much contact with NHS supply staff, except when equipment is being ordered, once decisions on type of equipment and manufacturer have been made by medical and technical staff. Eight out of the ten supply staff interviewed said that they had never heard of the company. The company advertises in several technical journals and in the hospital equipment and supplies journals. They produce limited quantities of catalogues which are distributed mainly to consultants and medical physics departments in hospitals. They attend few exhibitions in order to advertise their equipment, as the cost of exhibiting is prohibitive.

Trade Associations

The company does not belong to any trade associations and does not see any particular value in so doing.

Firm G: Anonymous

This organisation is part of a foreign group with companies in the UK and Germany as well as its home country. It manufactures patient monitoring equipment and distributes a variety of equipment and disposable products. The thirty staff employed in the UK are mainly sales, distribution, and service staff: seven salesmen and seven service and maintenance engineers. The UK division represents approximately 10 per cent of the total worldwide company. Approximately 95 per cent of the sales of the UK company are to NHS hospitals, with the remaining 5 per cent to industry and private doctors. The total worldwide turnover of the company is approximately £15 million per annum (1976 figures) and the UK turnover is approximately £1 million (1976 figures).

New Products and Developments

In the last two or three years the company has been developing a new range of defibrillators which are now being marketed, and also pre-gelled ECG electrodes which are also being sold within the NHS. The main general developments in the company's equipment have been in systems designed to increase information output from patient monitoring equipment. Where parameters of equipment are well established, as with patient monitoring equipment, the company concentrates on developing and refining products.

Business dealings with the NHS

The salesmen employed by the company travel around 250 hospitals on which they concentrate their sales efforts. They see mainly medical consultants and medical physics staff. The representatives demonstrate equipment, hand out technical leaflets, and monitor 'in use' testing of equipment in hospitals. They have less contact with supplies staff. Most of the equipment sold by this company to the NHS is for capital schemes, so that as well as medical and scientific staff, architects and engineers are sometimes involved in purchasing negotiations with sales representatives.

It is claimed that, despite some contact with the DHSS and the Scientific and Technical Branch, communications are not ideal. It is possible for the Department to issue hazard warnings on equipment without simultaneously telling the manufacturing company or consulting them in any way. The seven out of ten supplies staff interviewed during the project indicated that the company's equipment is purchased in their area but they did not show any positive enthusiasm for it. One or two mentioned that the equipment is expensive and that their service and maintenance has deteriorated in the last two years. The DHSS has purchased some of the company's equipment recently and although they did not give any details, the firm is aware that some kind of evaluation is being carried out.

NHS Paperwork, Ordering and Payment System

Most quotation forms from the NHS are standard and are administratively easy for the company to deal with, although they still contain questions about the company's compliance with national pay policy guidelines and whether equipment conforms to HTM8 safety standards. Both these queries are resolved centrally by the DHSS before hospital sales are negotiated.

The company has noticed an improvement in the length of time that the NHS customers take to pay for equipment received. It now averages sixty days between delivery and payment. The company offers quick settlement discounts only if asked and on the whole the NHS does not ask. However, on capital schemes some price concessions may be expected. For example, a region was given a tender amounting to £210,000 against a list price of £240,000 for the equipment. All delivery charges are transferred to the NHS except for very large orders. For example, the equipment for capital schemes is normally delivered free of charge. Because the company sells much of its equipment to the NHS for capital schemes, there are considerable storage and delivery problems. When capital schemes are delayed or fall behind in completion schedules, the company may be asked to hold on to stock which should have been delivered. This imposes additional insurance problems for the company because premiums on stocks of equipment held are very high and the company is covered to hold only limited stocks in their storage depots.

Service and Maintenance

The NHS service and maintenance situation is now very complex with the expansion of medical physics departments where hospitals are carrying out 'in house' servicing. This leads to ambiguous liability situations for manufacturers who are held responsible for upholding DHSS safety regulations on equipment. This is made difficult by more stringent equipment safety standards now demanded by the DHSS. The company has noted instances of hospital staff adapting equipment to suit their needs and leaving the equipment no longer conforming to the safety regulations. The rapid growth of medical physics and technicians in the NHS and the resultant expansion in 'in house' servicing should be investigated thoroughly by both the DHSS and the manufacturers who supply equipment.

Competition from Other Manufacturers

At present there is a total of approximately fifteen firms either manufacturing and distributing or just distributing patient monitoring equipment in the UK. The total NHS market is valued at £2,500,000 per annum so there is relatively little NHS business to divide between these firms. In 1975, at least three companies made a loss, one German distributor and two British manufacturers. There are only about six British manufacturers of patient monitoring equipment left after the crisis of the early 1960s when many went out of business. The company is one of the three manufacturers who together sell most of the monitoring equipment to the NHS. None of them is British.

Wholesalers and Distributors

The company does not use wholesalers to distribute its equipment except in Scotland and Ireland where agents are employed.

Advertising and Publicity

The company sells within a medically well-defined market and so advertises specifically to medical and scientific NHS staff. It has a 2 per cent advertising budget, spent mainly on advertisements in trade and professional journals, and on catalogues and literature to be distributed by sales representatives. Exhibitions are felt to have a limited sales promotion function. New products are launched by a combination of advertising and 'in use' testing carried out in hospitals by medical staff and monitored by the company's sales staff.

Trade Associations

The company does not belong to any trade associations and relies on sales representatives and other sources for market intelligence on the state of the industry. This means also that they have no direct representation to DHSS and the Scientific and Technical Branch as do the companies that belong to trade associations.

Firm H: Anonymous

Began in 1968 as importers of infusion pumps from the USA. In 1973 began to manufacture infusion pumps cheaper than those it was importing. It copied the American product, but after a number of law cases it was established that it had not infringed the American patent. The present product sells at under £500 in the UK. Although they manufacture in the UK, it sells mainly to a continental company with 90 per cent of its products exported and the remaining 10 per cent sold to the NHS. It employs forty-five staff in the UK and five abroad, as well as having a sales office and servicing outlet in Germany. The business, originally Swiss-owned, was sold to an American company a few years ago.

New Products and Developments

The new products developed over the last few years have been basically modifications of the original infusion pump manufactured by the company. The original pump is still on sale and a modified, gravity feed drip counter pump has been developed over the past three years and is not yet on the market. The company has asked the DHSS for financial help in the development of their work, but has so far not received any aid. The company completed the development of their infusion pump alone and started to sell to NHS hospitals in 1978. DHSS would not guarantee purchases of the pump by the NHS after it was marketed. The latest development is a volumetric pump, originally made in the USA, which is being sold widely in the NHS. It is the most important development so far in its field as it combines an accurate continuous drip feed and can be battery-operated. This is particularly useful in developing countries. Suggestions for innovation and development come from users in hospitals and from the company's research and development staff.

Business Dealings with the NHS

There is little contact between the company and the DHSS because new equipment is not sent to be tested. The DHSS asked only once to check a machine that was discovered to have a technical fault. The company have applied to the DHSS for a development grant, but has not received one so far. The company is pleased to note that, apart from issuing hazard warnings, the DHSS is now going to issue recommendations for manufacturers whose equipment has been evaluated positively. This is a bonus for manufacturers of medical equipment who can use these letters of recommendation in their advertising, particularly to overseas markets.

Sales representatives visit hospitals and make contact with nursing and medical staff but rarely see supplies staff. Two of the supplies staff interviewed said that they had never heard of the company, while another four said that they had recently changed to another manufacturer because of the company's involvement with law suits about possible infringement of patents. This is in spite of the fact that the rival company's pumps are more expensive.

Sales representatives demonstrate equipment and monitor 'in use' testing for the company. The average time taken for an 'in use' test is three weeks, after which the representative is expected to report back to the company with the user's comments and a possible sale.

NHS Paperwork, Administration and Ordering Systems

The company does not offer prompt payment discounts to the NHS and expects to receive payment sixty days after delivery of equipment. They do offer a bulk purchase discount: if an authority buys five pumps, they receive 2½ per cent discount, if ten pumps, 5 per cent discount. NHS authorities rarely buy more than ten machines at one time. Recently the company has been trying to interest regional scientific officers in regional bulk purchases but so far none of those approached has shown any interest. The company recently introduced delivery charges to the NHS as they could no longer afford to carry the cost themselves.

Service and Maintenance

The company estimates that it has service contracts for 50 per cent of the machines it sells, the other 50 per cent being serviced by the NHS. NHS servicing is in areas and regions where there are medical physics and electro-biomedical engineering staff. If an authority asks for help and instruction, the company will provide the expertise to enable them to carry out their own servicing. The company's service contracts are for one year. The company's contact with regional scientific officers has been mainly about maintenance.

Competition from Other Manufacturers

There is only one competitor selling infusion pumps to the NHS, and the market had been divided 50/50 until recently when the company reckons it has increased its share of the market to 70 per cent. Some supplies officers interviewed said that they had recently started to buy from the rival company.

Wholesalers and Distributors

The company divides its market into three territories in England and Wales, each with one of their own sales and service representatives. Scotland and North and South Ireland are each covered by agents who sell and service the company's products. This covers the sale of all infusion pumps; the oxygen monitors manufactured by the company are distributed and serviced solely by a large British company specialising in ventilation and respiration equipment. In total, the company distributes and services approximately 70 per cent of its own products. The distributors in Scotland and Ireland and the other large British company sell and service the rest.

Advertising and Publicity

The company does comparatively little advertising and publicity except through two journals, the *Hospital Equipment and Supplies Journal* and *Clinical Equipment.* They attend very few exhibitions, which are prohibitively expensive. Technical leaflets are taken around to hospitals by sales representatives. Direct mail advertising is not used. The bulk of advertising is done by sales representatives who distribute technical leaflets to medical and nursing staff.

Trade Associations

The company does not belong to any trade association but it is a member of the British Hospital Export Council.

Firm I: Vickers Medical Engineering (UK), Priestley Road, Basingstoke, Hampshire

Forms part of one of five groups within a large British engineering company. The total medical company turnover is approximately 1¼ per cent of worldwide company sales. The worldwide medical engineering division turnover for 1976 was approximately £4 million, of which the UK based sales was approximately £3.4 million. The worldwide total company turnover was £330 million in 1976. Medical division sales to NHS hospitals was approximately £2 million in 1976.

The medical division exports 45 per cent of its products at the present time, with most of the remaining 55 per cent of home sales being to the NHS. However, NHS business has shown little real growth in the last two to three years and this is being compensated for by an export sales drive and increased home sales to industry. The £2 million sales to the NHS is divided into approximately £1 million capital expenditure sales of incubators, ventilators and blood analysing equipment in the price range of £1,000 to £100,000 per item, and £1 million sales to the NHS is largely revenue expenditure which involves maintenance and service, rentals for hired equipment and low value supplies of disposable accessories for use with oxygen therapy equipment.

The medical division employs 130 manufacturing staff, 100 sales and service staff, and 120 management, clerical and administrative staff. Vickers acquired the business in 1966.

New Products and Developments

The company has a number of new product developments in the last two years which have come mainly from 'in house' research within the company. It has developed a remodelled controlled oxygen mask, a patient isolator system, more of which have been exported than sold on the home market, and a number of new paediatric projects. Some new ideas are brought to the company from specialists in the NHS by sales and service representatives. In addition, the company has developed blood analysis equipment, speeding-up processes and enabling equipment to carry out more simultaneous tests with fewer staff.

Most of the new equipment is being developed with export markets in mind, as the future market in the NHS does not look very promising for the company. This ties up with the comments of four of the NHS supplies staff interviewed who said that their areas had changed to another company's incubators in the last two years. Another ASO commented that his area's business with the company was now confined largely to the hiring of equipment because the company was retracting in the field of equipment sales. Since the start of the company's contact with the NHS in 1966, it has dealt mainly with medical and technical staff in hospitals, and contact with supplies staff has been confined to the level of ordering and administration. The company feels that its more significant contacts have been with the DHSS and in particular the Scientific and Technical Branch which overall has proved to be unrewarding.

In 1968 the company was concerned with the development of a range of analysis equipment called the M300 range. This was at the beginning of a general changeover in the medical field to automated analysis equipment: blood samples were fed into a machine which carried out simultaneous tests and printed out the results. The DHSS bought a machine from the company for evaluation and subsequently placed central contracts for it between 1972 and 1975. After the DHSS had made this arrangement, it circulated details of the equipment to the NHS regions and asked them to place orders. The first machine was delivered and working in a hospital in 1972. The DHSS evaluation at this stage consisted of testing the product for performance and safety standards specifications. In other words, it had acknowledged that the equipment was safe and could carry out tests claimed by the company.

In 1975 the DHSS stopped buying the machine on a central contract, after it had purchased 20. At the same time, the DHSS did not produce the official evaluation report that would assist the equipment production to be channelled into export sales.

In 1973 the DHSS and Medical Research Council were financing research and development on new blood analysis equipment at the Wolfson Research Centre in Birmingham. The equipment was expected to be highly automated and in 1974 a prototype was emerging. However, since a prototype of this kind usually takes three years to develop, the DHSS approached the company asking it to become the industrial partner in the development of the equipment. Up to this point the research and development had cost the DHSS and the Medical Research Council approximately £75,000. The company agreed to the collaboration and asked how many of the machines the NHS would need. The DHSS replied that it could give no sales guarantees except with the first machine, which it would buy and evaluate. The company then calculated that its own involvement with the research would cost it £2 million until the first machine was ready and that unless the DHSS could make a contribution to the £2 million, then the sum of money at risk for the company was £2 million less £50,000. Agreement could not be reached and the DHSS went to an American company for industrial support where it did not have to contribute financially to further research and did not have to guarantee any sales to the manufacturer.

Also in 1976, the company developed blood analysing equipment to sell principally to the American market. One was sold to the DHSS for evaluation. The DHSS used its own research and development funds to purchase this equipment. The region and hospital chosen for the evaluation were selected by the DHSS because regional contributions to both data-processing costs and the overall costing study could be made. However, the DHSS was not in a position to make a technical staff provision to carry out the tests, and as a result, clinical staff in the hospital were working evenings and weekends to maintain the evaluation and their own workload. In the meantime, other regions were interested in buying the equipment, but would not do so before the results of the evaluation in the test region are known. In September 1977, the evaluation report on this equipment was in final draft.

Since these experiences, the company has been sceptical of the powers and authorities of the DHSS in the field of research and development in new equipment for the NHS market. The company was concerned about the Collier Report and its implications for British industry. At present, the company is judging that it is best to give second priority to the NHS in favour of concentrating on export sales.

NHS Paperwork, Administration and Ordering Systems

The company has noted that there is a higher degree of standardisation in all types of forms, including quotation and order forms, used by the NHS in the last three years. A more serious problem for the company is the NHS administration of the rental of equipment, and it has spent the last eighteen months trying to persuade areas and regions to accept rental invoices for equipment on a three-month, or even a six-month basis, instead of the present monthly system. The main complaint is the excess of paperwork and administration involved for the company which would be able to reduce hiring costs if its handling costs could be reduced. So far the company has been unsuccessful in persuading areas and regions to change.

The average length of time NHS customers take to pay for both the purchase and hire of equipment is approximately sixty days and is not satisfactory to the company, which normally asks for payment within thirty days of delivery. However, the company does not offer quick payment discounts and the managing director is considering this as a measure to cut down on NHS debts to the company.

Bulk discounts are given on consumable sales, but discounts on bulk equipment sales are discretionary rather than automatic, i.e. on sales of equipment over £20,000, the company is prepared to negotiate a discount depending on the number of items involved. If the sale is for a single item of equipment, then the scope for discounts is very small. On the whole the company expects the NHS to take the initiative in asking for discounts but finds them modest bargainers, concentrating their purchasing efforts on the quality of the goods rather than the price. The company charges the absolute minimum possible in transport costs to the NHS, from their eight storage depots in the UK.

The managing director described how the company had lost a contract for oxygen ventilation equipment accessories through the maladministration of a supplies officer who had made a contract with the wrong manufacturer for the wrong accessories. The supplies officer, who had changed from one manufacturer to another, did so because of price considerations, only to find that the products of the two manufacturers were different although the descriptions are similar and that the accessories did not fit the equipment used in the area. This particular company had to explain the difference to the supplies officer, and its contract was renewed.

Service and Maintenance

The company finds that the NHS's own service and maintenance of equipment is concentrated in particular regions which have substantial medical physics departments. The extent of NHS 'in-house' service also varies according to the type of equipment. The company does not approve of NHS servicing equipment but does not have the authority to stop it except by disclaiming responsibility.

Recently the company restructured its sales and service organisation in the UK so that the two are linked and regionalised to give a more comprehensive and efficient service to the NHS.

Competition from Other Manufacturers

The biggest developments in electronic patient support ventilators have come from the USA in the last ten years. Until recently the company had the biggest share of the NHS market for paediatric incubators, but some of the supplies staff interviewed suggested a recent changeover to the NHS purchasing from another company. The most serious rivals for the NHS market in incubators are American companies and it is an American company which has 90 per cent of the world market as well as 90 per cent of the NHS market in ventilation equipment.

Wholesalers and Distributors

The company does not use wholesalers or distributors in the UK where it carries out all its own sales. However, in most other countries where export sales are made, the company uses distributors to a large extent.

Advertising and Publicity

At present, the company is aiming most of its advertising and publicity at the export market, as it is now their policy to concentrate sales outside the UK. This advertising is done with newly-designed brochures and catalogues, either distributed by sales representatives or sent directly through the post to medical and technical users of equipment. All the brochures are now printed in four languages. The company advertises in trade and professional journals but to a lesser extent.

Sales representatives visit medical physics departments and also see consultant heads of departments and arrange and monitor 'in use' testing of equipment. With the new linked sales and service structure, they are able to report immediately to service staff in the area if equipment needs attention. Sales staff rarely see supplies staff at any level of the NHS organisation.

Trade Associations

The company belongs to three trade associations and has used these associations to make representations to the DHSS. At present, the company is considering forming another association which it hopes will have more authority in confrontations with the DHSS and which will be more appropriate to its particular organisation.

Firm J: Wardray X-ray Products (Clerkenwell) Ltd, 15/19 Bakers Row, EC1R 3DT

A small British firm manufacturing X-ray accessories. Their products include X-ray cassettes, protective aprons, dark room furniture, and lead-lining protection for rooms housing X-ray equipment. It has been established and supplying hospitals for forty years. In 1976, 80 per cent of its sales were to the NHS, 10 per cent to industry and 10 per cent exported. The large capital schemes in the NHS are virtually coming to an end and the company is working on an export sales drive to counter this loss of business in the home market. The expansion in export sales is concentrated on Nigeria and the Middle East. Since 1976 their export sales have risen from less than 10 per cent and are at present up to between 17 and 20 per cent. There are approximately thirty staff employed, five administrative and clerical, twenty-four production staff, one technical representative and one sales representative. The total turnover of the company was approximately £500,000 in 1976. Since 1976 the company has made arrangements for storage and distribution of most of its products to be undertaken on a contract basis by an associated company, which also distributes X-ray film.

New Products and Developments

Within the X-ray market generally, the main development has been a tendency to move away from traditional dark room activities towards cassettes and daylight developing of X-ray film. In the long term it will mean a decrease in the production of dark rooms and of traditional X-ray film loading. The company has developed a cassette, which can take any type and make of film whereas large manufacturers make cassettes that will take only their own film, limiting their market.

Two or three years ago, the company began to make X-ray protective aprons using a lead and plastic material instead of the traditional lead and rubber. The material was developed by this company and one other. They have also developed a piece of equipment to enable hospitals to test their own X-ray equipment for electrical faults. It can be used to test other types of electrical equipment which are earthed. The company is selling, but not manufacturing, X-ray grids which are made only in Sweden and Japan. The grid consists of a metal plate covered with fine lines of lead and aluminium (80 lines per inch) and is designed to improve the quality of the X-ray picture. The grid is applied after the X-rays have penetrated the patient and the film, after which the film is sifted through the grid giving a clearer picture.

Business with the NHS

The company deals with all levels of the NHS. Their equipment is bought by regions for capital schemes and areas purchase equipment from their revenue budget. There are only two major suppliers of lead-lined protection for X-ray equipment and this company has about 40 per cent of the NHS market.

Although the company has been dealing with the NHS since it started, the managing director has never formally discussed the contracts or arrangements with DHSS representatives, but assumes that at some point early in the firm's development they were officially approved by DHSS. The managing director deals directly with architects, engineers and medical staff; his only contact with supplies staff is at the point at which orders are placed. The company has been asked to attend meetings on the National Supplies Vocabulary but has declined so far.

The Scientific and Technical Branch evaluates most of the company's equipment, but the time they take to carry out evaluations can seriously delay production. When the company began to manufacture X-ray protective aprons, the DHSS asked to test and evaluate the product, to which the company agreed and gave them samples. After six months, the managing director gave up waiting for the department's evaluation, carried out his own evaluation, and submitted the results to it for approval. In the meantime, a rival manufacturer was selling protective aprons made of the new material to NHS hospitals without DHSS approval. This was particularly upsetting to the company because DHSS approval is not mandatory for selling to hospitals and most manufacturers agreed to their equipment being evaluated in order to maintain goodwill. The DHSS have still not inspected or approved the lead and plastic X-ray apron, but in spite of this 50 per cent of all protective aprons purchased by NHS hospitals are lead and plastic and not the British standard lead and rubber which has not yet been changed by the DHSS. The combination of lead and plastic is far more durable and safe than lead and rubber which cracks and breaks more quickly in use. However, national standards of safety are the concern of the DHSS, and therefore it has to take the initiative. The managing director has sent them samples and asked for approval and offered his expertise and services but as yet has not had a reply.

Another example of the company's dealings with the DHSS occurred three years ago after the company had developed a piece of equipment to enable hospitals to test their own X-ray equipment for electrical faults. The equipment is quite versatile as it can test any electrical equipment that needs an earth. DHSS were actively involved in the evaluation and approval of this equipment and their recommendation contributed significantly to sales. They were, however, particularly occupied with minor details of the design.

NHS Paperwork, Administration and Ordering Systems

Quotation forms from the NHS are standard throughout the country, and order forms are standard throughout a region, although they vary slightly between regions. The problem with quotation forms is that they are not designed to give the manufacturer enough room to give sufficient detail on his products and there is generally no duplicate working copy supplied. This means that 80 per cent of all single quotation forms have to be photocopied by the company for their own use.

The managing director gave an example of an area supplies department sending out a quotation form for a spare part costing £3. Someone could have telephoned for the item, which is made only by this company, and it would have been sent free. In the event, the exercise must have cost the health authority in excess of £20, including administrative costs.

The company offers a quick settlement discount of 2½ per cent for invoices paid within twenty-eight days of delivery on all orders over £100 and a separate discount on bulk deliveries. For example, 100 illuminators ordered for a capital scheme would constitute a bulk delivery and the company would waive carriage charges and give 7½ per cent for a settlement within twenty-eight days. However, most of the quick payment discounts offered by the company to the NHS are not taken up.

Recently the company quoted prices for lead-lined doors and screens to a regional authority supplies department for a new health centre. They were then asked to make a separate quote for dry benches and were accepted to supply all the items. They then offered to deliver all the equipment at one time at a saving of transport costs of £60 per item. The regional supplies department did not accept this offer, ordered the items separately and lost £250 bulk delivery discount.

Service and Maintenance

The company does not sell anything that requires regular servicing so does not employ maintenance staff. Occasionally, items need repair or adjustment which hospital staff can do themselves with some telephone advice and instruction from the company. Even more occasionally, items are sent back to the company to be repaired.

Competition from Other Manufacturers

The company has 10 per cent of the protective apron market in the NHS, with 25 per cent of the market being held by another British firm, and 65 per cent of NHS sales going to a German manufacturer. The development of the lead-plastic material for protective aprons was made in Britain and the material is still made in Britain. A major problem has been the DHSS's reluctance to approve the material officially for British manufacturers, thus allowing the German company to gain a stronghold in the market. The British standard still applies only to traditional lead and rubber protective aprons, even though manufacturers' tests have shown the new material to be more effective, more durable, and cheaper.

Wholesalers and Distributors

Fifty per cent of the company's products are sold directly and 50 per cent via agents and distributors. The company's own field representative works in the south of England and wholesalers' sales representatives cover Ireland, the north of England and exports. The company values the services of wholesalers and distrubutors and although they might sell slightly more than the 50 per cent of their own products directly in the future, they will never dispense entirely with wholesalers' services.

Advertising and Publicity

The company has recently begun a national and international advertising drive under their own name and have just completed a new set of catalogues advertising their products and giving technical information. These will be distributed to the radiology departments, area supplies officers, regional X-ray engineers and export agents. They advertise in two journals, a monthly professional journal and a small trade journal, as well as in the *Hospitals' Yearbook* and the handbook of the Association of National Health Service Supplies Officers. The company does participate in exhibitions, but to a limited extent. Only one of the supplies staff interviewed had heard of the company so it is possible that its products purchased from revenue expenditure are obtained mainly from wholesalers. The company's research and development of products is carried out largely in the field, as is most of their equipment evaluation. Hospitals install and use a product and then suggest changes and modifications which the company works on. Most of the changes in X-ray accessories have arisen out of 'in use' observations and the needs of radiology departments. The X-ray scanner was a breakthrough in technology but will not replace traditional X-ray machines, only supplement them.

Trade Associations

The company does not belong to any trade associations and has no plans to do so in the near future.

Summary

Types of Manufacturing Organisation

Of the ten manufacturers of electromedical equipment interviewed in the project, four are small British companies, two are large British companies, one is a large American company, one a small American company, one a large Swiss company and one of another nationality.

New Products and Developments of the 10 Companies

All of the companies manufacturing medical equipment had at least two new products marketed in the last two years. General trends in electronic medical equipment have been towards cheaper, smaller equipment with an increased number of functions. There has been an increase in the manufacture of computerised patient management equipment. There is also a trend towards an emphasis on higher safety standards, both for patient and user of equipment.

Business Dealings with the NHS

All the manufacturers interviewed said that they had only marginal contact with NHS supplies staff, except at the time orders are placed. Their main contacts are with technical, medical and (very occasionally) nursing staff. Four firms said that they had been asked by DHSS to supply equipment to be evaluated at testing centres set up in response to the Collier Report. All expressed disapproval of the possible 'limited list' of manufacturers expected to emerge from the evaluations, including those who thought they would be on the list. The reasons for disapproval were:
(a) small firms might easily be bankrupted by not being included, and
(b) the evaluation of equipment would impose an artificially static sit-

uation on a continuously developing industry. For example, equipment tested by the centres might well have been superseded by new products and developments at the time that it is given a seal of approval by the DHSS.

One of the manufacturers interviewed complained of the length of time the DHSS takes to test and evaluate their equipment for sale to the NHS; equipment is submitted out of goodwill and politeness as it is not mandatory to have DHSS approval in order to sell equipment to the NHS, provided the equipment complies with the safety standards set out in DHSS document HTM8.

The manufacturers mentioned losing NHS business to competitors as a result of submitting new products to DHSS and waiting for an evaluation. As one manufacturer remarked, although the Scientific and Technical Branch of the DHSS is competent to evaluate medical equipment, it does not evaluate fast enough for the competitive market.

Two manufacturers said that they had approached the DHSS for financial help to aid their research and development of new products but had been refused. One British manufacturer has had bad experiences with DHSS since the 1960s. The company's research and development was misdirected on advice from the DHSS and then, when it appeared to be in accord with the needs of the NHS, DHSS refused to give it financial backing. To a large extent, this company is withdrawing from the home market, and concentrating its research and sales efforts on exports.

NHS Paperwork, Administrative and Ordering Systems

All the manufacturers commented on the high degree of standardisation of quotation and order forms now used in the NHS. They were full of praise for this aspect of NHS business, although three of the companies said that the space provided on the quotation forms for a firm's own detail on its products was not sufficient and also that duplicate copies should be provided for the company's own records. Two of the largest manufacturers said that they printed their own specially designed quotation forms as they could afford to and did not use the NHS ones.

There were differences of opinion among manufacturers on the NHS payment of accounts. Three companies do not offer quick payment discounts, and of those that do, four said that only half of NHS customers take advantage of these discounts. The discounts given range from 2½ to 3½ per cent for payment within 15/28 days of delivery, but on average the NHS customers take 2/3 months to pay for equipment. Some manufacturers offer bulk delivery discounts, particularly for capital schemes, and on the whole the NHS takes advantage of them. Most of the companies charge the NHS for deliveries; several have transferred these costs in the last two years as they can no longer afford to deliver equipment free of charge. Two large manufacturers do not charge for deliveries as the list prices of their equipment include transport costs.

Only two manufacturers mentioned the inconvenience of sudden buying at the end of the financial year when health authorities try to spend their revenue allocation so as not to incur financial penalties in the following year. This practice is dying out with the advent of regional strategic planning, the influence of regional scientific officers, and because the NHS has had the beginning of a rolling financial budget since April 1977. There was a general feeling among most of the manufacturers that NHS customers have become more businesslike in their purchasing methods in the last three or four years.

Service and Maintenance of Electromedical Equipment

All the manufacturers said that NHS hospitals were increasing their own servicing and maintenance of equipment with the expansion of medical physics and electro-bio-medical engineering departments in hospitals since 1975. Most of the manufacturers had some reservations about this change: there are few problems where the maintenance is carried out by expert technicians, but some said that the expansion of NHS 'in house' maintenance is not evenly distributed throughout the country. Three of the manufacturers have responded to this expansion by providing training schemes for hospitals and thus are able to control to some extent the quality of NHS staff who are servicing equipment, the type of equipment being serviced, and ensuring the safety of the equipment. Two manufacturers have developed testing devices to be sold to NHS staff to enable them to test certain types of equipment. All the manufacturers expressed concern that this expansion of 'in house' servicing might cause a lowering of safety standards and reduce the quality of their equipment. They approve of the DHSS plan to look at the service and maintenance situation in the NHS and particularly the attempts by some regional scientific officers to rationalise service and maintenance at area and regional levels. Only one manufacturer said that he was unhappy about the expansion of NHS 'in house' testing of his company's equipment.

Competition between Manufacturers

All the British manufacturers of patient monitoring equipment interviewed said that their biggest competitors are foreign owned multinational companies, mainly American but some German. In addition, 60 per cent of X-ray cassettes sold to the NHS are imported, and a German manufacturer has 60 per cent of the NHS market for X-ray protective aprons. It is estimated also that 90 per cent of X-ray equipment purchased by the NHS is imported.

The biggest developments in ventilation equipment in the last ten years have been made by American companies, and at present an American company has 90 per cent of the world market as well as the NHS market in ventilation equipment.

Approximately 95 per cent of blood gas analysis equipment is manufactured in the USA by American companies.

This situation substantiates the concern for British manufacturers of electromedical equipment expressed in the Collier Report.

Wholesalers and Distributors

Three of the smaller British companies interviewed use wholesalers and distributors to advertise, sell and service between 45 and 50 per cent of their equipment to the NHS. These companies, who do not employ sales and service staff, said that they would not distribute 100 per cent of their own products. Only one of the ten manufacturers said that they did not use the services of wholesalers at all, while seven said that they used agents to advertise, sell and service their equipment in Ireland, Scotland, and in export markets.

One company had arranged for a new product to be handled entirely by an agent who was to carry out a pre-sales launch, promotional advertising, sales, and after-sales service. This decision followed a successful campaign carried out by agents in France for this particular product. The advantages of distributors is that they can operate in areas of the country inaccessible to the manufacturer. They provide the sales and service staff that small firms cannot afford, and they advertise on behalf of the manufacturers.

Wholesalers and distributors also give a valuable service to the NHS, providing them with a variety of usually small items from different manufacturers on one order, and thus reduce NHS paperwork and administration. Wholesalers and distributors provide a localised service and so are often able to make quicker deliveries to NHS customers than manufacturers themselves. Sometimes NHS customers use wholesalers when they need an item urgently. Two of the manufacturers interviewed said that it is possible for the NHS to purchase goods cheaper from distributors than from manufacturers themselves, as many are given 20-25 per cent discount by manufacturers. The three small firms who said that they use distributors for up to 50 per cent of their sales were the ones least known by name to NHS supplies staff that place orders. The distributor thus may become better known by name to the NHS than the manufacturers themselves. On the whole, distributors concentrate on small medical items, while most large electromedical equipment is distributed by the manufacturers themselves.

Advertising and Publicity

Eight of the ten manufacturers interviewed employ sales representatives, the small firms employing one or two while the bigger firms employ up to ten on average. Almost all the manufacturers stressed the importance of sales representatives: they are expected to distribute technical leaflets and catalogues, carry out demonstrations, and monitor 'in use' testing of equipment in hospitals. All the manufacturers said that their sales representatives visit mainly technical and medical staff and rarely deal with supplies staff, except at the stage where orders are placed. Four manufacturers said direct mail advertising has become very successful and it forms an important part of their advertising programme. Most manufacturers of equipment advertise in professional journals, and four said that they advertise in the handbook of the Association of Health Service Supplies Officers, and in the *Hospital Equipment and Supplies Journal* which has a wide circulation among NHS supplies staff.

All manufacturers interviewed said that advertising through medical equipment exhibitions has become prohibitively expensive. Most of the smaller companies do not know the exact percentage of their turnover which is used for advertising but a large American company says that of the 2 per cent of annual turnover allocated to advertising and publicity, the largest part is spent on catalogues and leaflets distributed by sales representatives and on direct mail advertising to NHS medical and technical staff.

Electromedical Equipment Trade Associations

Six of the ten manufacturers do not belong to any trade association. One, already a member of several, is presently involved in forming another association. The other four manufacturers belong to between one and three trade associations. They say the main advantages of the associations are that they provide a way of keeping in touch with other manufacturers and, very importantly, giving the company formal access to the DHSS. In 1977 and 1978, several issues arose within the electromedical industry involving both manufacturers and the NHS which were discussed by DHSS and trade associations: the implications of the Collier

Report and of the resulting equipment testing centres that are generally disapproved of by manufacturers, and the concern of both the DHSS and the manufacturers with the present state of service and maintenance of equipment in hospitals throughout the NHS. They were meeting to discuss ways of rationalising the present system while maintaining a high standard of safety for both user and patient.

Part Three

OTHER SUPPLIES SYSTEMS

10 THREE BRITISH SYSTEMS

The supplies system in the NHS can only be assessed on the basis of its contribution to the achievement of health care in Britain and its degree of effectiveness when compared with supplies systems in other organisations. This part of the present study reports on some comparative studies. The resources for these comparisons were even more limited than those available for the main NHS supplies project and the information given in the following chapters is based on published data and fewer interviews, rather than a series of interviews and observations over 18-24 months available in the main study. Despite those limitations, the problems that emerged from these discussions reflected issues common to most procurement situations and helped to highlight strengths and weaknesses peculiar to the NHS.

As the NHS is a public service, it seemed sensible to compare its supplies situation with that in other public sector organisations. British Airways is a nationalised industry operating within the UK and throughout many parts of the world, and the scale and complexity of its operations seemed likely to resemble some NHS challenges. The Greater London Council has a fixed, relatively small geographical context, but the range and density of its obligations might throw some light on supplies policy suited to urban situations.

These organisations may all share peculiarities due to their public ownership, and ICI Ltd was asked to co-operate so that we might at least identify such distinctiveness, as well as learning something of the practices of private industry. In view of the size of ICI, we had to content ourselves with an examination of their Paint Division.

The other dimension of comparison had to be international as all the organisations involved may have been shaped by particular British situations. Brief studies have been made, therefore, of health care supplies in France and West Germany, based largely on published material but including some dozen interviews in Paris and Rheims in France, and Dusseldorf and Essen in West Germany.

British Airways

British Airways resulted from a merger between British European Airways and British Overseas Aircraft Corporation. In June 1976, formal agreement was reached between British Airways and staff unions to implement as soon as possible a rational system of central supply control, with other authorised supply units existing only where it was felt necessary. By August 1977, the centralisation of British Airways supplies was completed after all the staff required had been appointed in April 1977. Although British Airways deals with approximately one million different products, 50 per cent in value of all their purchasing is aircraft fuel. In view of this, it was considered that a central supplies department is the proper organisation for the purchase of fuel, uniforms, printing and stationery, and aircraft. Some other commodities, such as engineering supplies, are purchased by authorised personnel within the engineering division.

In 1974-5, the scale of supplies activity recorded amounted to a total expenditure of approximately £384 million, handled by approximately 628 supplies and supplies-related staff. By 1978, British Airways was spending approximately £600 million on supplies annually (excluding capital expenditure) and there are approximately 2,000 staff working on activities related to purchasing and supplies throughout the areas of the world in which British Airways operates. The new central supplies unit employs approximately 50 people.

The Organisation of the New Central Supplies Division at British Airways

In 1974, a study of the supplies situation in British Airways was started. One result was the creation of a new post of Head of Supplies and Mr J. Finnimore took up the appointment in September 1975.

A special report was requested from Productivity Services of British Airways about the optimum organisation for supplies. The key issues of the report are:

> The term supplies is used to cover contracts, purchasing and stock control and includes the disposal of equipment, surplus materials, spares etc. As a service function, the primary role of supplies is to provide least cost solutions and to seek a balance between service, reliability and price. Thus whilst the employment of specialist staff is likely to be the most effective way of providing the service, the requirements of the user are an important factor in determining how and where the activity should be performed.
>
> *Possible Organisational Arrangements.* The Head of Supplies is the Chief Supplies Official in British Airways and reports to the Executive Board of Management through the Finance Director. He is responsible for the satisfactory performance of the function irrespective of where

it is performed and in particular for the formulation and implementation of policy and procedures and ensuring that the function is properly resourced.

One of the Objectives of British Airways is: 'To earn and keep a worldwide respect for reliability, fair dealing, value for money, efficiency, initiative and good human relations from the community as a whole, customers, HMG, suppliers, agents and other airlines.' This requires:

a a consistent approach to all outside suppliers;
b a common face to any one supplier;
c ensuring that full but fair advantage is taken of British Airways' negotiating position.

Supplies activities can be organised in one of six ways, each of which relates to Head of Supplies in a slightly different way:

a *A Central Supplies Department* should be directly controlled by Head of Supplies and perform supplies activities for British Airways as a whole.

b *A Supplies Unit within a Group Function* should be an Authorised Supplies Unit (ASU) headed by a person fully engaged on supplies activities and directly employing its own supplies staff, physically located by agreement with user and would functionally report to Head of Supplies. It should serve only its own function unless otherwise authorised by Head of Supplies.

c *A Supplies Unit within a Division* should be an Authorised Supplies Unit headed by a person fully engaged on supplies activities and directly employing its own supplies staff, physically located by agreement with divisional management and should functionally report to Head of Supplies. It should serve only the division and its departments unless otherwise authorised by Head of Supplies.

d *A Co-ordinated Purchasing Approach* between two or more Supplies Units or users will take place where Head of Supplies sets up a committee or project group to examine specific commodities and undertake joint purchasing.

e *For Specific Major Projects* Head of Supplies will allocate an appropriate project team drawing from the total supplies manpower resource and other skills, irrespective of normal reporting relationships.

These will be ad hoc projects with a defined life span and the mechanism by which the Head of Supplies identifies these projects will be by involvement in the capital sanction procedure. This could be by inviting Head of Supplies to become a member of the Capital Expenditure Sub-Committee.

f *Local Purchasing* will be authorised by Head of Supplies where there is insufficient evidence to warrant the employment of specialists and consequently will be carried out on a part-time basis by staff primarily engaged in other activities.

As the British Airways organisation develops, an activity could be transferred from one category to another and the supplies organisation must be flexible enough to respond.

Control of the Function. The responsibility Head of Supplies has for the total function can be considered under three headings:

- supplies decisions, such as choice of supplier, recognising user constraints, price and commercial terms, and authority to order
- determination of the manpower requirements
- the monitoring of performance.

Co-ordination of the Function. A Supplies Management Committee (SMC) should be formed, chaired by Head of Supplies and comprising senior supplies management. It should have the following roles:

- a forum for discussing future supplies policies and procedures
- the determination of representation on outside bodies
- the identification and monitoring of co-ordinated purchasing
- the planning of supplies involvement in major projects
- the monitoring of stock control policies, procedures and performance
- supplies organisation development and harmonisation including the regular review of the organisational structures of all ASUs supplies grading structure
- manpower and career development
- the review of individual performance and potential
- the policy and procedures on local purchase arrangements.

This committee should be supplemented by a Joint Management/Staff Supplies Consultative Committee whose role should be similar to the management committee except in the areas of career development and individual performance and potential where the committee should not be involved in discussing individual cases.

Head of Supplies should review the total supplies training requirements in conjunction with the Supplies Management Committee and the Supplies Consultative Committee. The precise arrangements for these committees will be developed later.

Organisational Shape. The shape of the organisation (as proposed in Phase 1) is based on three premises:

individual accountability
a clear career path horizontally, diagonally, and vertically
compatible jobs in a simple structure.

The aim of individual accountability is the development of a skilled supplies function in which objectives are clearly set and responsibility delegated to the lowest appropriate level in the organisation. It requires the development of an individual performance review system specifically designed to meet the needs of the supplies function.

To ensure a clear career path requires that potential is appraised and information is available when manpower development is being planned.

The organisational structure should have a number of levels, each of which contains similar jobs and job titles. Analysis of the supplies function suggests no more than seven organisational levels, each of which should have a defined level of responsibility and work content. The existing multiplicity of structures should be reduced over a period of time and harmonised to reflect the agreed structure. The Central Supplies Department or any new supplies unit should immediately conform to the structure.

Economic benefits can be derived from some or all of the following:

opportunities for lower investment in inventories
systems standardisation and development
improved standardisation and development
improved availability of stock items
opportunities for joint purchase and using the bargaining power of British Airways
variety reduction, rationalisation, and standardisation of purchases
reductions in workload and administrative costs
better use and development of staff skills

Economic benefits have to be viewed from a British Airways standpoint as there could be instances where despite an overall benefit, one division or department may not find the arrangement beneficial. An objective should be to negotiate the purchase of a commodity at one point in British Airways although it may be called off, stocked, and used in a number of places.

The user must be satisfied that the location of supplies staff serving his needs is suitable and that he has a person clearly accountable for the activity in his area. The responsiveness required by users to meet day-to-day supplies demands is an important factor in deciding whether to centralise an activity or leave it locally. Day-to-day supplies requires meeting users' immediate operational needs for spares, services and minor equipment and includes stock and purchase records as well as placing and progressing orders.

The practicality of any arrangement is a prerequisite of change. The approach has been to identify benefits and to ascertain how practical it is to achieve these. Certain potential benefits may require changes in systems or procedures which until done could constrain any organisational change.

A Central Supplies Department is the proper organisation for the purchase of commodities across the group such as fuel, the provision of services such as uniforms, printing and stationery, and financially significant complex purchases or sales, such as aircraft. Any advantage in further centralising the supplies activities for a group function depends on whether the items purchased are common with the other users, and whether the formation of an additional ASU makes less than optimum use of staff. Where the items are specific to user and there is sufficient work to justify employment of supplies staff, the formation of an ASU within the group function should be the answer.

Of the £600 million spent annually by the supplies department, approximately £500 million is controlled directly by central supplies. Half of this £500 million is spent on one item, aircraft fuel. The other half of the £500 million, controlled centrally, is spent on catering for the staff and passengers, spares, aircraft and motor transport. The remaining £100 million not centrally controlled is spent by authorised purchasers as follows:

(a) Medical division supplies: £100,000 per annum.

(b) Passenger and crew subsistence, including emergency meals and subsistence: £53 million per annum.

(c) Advertising and publicity: £24 million per annum.

(d) Accommodation services: £26 million per annum.

The engineering departments have their own purchasing unit, but it is now part of an authorised system. The chief engineer controls the day-to-day system while the supplies department has functional management responsibility. Until this central supplies system came into operation, supplies staff in British Airways were confronted by non-supplies staff trying to do their own purchasing. This was particularly so with engineers and engineering supplies, and was perhaps equivalent to the situation in the NHS.

The catering unit of British Airways is also an authorised supplies unit, with the chief caterer running the day-to-day activities. The central supplies department, for example, deals directly with farmers for supplies of some food items.

The central supplies department does not see copies of all orders placed by authorised purchasing units but there is a check on all purchasing carried out by the Head of Supplies and the audit department.

Supplies Purchasing and Financial Arrangements of British Airways

Since the reorganisation, British Airways has a supplies finance accountant to give financial advice to the Head of Supplies, but the payment of invoices for goods received is carried out by a separate finance department in the company. However, the supplies department checks invoices and passes them to the finance department for payment and they are able to take advantage of payment discounts.

The Price Analysis System in British Airways Supplies

The central supplies department hopes to operate a price analysis system whereby the cost of manufacturing a supply item is used as a basis for assessing the price to be paid by British Airways. Supplies staff will estimate factory costs, sometimes with the manufacturer's help, and then estimate the manufacturer's overhead costs, including marketing and profit. The aim of the supplies department is to agree with manufacturers on a reasonable overhead cost for their product and the price to be paid. The Head of Supplies, who has been using this system elsewhere for the past ten years, is hoping to bring it into operation at British Airways as soon as possible. The system is usually applied to supply items accounting for 80 per cent of total expenditure, which is about 20 per cent of total items purchased. In the experience of the Head of Supplies at British Airways, once manufacturers become confident of the skill of the experts employed by the supplies department, they do not object to price analysis. However, this system can only operate within a purchasing situation where the buyer knows his own purchasing strength; he has to know exactly how much he buys in both amount and cost and from which manufacturers.

The British Airways Supplies Vocabulary

The supplies vocabulary at present in use at British Airways is based on the Air Ministry coding system and has a non-significant coding for items.

The Head of Supplies is waiting for a merger between two units to throw up a surplus of supplies staff, who can then work exclusively on a new vocabulary. Meanwhile, he has started preparing a full commercial catalogue, starting with aircraft parts.

The centralisation of supplies was completed in the middle of 1977 and it is not possible at this stage to give any indication of the total saving of staff. Savings achieved in 1977-78 amounted to £45 million on bulk purchase since centralisation. It is expected that the central supplies department will publish a report in 1979 outlining all the savings made since centralisation.

The Greater London Council

The Organisational Structure of GLC Supplies

The Supplies Department of the GLC is one of the support departments of the council and is responsible for the supply of goods and other services to the council's own departments as well as to the Inner London Education Authority. Its voluntary customers are the London boroughs and some rate-supported voluntary bodies in London.

The central departments at County Hall are largely administrative; most of the purchasing and distribution of supplies is carried out at the GLC's depots at Tottenham Hale and Southfields. The Southfields depot deals mainly with educational supplies: educational and office stationery, art and craft materials, office machines and books. This depot is also the main contracting centre for fuel oils and petroleum. The Tottenham Hale depot supplies furniture, building materials, metals, tools, cleaning materials, clothing textiles, electrical goods and food. It also operates a mobile showroom and clothing shop. In addition, there are large printing and reprographic services based at County Hall and the GLC has explored the possibility of selling surplus capacity. The motor transport supplies division designs and purchases vehicles and also repairs, services, and hires vehicles for a wide range of customers on competitive terms. The planning and development of capital projects is done by the Architect's and Engineer's departments of the GLC who use the supplies department to purchase some fittings and furniture.

Political influences can have dramatic effects on GLC purchasing. For example, a reduction in local authority spending may mean that the GLC Supplies Department has less extensive purchasing power to negotiate with suppliers. In spite of this, the Supplies Department is expected to make overall a small surplus or at least to break even on their annual supplies turnover, which is now in excess of £100 million. The breakeven or small surplus situation includes oncost charges levied by the GLC on all supplies in order to cover contracting, storage, and delivery of goods. The average oncost charge is 25 per cent, within a range of 16-45 per cent. The highest oncost of 45 per cent is levied on the supply of special uniform clothing which involves a high labour cost in fitting and alterations.

The GLC supplies catalogue has been redesigned as a looseleaf system so that it can be updated easily by users. The price section is looseleaf and is reviewed and updated every few months, and is also colour coded, with a change in colour every time a section is replaced. There are 10,000 copies in circulation; in some cases, only sections are distributed to specific users in order to save printing costs. The coding was designed approximately twelve years ago by a GLC systems analyst and is based on a simple six digit code to suit the computer input. The catalogue contains 15,000 items which can be redescribed or recoded as required.

Inflation and Purchasing Methods of the GLC

The GLC supplies department has a flexible purchasing policy, either storing or using call-off contracts, depending on the prevailing economic climate.

The GLC's Non-Captive Customers

Because purchasing policies vary between London boroughs, it has been difficult for the GLC to launch an overall advertising campaign which would be effective in all boroughs and in all departments within a borough. However, they have produced an information magazine since the beginning of 1977 which is distributed to many present and potential customers.

One of the features of the first edition was a special offer of a 9 per cent discount to customers on all bulk orders of electric lamps of a value of £700 and where a one-drop delivery could be made. While the discount recovered basic costs, contribution to overheads was less than average. It was hoped that the 9 per cent extra discount, added to the usual 35 per cent trade discount, would bring in enough new customers to allow the GLC, at the very least, not to make a loss on the deal. This campaign was launched because other suppliers of electric lamps were offering a 40 per cent discount and the GLC's 35 per cent plus 9 per cent discount added up to a total of 41 per cent discount on the list price (the additional 9 per cent being calculated on the list price less 35 per cent).

On the whole, the GLC concentrates its sales efforts towards the London boroughs where the situation is fairly fluid and difficult to quantify.

The London Ambulance Service is not a 'captive' customer and the GLC supplies department competes with the NHS supplies organisation to sell to it.

The Joint Supplies Board

The GLC, ILEA, and the London Boroughs have set up a joint advisory board to act as a supplies ginger group and it considers ways of purchasing to the best advantage of ratepayers. The board set up a study group whose aims are to consider user requirements and optimum levels of purchase. The commodities chosen for discussion have been left to the members of the study group but are likely to be joint user, high expenditure items.

Supplies Purchasing and the Finance System of the GLC

The purchasing finance system is integrated into the supplies department of the GLC, and all payments to suppliers are made in order of priority, according to the various discounts available. Approximately 20 per cent of invoices carry quick settlement discounts, ranging from 7-day to 14-day discounts to 28-day discounts. Discounts for payments within 7-14 days are usually for food items and the discounts for payment within 28 days are usually given by manufacturers of clothing and building materials. The computer makes payments to supplies according to the invoice coding carried out by the supplies department. There are also manufacturers' discounts for bulk one-drop deliveries, continuous business, and acceleration of the call-off of supplies on a contract.

Of the 94 per cent of supplies delivered directly, the supplies department carries out detailed checks on those invoices over £200, which amount approximately to 8 per cent of direct delivery invoices. In addition, there is a 5 per cent random sample check of the other invoices. All invoices for goods taken into store at GLC supplies depots are checked automatically.

Cost Analysis of Purchases

For a large number of supply items, the GLC asks manufacturers to provide a breakdown of the cost of their products. It is not made a condition of contract of purchase, but most manufacturers agree to it. The purpose of this is to give the GLC some basis on which to assess price increases asked for by manufacturers during a contract. The information is not used in order to make a contract, on the assumption that the competitive situation in which tendering takes place will afford the GLC the best prices.

For all supplies purchased by the GLC, including services and labour, firms are required to pay wages at least to the level of national agreements for the industry. There are standard clauses in all GLC contracts for supplies relating to fair wages and conditions of labour; the GLC never knowingly purchases textile goods from manufacturers who use outworkers or unregulated labour.

The Take-up of Supplies

The GLC monitor the take-up of supplies by their customers on call-off contracts and also ask some manufacturers to supply information. Some firms volunteer information on the progress of a contract where call-off is not matching initial estimates. On the whole, manufacturers do not complain when call-off is less than estimated on contracts for non-specific supplies, such as paint and cement, provided the short fall is reasonable. Where supplies have been made to GLC specification (usually items taken into stock), manufacturers do complain to the supplies department when take-up is falling behind schedule during a contract. Similar questions arise about price and estimated quantity for supplies not made to buyer's specifications. In the NHS, supplies officers are beginning to question manufacturers' claims that there is a precise relationship between estimated quantities to be purchased and the price of some supply items.

Manufacturers' Representatives

Firms' representatives normally call by appointment at the GLC depots. The depot dealing with clothing, textiles, food, furniture, and building materials estimates that forty manufacturers' representatives call on average every week. Most representatives calling are from firms selling building materials and furniture. These representatives do not sell or receive orders directly, because purchasing is centrally controlled by contracts and arrangements. Sometimes they visit outlying GLC departments trying to sell directly, but orders are scrutinised by the supplies department at the depots and are checked and queried by the purchasing staff. Representatives sometimes visit ILEA schools to try to sell to school staff. The head of a school can spend only 15 per cent of his annual budget outside the GLC supplies depots so there is not much scope for firms' representatives.

The GLC Supplies System and the User

Most supplies purchased by the GLC are checked and discussed for quality and price by the expert panels concerned with a specific product. User participation in supplies is widespread in school supplies, including teacher aids, and includes concern for the safety and innovation of educational supplies. The school meals advisers of ILEA have a food user panel to discuss the quality and types of food purchased by the GLC on their behalf.

Quality Control

The quality control checks on supplies for direct delivery cannot be carried out by GLC purchasing staff, except in respect of furniture. They have to rely on a feedback of information from users and customers. Supplies taken into store at depots are checked at regular intervals during a contract by purchasing staff and experts. They are also checked at the point of delivery by the stores staff. The buyer of the commodity is responsible for all quality control. Among the most frequent and carefully checked supply items are clothing and textiles made to GLC specification.

The GLC and Its Suppliers

Manufacturers apply initially to be put on the GLC prescribed list of suppliers, at which stage most of the vetting takes place. The firms who pass the GLC scrutiny and are accepted as potential suppliers are classified according to the type of product they sell, the size of their company, etc.

Usually the GLC keeps to term contracts, asking suppliers to tender on a competitive basis in a similar way to the NHS. Because of inflation, two-year contracts favoured by the GLC until a few years ago have been reduced to a one-year term, with prices fixed for six months.

The largest supplies division at Tottenham Hale purchase over half the total turnover of the GLC Supplies Department annually and recovers its running costs, which are in excess of £4 million, from oncost charges to their customers.

Imperial Chemical Industries Ltd

Imperial Chemical Industries Limited is a British-based international group of companies whose products go to almost every sector of industry, agriculture and medicine. It is one of the largest chemical concerns in the world with more than 192,000 employees and annual sales of more than £4,000 million in chemicals, petrochemicals, plastics, fibres, dyes, paints, pharmaceuticals, agrochemicals and non-ferrous products.

The company has manufacturing operations in Britain and Western Europe, and throughout the world in such countries as Canada, the USA, India, Australia, Latin America, Africa, Pakistan, Malaysia and Indonesia.

ICI has nine manufacturing divisions in the United Kingdom, each of which can be thought of as a big company in its own right, in terms of assets and turnover. The group's activities are diverse and its organisation reflects this. The emphasis is on decentralisation with as much autonomy as possible being given to the UK divisions and overseas companies. These are in different businesses and, within a common framework, each has its own individual organisation structures and methods. Each has a strong sense of identity—a natural consequence of what it does, where it is, how it started, and the customers it serves. Divisional and overseas loyalties are strong, resulting from the fact that each unit has considerable control over its own affairs. Each Division has its own research, engineering production, selling, purchasing, marketing and personnel departments, operating under a divisional or company chairman who agrees financial targets and is responsible to the ICI main board for achieving them.

Purchasing and Supply

ICI spends hundreds of millions of pounds each year (in 1976, £1.35 billion) on buying raw materials, equipment, packaging and fuels. A central purchasing department in London has responsibility—in co-operation with the divisions—for negotiating the principal ICI contracts for supplies to divisions, although more responsibility is now being delegated to divisions' purchasing and supply departments as their processes become more specialised. The biggest single example is the company's multi-million pound oil purchases which are carried out by Petrochemicals Division.

For many supply items, ICI makes central contracts that extend over several years with the minimum definition of quantities to be taken up during the contract. This makes ICI's aim of more than one supplier for each product purchased more easily attainable.

Paints Division

Among the smaller divisions, but one of Europe's largest paint makers and the UK's largest manufacturer of decorative paints. The division employs some 6,000 people at five main locations in the UK.

Location	Product
Slough, Berkshire	headquarters and works. Paints
Glasgow	paints
Hyde, Cheshire	plastics and plastics coating sheet fabric and films
Oldham, Lancashire	wallpapers and vinyl wall-covering
Stowmarket, Suffolk	paints

All these units are serviced by one Purchasing and Supply Department at two locations, Slough and Hyde. (See Fig. 10.1.) Of the total spent on process materials, two-thirds are against central contracts. For general and engineering materials, the figure is nearer 50 per cent.

Rate of Division and Central Purchasing Department

The purchasing organisation within ICI is split between the divisions and the centre, mainly by their slightly differing roles.

Central Purchasing Department

a buys over and above a certain annual expenditure
b buys certain specific items
c makes contracts.

Division Purchasing Departments

a buy items under a certain annual expenditure
b buy non-stock lines (items individual to that area of business)
c buy certain specific items
d buy within contracts.

The two sections work together to form the matrix of all the divisions of the company. This gives maximum purchasing power.

ICI and Suppliers

The buyer/supplier relationship is extremely important. ICI is a very large customer of many companies in many varied fields of industry. The company needs raw materials, services, engineering and general supplies to be bought in at the right time, the right place, the right quality and at the right price. To meet these criteria, ICI and their suppliers work together and negotiate at all levels for mutual profit. Of course, being such a large company, ICI divisions often supply each other with raw materials. (See Fig. 10.2.) Once a supplier has been accepted by the company, there is usually a fairly long-term relationship. Inspection and quality assurance tests, financial surveys, and personal visits are carried out by ICI to ensure quality and stability are maintained.

When large sums of money are involved, manufacturers are referred to the Central Purchasing Department where contracts are drawn up. Contractors and service suppliers are exceptions to this as they deal direct with the divisions.

Suppliers Purchasing and the Finance Arrangements at ICI

The purchasing section of the Paints Division has its own accounts staff who check and pass invoices, although invoices are paid by ICI's group sales and purchases accounts department. There are no problems in taking advantage of quick payment discounts as it is possible to make daily payments if necessary by computer. The division sends invoices to be paid twice a week to the Group Sales and Purchases Accounts Department, with carefully coded instructions indicating discounts available for quick payment. There are several other kinds of manufacturers' discounts, all of which are taken by ICI. These discounts are for continuity of business, one-off goodwill discounts, bulk delivery discounts, and fixed quantity discounts.

Price Analysis of Supply Items

The central purchasing division of ICI does not attempt to carry out detailed cost analysis of supplies purchased, mainly because in the chemical industry there are few cost secrets. Cost analysis takes place usually for engineering supply items, or for labour intensive services. For example, some high value, frequent purchase engineering items are cost analysed by the division's purchasing staff, and for services such as window and office cleaning and site cleaning, the division expects to know from suppliers how many staff are to be employed and what their hourly rate of pay will be.

Purchasing Evaluation

ICI evaluate their purchasing by open scrutiny, involving close links between each division and the central purchasing department. Meetings are held to review comparable prices, security of supply, and guarantee of quality. As a large and well established company, ICI tries to make as full use as possible of its large spending power. The volume of business available means keen competition to supply, which in turn means good service and competitive prices.

Conclusion

It is obviously true that each organisation is unique, and supplies policies

Figure 10.1: Paints Division Purchasing and Supply Department Organisation as from 1 April 1978

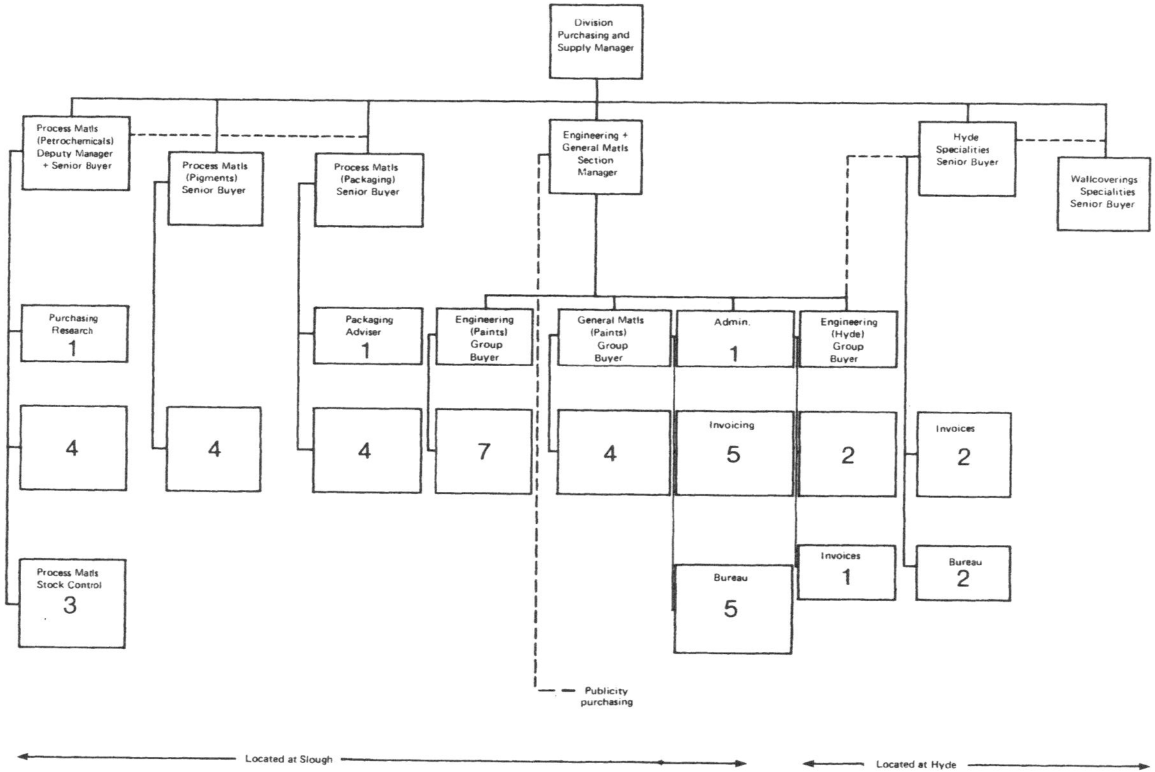

Figure 10.2: ICI Manufacturing Divisions—Interdependence

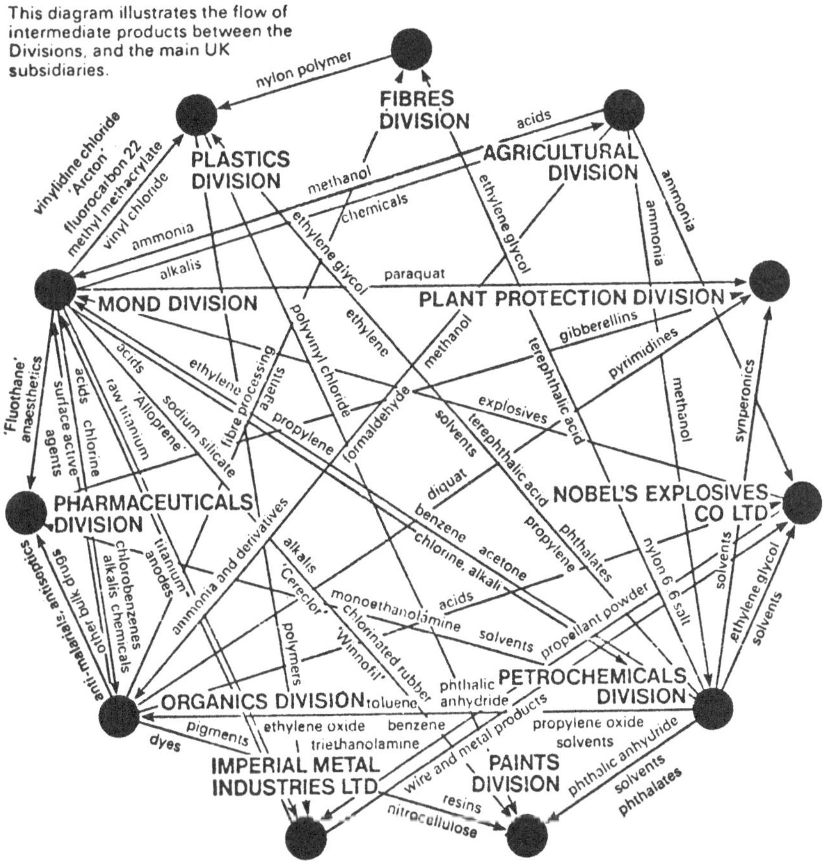

and procedures suited to one organisation are not necessarily appropriate to any other. But all organisations have many characteristics in common, and it would be absurd to dismiss any difference as obviously irrelevant.

The three British comparative studies suggest first more emphasis on active central operations than exists in the NHS, and it would be useful to have evidence that greater appropriate centralisation is irrelevant or impossible. Second, there seems to be a greater use of price analysis in negotiating with suppliers, and presumably it has been found valuable. Third, there is a more determined desire to mobilise the total buying strength of organisations, however dispersed they may be, in order to obtain better prices and services. Fourth, the GLC use of depots may be helpful to the NHS in major urban areas, especially London and is likely to repay careful study.

The considerable progress in NHS supplies in the past decade suggests that the major source of further improvement in the future will lie in successful supplies management in other organisations. These comparisons emphasised the somewhat excessive introspection of NHS supplies officers and of the DHSS. Perhaps more still is to be learned abroad.

11 HOSPITAL HEALTH SUPPLIES IN FRANCE

In a short visit to France in March 1978, I interviewed staff of the Assistance Publique, UGAP, the National Centre for Hospital Equipment, a trade association and a major regional hospital. Health services in France are a mixture of public hospitals and private hospitals, some of which are profit-making. Detailed information is available in some of the publications listed in the bibliography.

L'Assistance Publique

In Paris, there is a group of thirty-eight hospitals known as the Assistance Publique. These are among the most advanced hospitals of the country and are looked to for guidance by many other hospitals.

The Assistance Publique de Paris was founded in 1848 to administer all the public hospitals of Paris. It is a public corporation. Its thirty-eight hospitals contain 37,000 beds; 23,000 are for acute patients, 7,000 for chronic or convalescent patients and 7,000 for elderly or disabled persons. Most of these thirty-eight hospitals are located within Paris, and all of them are in the Paris district area. Besides these hospitals, the Assistance Publique runs several important general supporting services, in particular a central pharmacy and factory.

In 1976, 548,000 patients spent about 12 million days in Assistance Publique hospitals. Over 500,000 were acute patients. Thirteen per cent came from the French provinces and from foreign countries. With about the same number of beds, there were 35 per cent more patients in 1974 than in 1964. The main reason is the continually decreasing length of stay (reducing by about 3 per cent).

The Assistance Publique employs 58,000 people and 7,000 doctors. Eighty per cent of senior medical staff work on a full-time basis. There are 13,000 nurses. The Assistance Publique runs a programme of continuous professional training (35 schools attended by 20,000 persons on a full or part-time basis). Its educational programme cost, in 1974, about 140 million francs.

Its budget in 1977 exceeded 5,000 million francs, plus 500 million francs on capital investment. About two-thirds was for personnel, 11 per cent medical expenses and 10 per cent non-medical care (food, laundry, etc.). Ninety per cent of its income is provided by social security through the 'day-price' of hospitalisation which must be paid by every patient.

This price covers all expenses. The 'day-price' increases at an annual rate of 10-15 per cent.

The Assistance Publique has a central purchasing organisation which enables it to exert considerable influence over the policies of all other hospitals, most of whom operate independently in purchasing their requirements. There is understandably great competition among manufacturers, importers, and distributers to sell to the Assistance Publique, both for size of orders and for prestige. It purchases much of its requirements from the Union de Groupement d'Achats Publiques (UGAP). This is a public central purchasing organisation which supplies all kinds of equipment to government departments and public institutions.

The Assistance Publique lists the following costs for 'Industrial and commercial services' in its 1976 annual report:

		M Francs
Central Pharmacy	distribution	219.5
.. ..	manufacturing	65.9
.. ..	imports	30.0
Central hotel stores		59.5
Central butchery		48.2
Central supplies		75.2
Central laundry service		91.9
Garages and central workshops		30.9

The central authority of Assistance Publique consists of a government-appointed director-general and a board of directors, assisted by an elected medical advisory committee. The base of the structure is made up of the hospitals, each with its own director, budget, and elected supervisory council. Between these two extremes, five deputy directors assist the director-general in the discharge of his functions. A central service organisation supplies administrative support services (e.g. planning, legal, and statistical support) and provides for the pooling of certain activities (e.g. purchasing, ambulance dispatching, laundry, pharmacy) on behalf of the hospitals.

Important among the recent achievements of the Assistance Publique is the far-reaching modernisation and construction programme begun in 1965. Five entirely new teaching hospitals, ranging in size from 500 to 1,200 beds, have been built on the outskirts of Paris. Simultaneously, the vast majority of multi-bed wards in the older hospitals has been replaced by single to four-bed rooms; the remaining wards are being phased out and will have disappeared by 1980. The net result of this programme is the transfer of some 3,000 beds from the inner city, where hospital bed concentration is high and population is declining, to the increasingly populous suburban areas.

Along with plant modernisation, the technical quality of care has been upgraded. Highly sophisticated equipment for diagnostic techniques (e.g. CAT scanners) and therapeutic procedures (e.g. linear accelerators) have been installed in selected, very specialised departments of Assistance Publique hospitals. The importance of intensive care units has grown dramatically; at present they provide 8 per cent of short-stay beds, admit 10 per cent of acute patients, and account for 15.2 per cent of the cost of acute patient care, as compared with 0.8, 0.8 and 1.7 per cent respectively in 1965.

The factory that Assistance Publique owns produces drugs, disposables, and other material required by hospitals. It is under the control of the Central Pharmacy and is the only surviving production activity within Assistance Publique. The factory was opened in 1964. The Assistance Publique buys competitively from this factory or from private manufacturers. The factory has no monopoly rights. It makes what private firms do not want to make because of unattractive quantities or prices, or what the Ministry of Health does not wish private manufacturers to handle—e.g. drugs using heroin. The factory employs 160 people and has about 400 different products. It subcontracts to other manufacturers when it is not able to deal with an item itself.

The Assistance Publique publishes a directory of 1,200 drugs under their generic names, and encourages all doctors to use them instead of buying proprietary brands. There are 6,000 of such pharmaceutical products available in France. The factory is not subsidised but does not attempt to make a profit. Private manufacturers do not object to its existence. Private firms might complain that, although the factory may cover all its costs, it does not have to worry about capital and therefore profit (or absence of loss) was artificial. On the other hand, the factory had certain disadvantages. As it is in the public sector, it is subject to special laws which lead to some state employees being paid about 30 per cent more than private employees. It does not charge lower prices than others and does not try to charge higher prices. It cannot increase its staff and it cannot sack staff, and therefore its progress over the years has been achieved through greater productivity. It has one customer only, the Central Pharmacy of the Paris Assistance Publique.

The small factory looks somewhat chaotic and amateurish at first sight, but in fact everything is very carefully planned and designed, and some of the equipment—such as that for bottling distilled water and for making up special pills and drugs—is impressive when closely examined. Its building dates from the nineteenth century and was formerly used for making car parts.

The Central Pharmacy was established in 1810 in order to centralise the delivery to all Paris hospitals of certain drugs. In 1963, the old system altered and many of the services that had grown up, e.g. the laundry, were changed. That was not a political decision, but was made by administrators. The organisation now purchases, stores or produces drugs for the Paris hospitals. Apart from drugs, it deals with products such as radioactive material, certain medical materials (mainly disposables), various cotton goods used in hospitals, and X-ray film. It does not deal with equipment, only consumables. It is in competition with direct purchasing by hospitals, and that situation is very difficult to counter because each hospital director wants to be independent and sees purchasing as evidence of his independence. It fights back by making very careful studies of the market and deals effectively with suppliers. It promotes its sales by publishing catalogues listing the products of the manufacturers they deal with. It shows how many of the prices vary for identical products, with the highest prices charged by American multinational firms. The Central Pharmacy tries to educate doctors and nurses to ask for the cheaper products that the pharmacy makes. French manufacturers are very interested in the hospital market but they have many difficulties and in some ways it may be easier for multinational companies to obtain the business because most French firms in this field are small and more concerned with production than marketing. The Assistance Publique tries to give aid and preference to French firms, but it does not protect them.

The recession in recent years has had a serious effect on the market for drugs. Prices now are lower than ever before because of the decline in world business. As a result, the Central Pharmacy is able to sell drugs under their generic names rather than under the names of the manufacturers and this makes them cheaper. Foreign imports of drugs are also possible if their prices are lower. One other change comes from a more intelligent use of, for example, antibiotics. The demand for penicillin products continues to grow annually, but the number of specialised penicillin products is falling. The Central Pharmacy buys at the best prices and only produces where there is a need that can be met competitively. The Assistance Publique gives guarantees to manufacturers in respect of prices, payments, and deliveries, so they now seem to like Assistance Publique, although they were suspicious of it initially.

Finance

The construction of new hospitals, whether private or public, is subject to the approval of the Ministry of Health and Social Security. When approved, the government will supply subsidies for public hospitals of up to 40 per cent of the total cost and a further 30 per cent is available on loan without interest from a special social insurance fund. The remaining 30 per cent is usually borrowed from savings banks or from the ordinary financial market. Interest is paid out of running costs.

There is an elaborate insurance system in France covering more than 96 per cent of the population. Of every 100 francs paid in wages, employers have to pay another 40 francs to cover national health and social security insurance, and employees pay 10 per cent of their income for such insurance. The total income for the health insurance scheme was 28.5 billion francs in 1971; 25 per cent went to doctors for their fees and 33 per cent to hospitals. Every doctor is independent, but those working in general practice have agreed to charge a fixed fee for a range of approved services to patients. Thus the patient knows what he will be charged. France operates a complicated system of reimbursement for patients who have to pay their own medical bills and then claim them back from health insurance organisations. The patient usually pays 25 per cent of medicines obtained on prescription, 25 per cent of a doctor's fee, and 20 per cent of hospital costs. He can obtain private insurance to cover these additional charges. The hospitals have a daily charge which is fixed annually by negotiation with the ministry.

In 1971, French expenditure on public health and medical care equalled about 7 per cent of gross national product—over 50 billion francs; 43 per cent of the expenditure went to hospital costs. The average length of stay in a French acute hospital was 14.6 days in 1972, compared with 18 days in West Germany and 11 days in Britain. In 1961 the average length of stay in France was 21.4 days. In 1972, over 60 per cent of hospital expenditure went to pay wages and salaries. Fifteen per cent went to accommodation and food. Expenditure on pharmaceuticals and other medical needs accounted for 12.6 per cent of the hospital total budget. In 1975, it is estimated that the total health care expenditure in France amounted to 81 billion francs, 35.7 billion on hospitals (12.2 billion to private hospitals), about 50 million francs on other medical expenses, (of which doctors' fees would be 12 billion), and 41 per cent on medical goods of which all but one billion would be on pharmaceuticals, the remainder being ophthalmic and other expenditure.

Purchasing

Purchasing in French hospitals involves the pharmacy (concerned with certain sterile supplies as well as drugs) and a central purchasing department headed by the assistant to the lay hospital director (the *économe*). There seem to be few regulations and product standards to worry the manufacturer. But approval to purchase in a public hospital usually depends on a professor of medicine undertaking an evaluation study of the product and giving his approval. Disposable supplies are subject to regulations about sterilisation and they must be tested by a pharmacist. In public hospitals, purchasing is constrained by a fixed annual budget, and that reflects the kinds of treatment carried out. If there is any change in techniques or type of patient, there will be repercussions on the supplies ordered.

Every doctor in a public hospital is asked to state his supply needs each month. The supplies officer consults doctors and other specialist staff about requested items but the decision to order is made by the officer. In Paris and Lyons, where the Assistance Publique exists, orders are placed with the Central Pharmacy and that office negotiates contracts with suppliers on the basis of tendering. In exceptional and urgent cases, the hospital will order directly from manufacturers or distributors. The Central Pharmacy has an advisory committee made up of members of staff of major hospitals and it assesses the quality of products and recommends the firms that should receive orders.

The demand for medical equipment in France is increasing at an average rate of 10 per cent a year and under the provisions of the Sixth Plan (1971-75) the government invested a total of 3.5 milliard francs (about £350 million at Frs 10 = £1) in the public health sector. Of this figure, 320 million francs were to be spent on building new hospitals and modernising existing ones, and 220 million on improving medical training facilities. In 1973 the Ministry of Health budget reached a record level of just over 2 milliard (about £200 million).

The decision to purchase involves all the familiar processes of making the product known to both doctors and purchasing officers. Usually, if a doctor asks for a product it is bought, so salesmen endeavour to influence the doctor. To do that, salesmen must have a thorough knowledge of the product and its use. There are also, of course, money problems. With rigid accounting rules in public hospitals, it is sometimes difficult to persuade bureaucrats to find money for new products and sometimes capital funds are diverted to consumption expenditure. Some products are bought through public bids (tendering), but most are bought conventionally. Hospital groups may undertake some joint purchasing. That may be spreading slowly to private hospitals, who seem to be willing to collaborate if better prices can be obtained, hence improving profits. About one-third of sales to hospitals are made through wholesalers.

UGAP

One interesting and important organisation concerned with all public sector purchasing in France is the Union des Groupements d'Achats Publiques (association of public purchasing groups). Set up as a public service group in 1968, it exists to serve any public organisation, such as government departments, nationalised industries, local government authorities and mixed public/private organisations if they provide a public service. It also acts for hospitals. UGAP started informally in 1966 when total sales for the year were 305 million francs, and by 1976 sales had risen to 1,207 million francs: an average annual increase of just under 15 per cent. It is an independent public body and does not receive any income from the state and must balance its budget. It obtains its income by charging an average of 5 per cent or 6 per cent on the price of the purchases it makes on behalf of its clients. That percentage varies with the kind of product. It now has fifteen regional offices and the headquarters is in Paris. Twelve of the regions have their own stores where goods may be bought. Either they buy from the manufacturer and send it direct to a client, or they take it into stock and then deliver it as required. If they stock the item, they may charge a margin of up to 15 per cent; if there is a direct sale, the average charge is only 5 per cent, as their costs are considerably lower. If they buy very expensive equipment, they may only charge 2 per cent.

They may buy through contracts awarded after tenders have been invited for definite amounts and prices, with specified products or materials. Or they may have a contract with a supplier under which they simply agree to supply as required those items whose demand cannot be predicted, such as a particular type of operating table. Medical preferences are very important in determining products and hence increasing variety. UGAP will quote a total price for equipping a complete hospital or ward. They do not construct buildings.

Its prices are lower than other suppliers, even with its percentage increase. Nobody is obliged to buy from it. It believes that it eases the problem of buying for its clients by ensuring that they have a full knowledge of what is available. UGAP works very quickly, and suppliers like to do business with it because their money is guaranteed and they tend to pay all their bills within forty-five days, whereas some public bodies, especially hospitals, can take nine months. UGAP, of course, is then left with the problem of collecting money from hospitals. It does not work on commission. It buys and owns the product that it then sells to somebody else.

UGAP also supplies technical aid to clients, especially hospitals, and has some expert staff. UGAP could buy for the army and other defence services, but does not at the moment and has not been asked, largely because of the numerous special requirements of the army, even in such items as typewriters.

UGAP employs about 800 people throughout the country, does not deal in food or other consumables. Its director says that:

> Its fundamental aim is to lighten the costs to taxpayers in a period of intense effort to equip and modernise public services. It had 18,000 clients in 1968 and 41,100 in 1976. Some of them use UGAP for all purchases, some only use it occasionally. It can exert its growing power to buy competitively and it aims to act as a large merchant able to offer goods of the right quality and price when required by buyers. It deals with over 2,000 suppliers, more than 20,000 articles, and a million units.

UGAP places contracts after inviting tenders to supply goods in accordance with its own technical specifications. It publishes a five-volume catalogue. In 1976, 55 per cent of its deliveries were to schools and colleges, 30 per cent to local government, 10 per cent to other ministries and public bodies and 5 per cent to other organisations.

The National Centre for Hospital Equipment

This centre (Centre National de l'Equipement Hospitalier) was set up in 1973 by the Ministries of Health and Industry. It originated with an official committee that proposed that France should establish an organisation along the lines of those already in existence in other countries, to provide French suppliers and hospital personnel with an opportunity to meet and pool their efforts with a view to improving hospital equipment. The centre states in one of its publications:

> The members of the committee, especially those representing the Ministry of Health, were convinced of the need for public and private hospital establishments to be kept regularly informed about available equipment. Clearly, with the continuing development of equipment

used in treatment and diagnosis which is advancing particularly rapidly in some branches, it is difficult for all but the largest of our very many establishments to keep fully abreast of the availability, usefulness, capabilities and costs of the various products on the market.

The committee found that one of the factors restricting the development of French manufacturers in the bio-medical field was the excessive variety of equipment, which was largely attributable to the fact that, although they did not have all the necessary information at their disposal, individual establishments or indeed departments were responsible for ordering and tended to specify purpose-built equipment. This made standardisation impossible and prevented a high proportion of suppliers from developing their activities much beyond the scale of a cottage industry. Hence the proposal to rationalise equipment as far as possible, both to help the manufacturers to establish themselves on a genuine industrial footing, and to reduce costs.

These findings led to consideration of the establishment of a national hospital equipment centre whose tasks would be to keep hospitals informed about equipment available, to improve knowledge of requirements and to facilitate rationalisation of production.

In the longer term it was hoped that the centre would carry out studies of future requirements in our hospitals and participate in the planning of new equipment in the context of research and development programmes carried out in the public sector.

The centre's stated aims are to:

1. undertake studies of the optimum use of materials and equipment,
2. ensure liaison between industrialists, hospital administrators, and users of equipment and materials,
3. join with others in working out standards and rules ensuring the maintenance of quality of products,
4. co-operate in experiments in hospitals and in all laboratories or organisations approved by public bodies,
5. study all appropriate attempts to improve the maintenance of equipment, and eventually to take part in such attempts or to promote them,
6. ensure that national information policies on hospital management are maintained.

Membership of the centre (legally, a private company) is open to public authorities, public hospitals, companies manufacturing hospital equipment in France, and other non-profit-making bodies interested in hospital equipment.

The centre's income in 1977 amounted to 11 million francs. Member hospitals paid 3 francs per bed, firms paid 2,000 francs plus 0.03 per cent of turnover, and other organisations paid 500 francs.

Its chief function is to obtain and disseminate technical information on all aspects of hospitals, including personnel, materials, laboratories, and equipment. Its activities vary:

> The Centre may act as consultant; under contract, to any hospital on request to advise on the installation of furniture or technical equipment or to assist in the preparation of contracts placed by hospital managements. It may provide services under the same conditions in connection with any technical or administrative enquiries or checking procedures involved in such transactions. It may also provide such services to foreign hospitals or public health administrators. It may also act as consultant to industrial or commercial enterprises, project overseers, or design offices in connection with hospital equipment problems.
>
> At the request of the Ministry of Health, it may be brought in on any construction project initiated or carried out under the supervision of the central administration department responsible for hospital building. The national centre is required to keep documentation on all matters falling within its terms of reference, to be kept up to date and available to users. The centre may publish specialised reviews, information bulletins, memoranda or monographs on any subject within its sphere of activity.
>
> The National Equipment Centre staff is now over fifty, which enables it to react efficiently to inquiries from interested hospital organisations on French hospital equipment.

A French Hospital

I was able to visit the Centre Hospitalier Régional et Universitaire at Rheims. The centre comprises several hospitals. One, the Hôpital de la Maison Blanche, is a children's hospital built with American funds in 1935. In 1976, a new hospital, the Robert Debré Hospital, was opened. In 1958, it was decided to create a number of regional centres that provided both advanced medical treatment and a medical school. There are seven main hospitals in Rheims forming the centre and they are administered by a director-general with seven assistants plus a director for each hospital. The regional centre has a total of 4,000 beds.

The director of each hospital acts as link between the director-general on the one hand and each of the hospitals concerned. None of the directors are doctors. There is no senior doctor, but there is a medical committee, and the chairman is influential.

The budget for the hospital is fixed by norms laid down by the Ministry, but the prefect of the region determines the daily rate to charge to patients in each region. These daily rates vary considerably between different kinds of treatment. The cheapest rate is for non-residential psychiatric treatment and that was 252 francs from March 1977. For surgery it is 623 francs, for maternity 597 francs, chronic illnesses 342 francs, for intensive care it is 1,679 francs and for cardiac treatment it is 2,966 francs. Under the social security scheme, the patient is only responsible for 20 per cent of the total charges, but 20 per cent of nearly 3,000 francs a day is clearly a considerable burden.

All the hospitals in the region buy food jointly and the *économe* in each hospital specialises. They have annual contracts with suppliers in most cases but some contracts may only be for six months: suppliers object to committing themselves for a long period, as happened last year in the case of sugar, when there were major international market problems. Under their contracts, the hospitals guarantee to buy a fixed amount within a margin of about 10-15 per cent. The price in the contract is fixed for the year.

The food for all the five hospitals in Rheims is delivered to the main stores at the Debré hospital. They have one monthly delivery for most goods, but perishables like fresh vegetables are delivered twice a week. The delivery arrangements are imperfect, but they are the only real problem in the supplies field.

The senior nursing officer has about 700 nurses under her. She is concerned with buying surgical gloves, catheters, syringes and surgical needles. They are listed in local catalogues and she buys at the best available price. Sales representatives come to her with new products and she sees them all. She is given a quantity of a new product to test and then if it is satisfactory the product is bought on a normal contract. She consults supervisory nurses about products tested in this way and she keeps a book in which their brief comments are recorded. They come to see her quite frequently and she does not have committees for this purpose. If the quality of products after delivery is not up to specification, she reports the matter to the supplier and he will replace them. If she is not satisfied, they do not argue with the supplier but do not use him again after the contract has run out.

There is a group purchasing scheme for all hospitals in the department.

It includes all kinds of medical goods. She is free to buy outside the contract, but never does so. If there is a disagreement among the doctors as to what should be bought, the majority decision is accepted by all doctors. Contracts for the region are made by the chief *économe*; he is part of the prefect's staff and joins him and other administrators and doctors in making the contracts. There are no national contracts and each region and department makes its own contracts.

As far as the internal distribution of stores is concerned, nurses send in their order each month for what they want and it is delivered to a senior nurse for use and distribution. There are some local stores. Drugs are dealt with in a similar way.

The Debré hospital was opened in 1976, but has been developing over many years. It has eight floors and is extremely modern and well-equipped. They have rooms with one, two, or three beds, and there are no large wards. Some think the hospital is too large and that patients and visitors find it enormous and frightening. On the other hand, they do have the benefits of the whole range of medical specialisation. All their food is cooked on the premises in very modern kitchens and delivered cold to floors, where it is heated. Patients are asked to order their meals the day before from a menu with a very wide choice. They have very extensive freezing facilities and by using those carefully they are able to ensure that enough food is prepared in advance so as to enable them to manage with a very small staff at weekends. The most intriguing piece of equipment was a robot delivery trolley for food. This does not run on rails and does not have anybody controlling it directly, but it is guided by wires laid in the floors. The trolley can move to where the covered trays of food are prepared for the patients. The trays are stacked on the trolley, which then moves automatically to special lifts and can go up to any of the eight floors, move out of the lift, and stop in the parking area from which the food is collected and distributed manually. These are electronic devices and are programmed to work as required. Batteries are recharged every day. The only time they broke down in two years was when the Minister of Health came to open the hospital officially.

Conclusion

The health care supplies system in France differs in a number of ways from both the British and German, but common needs lead to many similarities. Perhaps the most outstanding difference is the apparent lack of discontent and argument. That impression is based on little knowledge, but a short intensive bout of interviewing in Paris and Rheims and a careful study of relevant publications may reveal a general tendency as well as more extensive inquiries. Such a state of satisfaction is not surprising, given the high priority for health services in national economic plans. The best French hospitals, especially the regional centres, must be among the best in the world. Within each hospital, there is a buyer or a group of buyers free to buy in any way they please within the constraints of hospital budgets. There is no hierarchy of supplies officers. The suppliers are not so content, but their complaints are due more to the general economic conditions of recent years than any peculiar vices of health services. Apart, that is, from the disgraceful delays in payment by hospitals, but even that is predictable and can be allowed for in costing and pricing. However, the contentment of supplies officers and suppliers is not the only criterion for assessing a supplies system. One looks for evidence of concern for achieving better results in all senses. French hospital supplies are supported by a wide range of useful supportive organisations, particularly UGAP and CNEH and the influence of the Assistance Publique and of the Ministry of Health. The School of Health at Rennes, the many professional societies, the social insurance institutions and academic studies all play their part. But they are all voluntary bodies, generating a considerable structure of bureaucracies that must consume many resources merely in existing and in relating to one another. Whatever the merits of apparent independence and the historical explanation for present policies, there can be no grounds for believing that the optimum arrangements have now been found.

12 HOSPITAL SUPPLIES IN WEST GERMANY

I visited Germany in March 1978 and interviewed members of the following organisations:

1. Deutsches Krankenhausenstitut, Düsseldorf,
2. Evangelical Hospital, Kirchfeldstrasse, Düsseldorf,
3. A firm supplying surgical goods.
4. Koch und Stergel, X-ray equipment manufacturers, Essen,
5. Evangelical Hospital ('Florence Nightingale'), Kaiserwerth, Düsseldorf.

A number of important issues emerged.

1. The hospitals obtain most of their income through charging a comprehensive daily rate to patients which is recoverable from the social insurance system. At present the daily rate is 150 DM. The rate has to be approved by the ministry, and 8 per cent of the rate is to cover the cost of capital equipment. The total cost of leased hospital equipment will be considered in revisions of the daily cost, whereas only a proportion of capital investment is considered. Private insurance exists if an individual wishes more treatment and if his monthly income is more than 3,100 DM he can opt out of the social insurance scheme. The daily rate covers all costs (apart from one mark for each prescription) and is payable to any recognised hospital. Thus the private hospitals, whether profit-seeking or not, obtain nearly all their income from the social insurance system that is supervised and subsidised by the state.

2. Annual exhibitions of hospital supplies are held in about twenty large cities, and a national exhibition is held every other year. The 1977 International Hospital Exhibition held at Hanover had nearly 1,000 exhibitors. The only government involvement is within the framework of ancient German laws requiring local authorities to ensure that there are open public markets for all goods. There is a national product evaluation service for all goods, run by an organisation similar to the National Consumer Council.

3. Each of the hospitals visited had about 600 beds and had been built since 1973, although they were old foundations, one of them tracing its history back for over 150 years. That hospital employed four supplies officers or buyers (*Einkaufer*) who dealt with all products except drugs, which were bought by the chief pharmacist. The chief buyer had

some difficulty in calculating total annual purchases, but after a number of consultations said they amounted to about 4 million DM, half of which were spent on drugs and about 1.5 million DM on food. The hospital had three stores, one for food. He thought he dealt with 900 suppliers annually. There were few written contracts and orders were placed as required. They paid within days of receiving an invoice and usually obtained a discount of up to 2 per cent for prompt payment. Most goods were bought initially in small quantities and tested through use. A committee of users evaluated products. The hospital was a member of a Düsseldorf group of 18 hospitals that undertook joint buying of some goods required in large quantities, such as paper.

4. Both hospitals said that they had no problems over supplies.

5. The surgical goods dealers handled many kinds of orthopaedic appliances, including specialised imports. It was a private company, established about 1900, employing 36 people; it sold to about 1,000 hospitals and to other dealers as well as directly to the public through three shops. Total turnover was expected to be about 9 million DM in 1978: sales in the first two months of the year were 25 per cent higher than in 1977 and the managing director was puzzled by such an increase. It may be due to government money being spent earlier in the year than usual, but the reason was likely to be different in each *Land* and they sold throughout the country. Hospital administrators liked to buy through merchants as it reduced the number of order forms and invoices they had to handle. But the dealer had to maintain personal contacts with hospitals, including doctors and nurses. There was no difficulty in seeing doctors if the firm was long-established but it was very difficult for new firms. They had few formal contracts but there was a growing tendency to order, say, six-months' supply of syringes and then to place a similar order. Tenders were increasing and contracts were more popular, mainly because one hospital had reported many advantages from that method of buying over the past six years. Up to 10 per cent on unit costs could be saved by bulk-buying on long contracts with reduced distribution routes, partly because the dealer could then obtain better prices from manufacturers.

New products were important to the business and it was one of only four or five German dealers who imported specialist items. The managing director visited many medical exhibitions and attended medical conferences to learn about new research work, in Germany and abroad. Foreign countries tended to be more innovative because Germany had concentrated on rebuilding its industry since 1945. British goods were bought and British prices were not always too high.

The firm responded to demand from hospitals and also offered unrequested new products. They had co-operated on two or three occasions with doctors in developing new products, including a special clamp used by one of the pioneers of open heart surgery twenty-five years ago.

There were few problems in hospital supplies. Most of their business was in surgical instruments and there were few maintenance difficulties: bigger hospitals now tended to have their own maintenance engineers.

The managing director was a member of the board of directors of the German Surgical Trade Association, and their main function was to exchange experience and information. They negotiated with government over technicalities in new legislation but there was no point in talking about tax reductions. He was also one of the two German representatives in a European surgical trade association that was established about 12 years ago to exchange information and to give advice about products and agencies. Prices were not discussed in the German association as that would be illegal, except where several firms were preparing a joint tender. He thought there would be less hospital building in the next few years as there had been too much in recent years: some hospital departments were now closed through a fall in demand, largely due to unemployment and the desire to delay treatment, or to get back to work as quickly as possible.

6. The X-ray manufacturing firm was now a subsidiary of the French Thomson group and its CGR Company. It employed over 1,000 people, and its total annual sales were about 100 million DM in Germany. It sold about 9 main X-ray products, plus generators and extra parts. The smallest X-ray cost 50,000 DM and with necessary extras (including generator) the total cost was 200,000 DM. Its most expensive complete equipment cost 1,000,000 DM. It dealt with about 1,000 hospitals. Its main competitors were Siemens and Phillips. The firm exported to UK, Ireland, and Eastern Europe. Most other countries were supplied by the French parent company. There were few X-ray imports. Sales had been stable in the last two years despite cuts in public expenditure. Over the past ten years, annual increases in sales had averaged about 10 per cent. Sales to hospitals were in response to invitations to tender. Prices of the three main firms were similar so success depended on quality, reputation, medical opinion, and financial facilities. Salesmen visit hospitals and private clinics regularly to keep in touch and especially to give information about new products. Salesmen were usually graduates with relevant electrical or electronic qualifications and were much involved in details of installation problems after orders were placed. The firm employed about 100 salesmen. Orders were by written contract,

and deliveries were made between one and twelve months as products were only made to order. The firm provided annual maintenance contracts as the equipment was too specialised for hospital technicians. It might wait one or two years for payment of the largest items. No discount was offered for prompt payment as a general rule.

New products tended to be improvements on existing ones in response to requests from doctors. One recent development had involved making a partially automatic machine fully automatic that was able to X-ray patients from all positions. The firm had to have a full range of products to be competitive, and thus were able to meet all the X-ray needs of most hospitals. It undertook fundamental and applied research, both within the firm and sponsored it in hospitals. It had no plans to diversify. It was a member of a trade association. They attended medical conferences. Future growth was likely to be small but ultrasonics were growing. My informants were a group of three young sales representatives.

Conclusion

The limitations of desk research and a brief field visit are obvious from the above report. At the interviews I was dependent on the knowledge of the informants and on their willingness to disclose it to me. I believe they were all free from the concern for secrecy that is common among British informants, but I was surprised at the general lack of readily accessible basic data. Neither hospital supplies officer knew his total annual expenditure nor the number of suppliers dealt with without complex consultations and the figures given were clearly imprecise. The method of regular quarterly visiting used in the main British study seemed justified by the superficiality of the German information. The X-ray manufacturers were probably represented inadequately by the relative inexperience of my informants, at least as far as company strategy is concerned.

Despite these inadequacies, all the information obtained contributes to a clear picture. Germany is a wealthy country wedded to a 'free market' philosophy that accentuates the individual role of each hospital and thus naturally the purchase of hospital supplies is seen as a separate, independent activity for each hospital. As a result, there are no problems—because there is little or no attempt to optimise purchasing in terms of price or product innovation. Moreover, the apparent 'free market' in health services is a myth, as the health system and the associated industries are dependent on an elaborate social insurance scheme that is not self-financing. One authoritative estimate is that the total deficit amounted to 2,047 million DM in 1966. Public subsidies for hospital building were approximately another 2,000 million DM in 1972. 'It means that the State via the *Länder*, with Federal Government approval, may finance out of taxation 15 per cent (investment and maintenance costs) of hospital care. The remaining 85 per cent (running costs) will be covered by health insurance.'[1]

The pressures of rising health care costs, particularly in recent years of economic recession and unemployment, have begun to encourage hospital supplies officers to buy on longer-term contracts and to take part in some joint purchasing but it is probably a very small proportion of total purchases. There is little prospect of a national health service evolving into the British form and thus there is no prospect of any kind of national supplies system. But the unavoidable partnership with suppliers is a reality, however unconscious to most participants, and the higher social status of industry may make it easier to create closer links that will have benefits to both sides as economic conditions or rising health costs encourage more rational collaboration.

It is wrong to view West Germany as a private enterprise society, with its nationalised industries, social insurance schemes, state welfare expenditure and guaranteed minimum wage. Its health care services will continue to flourish within a diversified ownership structure, but its functioning should become more rational over the next decade or two.

Note

1. A. Maynard, *Health Care in the European Community*, Croom Helm, London, 1975, pp. 39-41.

Part Four

DANGERS AND OPPORTUNITIES

13 THE PRESENT POSITION

The main value of this study will be the quality of its proposals for the future. Those proposals must emerge from a careful appraisal of the present situation and that independent appraisal may be of some use in itself. The focus of our attention has been the relations between the NHS and its suppliers. That can only be understood after an appreciation of the function and needs of each party to the relationship. We have not examined the whole of the NHS nor all suppliers and our conclusions can only be generalisations, and many will assume some significant disadvantage from the location of the twenty organisations within the London area. Such a case needs to be carefully made and assessed before it can be accepted. From my limited knowledge of the NHS and firms outside London, I am not aware of any significant peculiarity of London in respect of supplies.

The NHS supplies situation can be readily grasped from the summary at the end of Chapter 7. All the NHS officers we met were busy, energetic, concerned and heavily involved in their work. Some were unduly depressed by local circumstances, one or two so excessively sensitive that any question or comment was seen as criticism, or as stupidity arising from ignorance so vast that communication about NHS supplies was impossible with anyone outside NHS supplies. As we were not trying to appreciate every subtlety of their work, but simply trying to understand it broadly and from a special concern with the NHS and its suppliers, such a limitation of researchers does not seem crucial and may be compensated by other knowledge. Readers will judge for themselves.

Our initial study of NHS supplies was in 1969 and there has been considerable improvement in the average quality of the NHS supplies officers we have met and there are major technical changes in NHS supplies that would seem to ensure greater efficiency in the future; the obvious examples are in training, the use of computers, the NHS Supplies Vocabulary, central stores and product evaluation. However, most people concerned with NHS supplies, insider or outsider, must be impressed with the obstacles to full effectiveness that are largely self-imposed and susceptible to self-reform. There has been obvious and serious concern with the organisation of supplies at least since the Hunt Committee was set up in 1966 and yet the strange failure to grasp clear opportunities for improvement persists. There are certainly conventions of many kinds that prevent DHSS taking the lead and ensuring that there is a truly national supplies system for the NHS; none of them justifies the absurdities that have led to the slow lurching from Hunt in 1968 to the Sunningdale conference with suppliers in 1971 to Collier in 1976 and to Salmon in 1977, almost certainly leading to a supplies board in 1979 that will merely consolidate the delicate game concerned with authority and power that has been played for so long.

A national supplies system can take many forms and there is no need for a soulless uniformity imposed by a dictator in Russell Square. There are local needs and circumstances that must be handled locally. But there are common needs that justify common, national solutions. The payment of accounts is an obvious example, and the cost of useless variety in accounting methods could be calculated in part by the value of lost discounts for prompt payment. Similarly, consultation with users, order forms, delivery and stores procedures, quality control, division of supplies responsibilities between region, area, district and sector, and information about new products would all appear to be better tackled as national problems with national solutions, simply because every ASO seems to share similar difficulties. The obvious path to progress seems to be through internal reorganisation, and through improving relationships between DHSS, regions and areas, and between supplies officers and finance, catering and engineering departments. But the obvious path is seldom the best route and it may be helpful to start from different assumptions and to seek different goals.

The first and reasonable assumption is that the NHS supplies system is imperfect because it has not been organised on the basis of systematic knowledge gained from objective enquiry. The absence of much elementary knowledge, such as the quantity of goods purchased in one year, is one symptom, although it must be established that such data is worth collecting. But the absence of such information is not the consequence of a rational decision. Instead, decisions are often made on the basis of argument and unsupported opinion, as it is clear from several reports referred to in earlier chapters.

We cannot put the clock back and we cannot start with a clean slate. There is an NHS supplies system and it works: patients do receive care and recover from disease and to do that they need hospitals with beds, food, operating theatres and electromedical equipment. But there is no evidence that by chance the optimum supplies system has evolved. Literally, we do not know how good it is. Nor how bad. Perhaps both conservationists and reformers can unite to seek methods of evaluating the present situation. But evaluation must be preceded by the selection of appropriate criteria and we must seek some objective guidance if argument is not merely to be diverted to a different focus. An attempt to define general criteria for evaluating supplies systems was made in Chapter 2. Criteria more relevant to the NHS must clearly include the welfare of patients. Less obviously, they should include the welfare (in the widest sense) of staff, the efficiency of the NHS as a whole and the impact of the NHS supplies system on suppliers.

Criteria about the welfare of patients involve consideration of the availability and suitability of existing products and services, and there is evidence of considerable efforts to consult users and, indirectly, consumers. The quality of such consultation varies and almost certainly would gain from the application of appropriate consumer research techniques used by some sophisticated consumer goods manufacturers. These attempt to deal with defined problems, involve the need to consult genuine samples of consumers, the formulation of objective questions, the systematic recording of answers and the statistical analysis of answers. We found no evidence of such techniques in the NHS.

There are more complex criteria of consumer welfare that are largely ignored by many advanced survey techniques. They understandably concentrate on the value of existing products. The most significant question for evaluating health care systems is whether the necessary products exist. This is a particularly interesting problem for electromedical equipment because of the apparently limitless opportunities for mechanising existing medical treatments and for developing new techniques, such as tomography. There is no organised process within the NHS for identifying needed products nor for determining priorities in developing them, although the Scientific and Technical Branch makes some attempts with inadequate resources. Product innovation is regarded as the primary responsibility of the manufacturers, and the decision to initiate has been taken by them. But our manufacturers tend to produce new products that are developments or extensions of existing products: strategic decisions to enter new product fields are rare and other research does not indicate any simple process or pattern.[1]

The welfare of suppliers is equally important because they must be able to fulfil their primary function of making available the goods and services the NHS needs. They are supposed to do this in the face of foreign competition both in the NHS market and in foreign markets and they are expected to help the British balance of payments. They are private businesses but depend on public funds. They cannot revert to 'free competition' even if they wished to do so because the upheaval of such a revolution would threaten the provisioning of the NHS. They cannot be nationalised because no government has had a mandate to do so and if they did, there would be problems of continuity of output as well as about the role of foreign firms, both those producing in Britain and importing into Britain. Thus suppliers need more certainty in NHS purchases and the NHS organisation and policy has to be adapted to help their functions as well as the activities of the NHS. Such problems exist for both parties in selling and ordering methods, documents, installation, information, servicing and product development and innovation. Finally, there are wider social and political needs: reducing costs of health care, promoting exports, maintaining employment, increasing productivity, and ensuring economical distribution. If these various considerations are brought together and we assess the problems of the British health supplies system as a whole, we can begin to see the kind of proposals that would be useful to all in the future.

The most important need is genuine collaboration between the NHS and suppliers. The DHSS has a formal responsibility to do this but its repeated actions demonstrate that it cannot bring it about; by convention, Treasury rules, political timidity and perhaps legal constraints it persists in seeing the NHS and suppliers as different responsibilities, with suppliers very much as afterthoughts. The Collier Report and the Salmon working party excluded suppliers instead of bringing them in in order to ensure that studies and proposals would be based on an appreciation of the total situation. That attitude has frustrated progress in many fields, despite the excellent work of the Industry and Exports Division to provide day-to-day service to manufacturers and exporters.

Some independent forum is needed: perhaps a simple joint committee or an advisory group of interested academics maintaining an orderly flow of advice to both parties for separate implementation or a new research institute for health supplies that would combine both research and implementation. The initiative cannot be left to the DHSS. Perhaps the supplies officers will seize the opportunity to demonstrate their ability to cope with the most challenging responsibility of management: constructive innovation.

Having devised an integrated mechanism for dealing with common problems, one of its perennial tasks would be devising and sustaining a strategy for new product development. We need to discover what activities can usefully be helped by mechanisation and then how the products can most sensibly be made, developed and scrapped when appropriate. That does not necessarily exclude variety and competition if they are wanted. Within the NHS, there must be a greater emphasis on specialisation among supplies officers and a central supplies staff bringing about a proper distribution of functions that bypasses the irrelevant NHS administrative structure. It should be concerned with all those matters that the Collier Report said it would have dealt with if it were trying to devise an ideal supplies system for the NHS. Out of that should come a rational contracting process, based on firm commitments to suppliers so that they can work economically throughout the year and expand exports whilst satisfying home demand. Before attempting to be more precise, foreseeable developments in health care must be considered.

The Future of Health Care

It is impossible for one person to know enough about medicine, sociology and industry to be able to predict how health care systems will develop and what their industrial requirements will be. But even a superficial review of some relevant trends may indicate some glimpse of the future.

The large, fully equipped hospital is unpopular and not necessarily essential to either treatment or economy. The considerable range of size among effective hospitals suggests that little is pre-ordered in this field, and much that exists is the haphazard consequence of arbitrary prejudices. Smaller hospitals are favoured by most, they should be more efficient, and the relative ease of transportation in a small country suggests that the advantages of proximity between specialisms could be provided within say, twenty miles instead of twenty hospital floors, without unacceptable penalties. Only detailed, continuous study will give the right answers.

People are spending shorter periods in hospital in acute cases. It is clear that hospitals must not continue to be used as unsatisfactory homes for the aged or the incurables. In many clinical spheres there are opportunities to return people to their homes more quickly providing that the homes are suitable and that professional help is taken to the patient's home. There is likely to be an increasing number of health centres, day hospitals, local clinics and fewer hospitals, with an increasing range of small-scale electromedical equipment that is portable, labour-saving, easy to use and safe. They must make minimal demands on maintenance engineers and servicing costs.

We should see an extension of links between the NHS and suppliers into a conscious effort to identify needed products, carry out research and apply findings both to develop existing products and to innovate, defining optimum output levels and establishing a distribution and storage network that takes account of the needs of NHS and its suppliers.

Some suppliers will wish to remain independent at all costs, whatever that means when they are almost entirely dependent on a public service, but others would welcome becoming 'manufacturers under licence' to the NHS, forging a different relationship that provided greater stability but requires ever higher standards of performance.

The Way Ahead

Some of these unexceptionable forecasts can be supported from trends outside health care systems and some helpful mechanisms can be found from our comparative studies.

The improvement of the NHS supplies system is not simply a rational problem. That would indicate a need for a centralised organisation that would emphasise uniformity and efficiency before any other consideration. But sensible changes must be acceptable to as many people as possible if they are to co-operate in designing and implementing reform. That consideration must not exclude inaction nor allow a tiny minority to veto progress. There seem to be widespread assumptions about excessive sensitivity and hostility to change among supplies officers but that has not been proved. Naturally, they will oppose another round of 'musical chairs' and the nonsense of moving officers to optimum appointments by cumbersome conventions of committee selection. Even within the constraints of existing structures, some useful reforms are possible. The major weakness of an impotent directive force can be overcome by voluntary collaboration, bringing together the existing national contract mechanism, the inter-regional consortia and the planning mechanisms developing within the regions and areas. The first necessity for intelligent progress is the production of firm minimum purchasing requirements that will lead to guaranteed orders to manufacturers. Only the most elementary encouragement is needed.

One variation (or extension of that when it is operative) is the creation of a national purchasing agency on the lines of the French UGAP organisation, an entirely voluntary service that will provide information, accept orders for some or all of a client's purchasing and obtain goods through long-term contracts with designated suppliers. Halfway between a compulsory nationalised service and an entirely voluntary service would be something similar to the Assistance Publique or at least its supplies component. The obvious testing ground would be the four contiguous Thames regional health authorities. They could without undue difficulty create a rational system of contracting, distributing, and manufacturing (where needed) of the whole range of health service supplies in their operational area or appropriate parts of it.

Whatever formal changes may emerge, there is a clear need for a more effective information system about available products and services. A beginning of such a system exists in a number of scattered places: the DHSS Hospital Building Division, the Hospital Centre of the King's Fund, the information services of the Department of Bio-Engineering of Northwick Park, the NHS Supplies Vocabulary and the files of supplies officers. It should be possible in these computer days to list and grade all available products, feeding in consumer reports on use, delivery, price and maintenance. Any supplies officer should have immediate access to such a service that would economise on ordering, delivery and storage at least to the extent needed to pay for itself. The French Centre National de l'Equipment Hospitalier should have some relevant experience to contribute.

We certainly need a more careful review of the central stores programme before it goes too far beyond its present thirty to the point of national coverage. Studies of net advantages are needed from the viewpoint of the stores, the hospital, the patient and the supplier. The excellent studies undertaken by the Operations Research Branch of the National Coal Board do not seem to have been sufficiently all-embracing to prove that the present development is the best one. The answer may indicate the need for fewer stores and a more ambitious scheme that would serve a range of public services, on the lines of the depots of the Greater London Council.

The quality of a supplies system can be measured in part by the prices it pays for good products delivered as and when required. The absence of a price evaluation procedure within the NHS means that every supplies officer is working at a serious disadvantage. Moreover, the experience of British Airways, and of British Gas, is likely to show that the professionalism exemplified by the informed power of such a mechanism improves relations with suppliers and produces better service.

What about the opposite policy? Would the NHS be better off by a return to pre-Hunt days when each hospital management committee did as it thought best, with a minimal national contracts policy? Presumably, examples are to be found in many countries. My limited studies of the West German situation indicate that there is virtually no attempt to interfere with the market mechanism, apart from limited joint buying by local hospitals. The USA seems similar but the joint buying arrangements are probably more extensive. There are also the activities of such bodies as the Hospital Corporation of America. In a letter to me on 20 October 1977 the Vice-President, Materials Management, wrote:

> Hospital Corporation of America and its subsidiary Hospital Corporation International purchase supplies through a method called Group Purchasing. It is not centralised purchasing as you think of centralised purchasing for a manufacturing company with many branches, but we at the central headquarters negotiate supply contracts then each hospital orders from that contract. The advantage to the hospital is (1) volume discounts regardless of the size of the hospital (2) not having to negotiate with every vendor.
>
> The central office also serves as a consultant to the hospital on Materials Management problems—such as excess inventories, distribution of supplies within the hospital, etc.
>
> All equipment purchasing is done by the central office for all new construction, renovation and/or addition and serve as consultants to each hospital on capital equipment purchasing.
>
> For the calendar year 1977—supply purchases under contract will exceed 83,000,000 dollars and 45,000,000 dollars for equipment.

The German and American situations would seem to reflect the buoyancy and prosperity of wealthy market economies, and where they work there are only ideological grounds for proposing change. In trying to be objective, however, it is important to remember that the state in both countries has an influential role in sustaining social security systems and in Germany provides extensive funds for hospital building, which in turn sustains large purchasing programmes. In Sweden, a company named LIC was set up thirty-five years ago to procure health supplies for hospitals. It now has as members twenty-three county councils, four municipalities, the Swedish Red Cross, the University of Gothenburg, four charities, and the Federation of Swedish County Councils. Its nine divisions are concerned with the manufacture or purchase of a wide range of products including linen, furniture, stationery, transport, medical apparatus, disposables, dental products and hearing aids.

Whatever the variations between countries, there is clear evidence of significant public financing of health care systems and their procurement management. Sometimes the relationship between public and private organisations appears to be complex and probably costly. Britain may be unique in having a national health system operating a deliberately fragmented supplies system that does not appear to have any advantage over a co-ordinated system that, if intelligently designed, would probably be acceptable to nearly every supplies officer and supplier.

Recommendations

One of the aims of the original research proposal was to formulate proposals for change based on insights that might be obtained from this study. The following recommendations are made to fulfill that obligation. The complexities of implementing them are fully appreciated although the necessary brevity of statement must make them look naive. But they could be useful, they are practicable, and they could be introduced quickly if enough critics exerted themselves and if enough senior officers in the NHS and DHSS encouraged them.

1. A NHS Supplies Corporation should be established to take over full responsibility for supplies throughout the NHS. It should be a public corporation with a board appointed by the health ministers. The staff of the corporation should be all NHS supplies staff and the relevant staff of DHSS and of the Welsh, Scottish and Northern Ireland health authorities: its board should include representatives of specialist manufacturers and of supplies officers.
2. All supplies staff should continue in their present posts. They would have a new employer and work under new conditions of service to be negotiated. In time, a national career structure would be introduced after negotiation and agreement with the Association of NHS Supplies Officers and interested trade unions.
3. The corporation should, from an agreed date, have the sole right of purchasing for and supplying the NHS, and it will delegate this right to appropriate supplies officers and to others, such as local administrators or contractors.
4. The corporation should introduce a single procedure for seeking tenders, ordering, and paying for goods and services for the NHS, incorporating the NHS Supplies Vocabulary and the appropriate use of computers.
5. The corporation should wherever appropriate negotiate contracts with suppliers for minimum guaranteed purchases over specified periods for stated prices, incorporating the assessed needs of the NHS; where essential the corporation should manufacture needed products.
6. The corporation should have a new products policy that would maintain a continuous scrutiny of NHS need and then undertake the necessary research and development work, in conjunction with selected manufacturers.
7. The corporation should have sufficient funds to work on long-term

purchasing programmes, up to ten years, and should be able to lend to or invest in supplier companies, through the National Enterprise Board.

8. The corporation should maintain a comprehensive information and consultancy service for the NHS on all supplies matters.
9. The corporation should have powers to undertake similar functions throughout the world in order to build up sufficient demands for needed products that would lead to optimum output levels.
10. The corporation should be established immediately but it should only use particular powers after voluntary co-operation has been negotiated with existing health authorities and suppliers.
11. The corporation should form part of a network of similar public sector purchasing organisations and should seek to promote such a network.
12. An independent monitoring and research mechanism should be built into the organisation of the NHS Supplies Corporation and be part of a similar mechanism for all public sector supplies.

Note

1. Cf. C. Freeman, *The Economics of Industrial Innovation*, Penguin, London, 1972.

14 PRACTICE AND THEORY

Providing the NHS with the supplies it needs is only one of many examples of purchasing by public bodies from private manufacturers. Public purchasing raises many issues and it may be helpful to conclude the study of NHS supplies by placing it in the wider context of the relationship between the public and private sectors of the modern economy. Many economists doubt the ability of governments to buy so as to optimise individual satisfactions and theorists can raise many questions that invalidate most assumptions about public purchasing. The Collier Report, for example, assumes that Britain's favourable balance on international trade in medical equipment reflects some desirable arrangement of economic resources, and that the existence of many similar versions of a piece of medical equipment is undesirable and reflects a misuse of resources: these views are debatable.[1] However, public purchasing has existed for centuries and there are no grounds for assuming it will disappear. Nor is it necessarily true that whatever principles may be relevant to optimise individual preferences will be useful in appreciating the many different and complicated issues in public purchasing. It will be sensible to consider the problem from the perspective of its function in the modern economy and the ways in which government should manage it.

In his comprehensive legal study of public purchasing, Colin Turpin concludes:

> as long as the present economic system endures and governments rely upon private industry for many of their needs, the necessary control to be applied to contracting firms, as well as the necessary autonomy to be assured to those firms if they are to accomplish what is demanded of them, are best defined and regulated by contract . . . it is . . . a kind of treaty, by which the conditions of a relationship of interdependence are established.[2]

That not unsurprising conclusion for a lawyer begs many questions. It assumes that we know what 'the present economic system' is and that it involves such a distinct separation of government and supplier that a contract is sufficient as well as necessary to 'a relationship of inter-dependence'. For example, the problem of the non-competitive contract for unique products has led to agreement on the average rate of profit of British industry being built into the price (18 per cent in 1978) and that principle has been extended to the voluntary price control over pharmaceutical drugs administered by DHSS. This is a curious version of the market economy that he implies constitutes our 'economic system'.

Governments have tended to promote industrial efficiency through their purchasing whenever possible or whenever they feel it sufficiently important to make the attempt. *Public Purchasing and Industrial Efficiency* was the title of a 1967 White Paper and it noted the advantages of economic production, variety control, standardisation, quality control, and co-ordination of purchasing, and showed how progress had been made. Other initiatives followed, particularly in local government, although the role of nationalised industries were excluded from a general public sector programme. A more ambitious initiative at the same time came from Robert Maxwell, MP, through the Labour Party (*Public Sector Purchasing*) and many of his minor proposals have influenced policy since then. But the principles have been modest and they respected the strict distinctiveness of the two parties.

The Treasury has a Procurement Policy Committee on which all buying departments are represented. 'The best value for money' is the guiding rule – not 'Buy British'. In fact, an EEC directive requiring all prospective public purchases over about £170,000 to be advertised in the official journal of the Community came into force in July 1978, although transport, water energy and telecommunications authorities were excluded initially.

Defence Procurement

Special problems exist over defence procurement for obvious reasons, and some extensive innovations have been introduced in recent years that could have lessons for public procurement as a whole.

The present system of defence purchasing was set up as part of a general reorganisation of major government departments in 1970. The rationalisation of the whole function of defence procurement was one of the government's intentions.[3] To that end a project team was set up under Mr Derek Rayner (then a senior executive of Marks and Spencer) with the following terms of reference:

> To make recommendations, in time for new arrangements to be implemented by 1 April 1972, on:

(a) How best to organise the integration of all defence research and development and procurement activities, under the responsibility of the Secretary of State for Defence: among the possibilities to be considered should be the establishment of an agency within Government.

(b) How best to handle, in the light of (a), the Government's relations with the industries concerned, including its responsibilities in support of civil aircraft projects and other civil aerospace activities.

The project team should pay particular regard to the need to meet essential defence and civil requirements in the most economical and efficient way.

The main features of their recommendations, which were accepted by the government, were:

(i) There will be a single procurement organisation headed by a chief executive responsible to the Secretary of State for Defence. It will be known as the Procurement Executive and will combine the existing responsibilities of the Ministries of Defence and of Aviation Supply for the procurement of defence equipment.

(ii) Directly under the chief executive, there will be:

  (a) three controllers for Sea, Land and Air Systems who will also be members of the Admiralty, Army and Air Force Boards respectively;

  (b) a controller for guided weapon and electronic systems;

  (c) a controller for research and development establishments and research.

  The chief executive and the four systems controllers will be accounting officers for their respective Votes. Reporting to the chief executive through a secretary will be four controllers responsible respectively for policy, finance, personnel and sales.

(iii) Responsibility for policy towards the aerospace industry and towards civil aerospace research and development, and projects, will be transferred to the Secretary of State for Trade and Industry, who will call on the sources of the civil programme.

(iv) The users will be responsible for determining in the light of all available information their requirements within their overall priorities and the resources available. The procurement organisation should have its own Votes for its procurement activities and should not be required to recover the costs of either research and development or production from its defence customers; but procurement on behalf of the Department of Trade and Industry and other departments will be paid for on their Votes.

(v) There will be a ministerial aerospace board consisting of the Secretary of State for Defence and the Secretary of State for Trade and Industry to oversee the collaboration between the two departments and to be the authority for instructions and policy guidance to the procurement executive on civil aerospace matters.

(vi) The ministerial aerospace board will also be responsible for the co-ordination of space procurement policy; for this purpose the Secretary of State for Education and Science and the Minister of Posts and Telecommunications will also be members of it.

In the course of its report, the project team noted that defence procurement involved an expenditure of over £1,000 millions annually and directly employed 52,000 people.

The report noted:

(i) Any organisation spending large sums on procurement must take the blindness out of its activity by having strong teams of scientists and other professionals who can understand the problems which confront it and can help at the various stages of procurement. All of these establishments are to some extent, and many of them are very largely and intimately, involved all the time in projects and project management; in this they are quite unlike the ex-DSIR establishments. Our main concern in this area is to build up the concept of partnership between the establishments and industry and to reverse the tendency of some of the establishments to undertake design work intra-murally. Much of this would be better done by outside suppliers, who generally have greater access to civil technology and more experience in matching design to production practicalities. Unfortunately, we have in some areas brought about a situation in which industry has lost, or has never even achieved, the capability to design for itself. We believe that this is a situation which is unacceptable and that, in the national as well as the defence interest, a deliberate and sustained effort must be made to change it.

(ii) A procurement organisation will always, in the final analysis, be as good or as bad as its suppliers. But it is vain to attempt to remedy suppliers' defects by carrying out tasks which properly belong to them such as quality assurance and detailed design supervision. One must also be wary of falling into the trap of treating second-rate suppliers as cost-effective simply because they quote lower prices. Lack of profit is in no sense a yardstick for judging whether the purchase price represents value. In commercial life, suppliers who do not make a profit are rightly considered less effective in giving value for money than those with good profit records, except in short term one-for-all transactions. The total price is what matters and low costs and high profits are a better national bargain than the reverse.

(iii) More active steps must be taken to educate defence suppliers with an understanding of the users, their future needs and the environment in which they live. The recent presentation by the Army which gave defence suppliers an opportunity of learning about the long-term requirements of the Army has been widely commented on, and entirely favourably. This kind of presentation should be given regularly by the Operational Requirement Staffs of all three Services in co-operation with the Systems Controllers proposed later in this report.

(iv) In developing the new organisation, we have tried to observe the following simple statement of principles:

(a) the organisation must be fully and obviously user orientated, but charged with the task of assisting its customers in their decisions and in building up the strength of its contractors;

(b) it must be organised and staffed on a basis that recognises the specialised nature of defence procurement;

(c) it must offer a full career in defence procurement and ensure that those engaged have a sense of involvement and participation in the ultimate objective of providing the Services with the best equipment that the resources of the nation will permit;

(d) it must avoid giving conflicting responsibilities to its divisions, and to individuals except at the highest level;

(e) it must distinguish more sharply in its structure than the present procurement organisations between responsibility for the management of approved programmes and the supporting staff functions;

(f) it must be able to take advantage of the opportunity that the creation of a unified procurement organisation will bring to rationalise the defence research and development establishments in the general defence interest;

(g) it must achieve a physical co-location of staff who need to work closely together;

(h) it must balance continuity with change and provide a framework which will allow further evolution to take place within it to take account of the lessons of experience or of changed situations.

(vi) With limited research, development and production resources, there will inevitably be conflicts between the demands of the three separate Services on these. The procurement organisation must in our view be a single entity and research, development and production resources must likewise be treated as a unity within the Ministry of Defence and in relation to the Treasury and the Civil Service Department. In these circumstances, individual Controllers must not, in our view, be liable to such direction from individual Service Boards as to conflict with their task in the procurement organisation or override their responsibilities to the Chief Executive.

(vii) It has been abundantly clear to us that the present arrangements for in-service support of equipment do not in all respects meet the users' requirements in any of the Services. The proposals in this report do not deal fully with those responsibilities of the procurement organisation which cover the efficient and reliable operating capability of weapons and equipment once they are in operational use. As we have already stated the new organisation would have to accept from the outset a responsibility for every item of equipment, whatever its origins, from its conception until it is finally phased out of service. Its minimum role must be to deal with problems arising in service requiring headquarters or establishment expertise for their solution, and arrangements must be such that support is available as rapidly and directly as possible. The users should be encouraged to discuss with suppliers their in-service problems so that the suppliers are fully informed of defects and shortcomings by those who are in the best position to do so. To look beyond this at the differing ways in which in-service support, the supply of spares, etc., are and might be carried out would require a further major study. But we do not believe that our proposals close any options in this area.

By 1976, the procurement executive was spending £1,500 millions annually on equipment and employed over 55,000 people. It placed about 68,000 contracts a year. It dealt with about 4,500 suppliers but most of its business rested with 200-300 companies.

One major problem in defence procurement was the complexity of equipment and the largely non-competitive environment. That has led to sophisticated procurement techniques apparently unique to the procurement executive and has the backing of industry. Among these techniques is 'equality of information'.

(i) Equality of information, or, in other words, the right of the Procurement Executive to have access to all the information in the contractor's possession which is relevant to the pricing of the contract at hand, was a radical innovation by any standard when it was adopted generally in 1968.

(ii) It means that a fixed price contract can be costed for anything up to three years after it has actually been completed. This enables the Procurement Executive to learn the actual costs in order to assist the pricing of follow-on contracts and also to refine its estimating techniques in the light of experience – points upon which the Procurement Executive places considerable importance.

In addition, Standard Condition 50 gives either party, Procurement Executive or contractor, the machinery for appealing to the Review Board if in the light of post-costing the contractor considers that he has made an 'unconscionable' loss, or if the Procurement Executive believes him to have made an 'excessive profit'. It is probably worth noting here that in the first case referred to it (an 'unconscionable loss' case) the Review Board decided recently in favour of a contractor.

The story goes back to 28 February, 1968, when the Chief Secretary of the Treasury told the House of Commons (following enquiries into the highly publicised affairs of Ferranti and the Bloodhound missile and of Bristol Siddeley and the Orpheus engine) that the government and industry had agreed on these two important principles and furthermore had agreed on a new profit formula to be applied to government non-competitive contracts, and to the setting up of a Review Board for Government Contracts.

The new profit formula was designed to give contractors a fair return on capital employed, that is to say a return equal on average to the overall return earned by British industry.

One other interesting development concerns quality control.

As a result of the work of the Raby committee which has been set up to investigate the workings of all nine Government inspection agencies it had been decided that a defence Quality Assurance Board should be set up which would have overall control of all the inspection agencies. The Boards first met in April 1970 and its first Chief Executive, the Director General, was appointed in September of the same year. Perhaps the most important task was to place increased responsibility on suppliers themselves for the quality of their own products. One cannot be sure but it is likely that at least some of the changes which were proposed in the Rayner Report for quality assurance would have come about as a natural result of the work of the Quality Assurance Board (DQAB).

However, the Rayner Report endorsed the findings of the Raby committee.

A basic requirement of the '6/49' conditions was that firms should be 'approved'. (There were exceptions to this rule upon occasion). Approval in this context usually meant that the firm concerned was the possessor of an inspection system of a composition, and with equipment, suitable for the class of work which was to be carried out. It was also required to have as the head of its inspection department a Chief Inspector, independent of production, who was personnally approved as being suitable to control the department. There were a number of subsidiary requirements which included a marginal involvement of the purchasing department. This mainly ensured that orders were placed only upon 'Approved' companies, that copies of the orders were made available to the inspection department for control purposes and that all those orders were endorsed 'Subject to 6/49 Conditions'.

The principle involved is this:

The customer, the Government, is prepared to pay the supplier for a product to meet certain agreed requirements. The supplier agrees to do so. It is then clearly his responsibility to ensure that the supplied product conforms to the agreed requirements. Why, then, should the customer have to expend any large amount of effort and money to verify that the supplier has met the requirements? It is the supplier's responsibility so he must take all reasonable steps to ensure conformance. The customer will satisfy himself in the first instance that the supplier has satisfactory systems of control and then it is up to the supplier. Just a simple philosophical point. It is the essence of the new system.

It will be clear that very close relations exist between the procurement executive and its suppliers. Detailed regulations exist for all aspects of the contractor's standards and procedures. He has to be inspected in detail over at least two days. He is responsible for ensuring that all purchased material or services conform to contract requirements.

All these activities are supported by an extensive research and development function carried out in twenty-five service establishments and in firms and universities under contracts. It has been said that all the establishments are devoted to one prime task: 'assessing and widening the range of possibilities and the promise of change and supporting its application to a military capability'. Defence research is the largest single research and development operation in the UK and is thus responsible for giving industry a steady and massive technological push. All defence research and development cost £350 millions in 1976.

The Royal Ordnance Factories are now part of the Procurement Executive. Their annual turnover exceeds £100 million and they employ about 18,000 people in eleven factories. They manufacture guns, heavy armoured fighting vehicles, engineering equipment, ammunitions, bombs, and guided weapons. A substantial portion of its output is exported.[4]

The process of contracting begins with a statement known as a Staff Target. It

> expresses in broad terms the function and desired performance of a new weapon or equipment. This will be the product of earlier research programmes the object of which will have been to identify promising lines of approach and sometimes of pre-feasibility studies carried out by industry. It is practice at this stage to circulate Staff Targets to industry in order to acquaint firms with intentions and to gain the benefit of any comments they may have. There follows a feasibility study stage which seeks to identify the most cost-effective solution in equipment terms to the stated military need and the culmination of which is the definition of a Staff Requirement.
>
> Once the staff requirement has been defined, the need is to define the project which is to meet that requirement in as much detail as possible in order to reduce to the minimum the areas of uncertainty. At this stage we cannot normally afford to prolong competition and the task therefore, in the project definition study, is to explore with a selected contractor areas of technical uncertainty, draw up a comprehensive costed development plan, establish the timescale for com-

pletion of the project and estimate the unit production cost. All past experience confirms that money spent at this stage in accurate definition will more than pay its way in helping to reduce subsequent delays, escalations in cost and technical set-backs. The Downey Committee on Development Cost Estimating recommended that on major projects up to 15 per cent of the total development cost should be spent on this process of definition.

Contract policy. It is general government policy to award public contracts whenever possible on the basis of effective competition as a means of securing the best value for money. For a number of reasons, however, this may often not be practicable. This is particularly so in the defence field where competitive tendering is often ruled out for more than three-quarters of our business.

The scope for competition in defence procurement is also limited by the need to see, so far as possible, that the competent firms have sufficient continuity of the sort of work to which they are particularly suited to maintain an adequate and dedicated defence capability. This is a very important feature of maintaining our industrial base.

Collaboration with other NATO countries. The problems of defence finance are aggravated nowadays by the steadily increasing cost and sophistication of current weapons. Some studies we have done have estimated that because of increasing complexity the real costs of equipment leaving aside inflation are rising by some 6 per cent per year. The cost of both development and production is increasing and because fewer weapons can be afforded the smaller production runs drive the unit costs of production still higher. There is an obvious interest therefore in finding ways of reducing development costs and securing the advantages of long production runs. This means looking for ways of sharing development and/or combining production. This process is loosely described as collaboration but it is important to realise that there are a number of different forms of common procurement.

First, collaboration on individual projects. Collaboration in development admittedly tends to add to the total cost because of the need for close liaison between the partners, cross-checking of work, extra prototypes and so on. In a major bilateral project the addition to the cost might be around 20 per cent. But even if the total cost increases to this extent the cost to each partner would be only 60 per cent of what it would have cost them to carry out the programme alone.

What about the quality of our relationships with industry? We have continued to foster working relations and need to improve contacts at the higher levels. At the highest level we have the National Defence Industries Council under the chairmanship of the Secretary of State for Defence. This body provides an opportunity, once or twice a year, for top managements of the defence industries and their trade associations to meet the top management of MoD as a whole, to discuss mutual problems of defence supply and procurement.

The PE has also instituted a programme of meetings with the boards of the major suppliers. The meetings allow us to look ahead with individual companies and to discuss matters of policy without being unduly influenced by the need to solve immediate problems. They provide an opportunity, which ordinary meetings can seldom do, to cover the whole field of our relations with each company at one sitting and to put over general points about current performance or about the future outlook.

Relevance to Health Services

There are of course many special characteristics of defence procurement that may make its experience irrelevant to health services procurement: it is on a vast scale, much of it is necessarily secret, some of it is dangerous, and it involves the policies of many other countries. But some similarities exist: it is based solely on expenditure by government, there are unlimited opportunities for purchasing, new and untried knowledge is involved, and the expenditure may lead to political controversy.

The essence of defence procurement policy is the concept of identifying a clear need and then ensuring it is provided. The NHS does not operate on that basis. It does not have a central procurement executive to carry out this essential task. It operates on the opposite principle: let industry try to guess what we would like and we shall then allow over a hundred independent buying authorities to decide whether they want such products. However, defence procurement is not based on the whim of a central dictator: an operational need is identified and that must involve examination of the needs of operational units and consultation about their requirements.

Thus a NHS procurement executive would have to begin with an attempt to scan medical practice and to detect needs. As not all would be met, a second stage would be the setting of priorities, perhaps on a rolling five-year programme: as some priorities are met, others would be added and the new structure of priorities would be reviewed each year and another five-year programme defined.

The next requirement is a positive effort to acquire expert knowledge about the ways of manufacturing and using the product or equipment so as to be able to specify precisely what is required and thus be able to monitor what suppliers do and how the health service uses what is supplied. The elements of such a service exist but it is dispersed and unintegrated.

The third requirement is a relationship of deliberate trust and partnership with suppliers. That exists on similar lines to defence procurement in respect of pharmaceuticals supply but it is not now extended to all suppliers. The benefits of a partnership based on joint design, precise specification, secure quality assurance, and price review based on 'post-costing' would be considerable. There is an implicit assumption in much public purchasing that uncertainty and insecurity keeps suppliers on their toes and ensures efficiency and economy. Those considerations may apply to a perfect market with many identical products and suppliers and where buyers are indifferent to the survival of suppliers. But as in defence, health services depend on innovation, reliability of delivery and quality, and need therefore to ensure the continued existence of at least the best suppliers.

The NHS is not the same as the armed forces and what may suit them may be irrelevant. But there are similarities between all public services, and the increasing demand for health care and the virtual impossibility of the NHS generating any significant income from its activities places the NHS in a special category alongside the forces. The Post Office and the other nationalised industries can be self-financing if governments so wish. The NHS could be but there is no serious support for such an absurd return to the administrative complexities of social insurance as practised in France or Germany. The demand for a 'free' health service is so great that no British political party can ignore it, although fiscal expediency will require some charges to be made occasionally.

The chief difference is the scattering of purchasing power throughout the NHS and that dispersal is defended because it is thought to exemplify local autonomy. It does not. Power remains with the minister if he chooses to use it. If he will not or cannot, the NHS itself should voluntarily develop its incipient integration of purchasing and set up the structure that professionalism, economy, and patient care all indicate as necessary. That extension of current trends must take advantage of the improving relationship with suppliers that has evolved in the past decade, and build it up with a rational partnership.

The Theory of Inter-organisation Management

There is nothing so practical as good theory and it is right to translate some of the conclusions of this study into theoretical consequences. Theory is a summation of experience and provides a tested guide to future action, especially in unfamiliar situations. Theory is thus not the same as speculation.

All the standard definitions of 'organisation' assume that its internal structure and operation are paramount, and that management must concentrate on improving internal performance. Consequently, the aim of the organisation seems often to be self-sufficiency and self-survival. Presumably much organisational thought is derived from the crudities of the classical market theory of economics and from associated misconceived analogies with Darwin's theory of evolution – 'the survival of the fittest'. But if these prejudiced assumptions are set aside and we try to understand the organisation by observing what happens, it becomes obvious that the crucial conditions of effective activity are adequate relations with the world outside its own boundaries. From that wider perspective, the organisation is seen as a collective point for a group of resources: capital, raw materials, customers, labour, and knowledge in particular.

In order to ensure an adequate flow of resources into it and a satisfactory flow of goods and services out from it, the organisation has to be closely concerned with networks of relations with many other organisations. These external relations are more important than internal ones. An organisation may be very efficient internally but still collapse if it cannot obtain supplies or an income. Once these are assured, at least in the short run it can survive even though it operates below optimum efficiency, as so many organisations obviously do.

Management in these extensive dimensions becomes a simultaneous process of internal-external operations that have also to be designed on several different time-scales. Today's raw material is virtually useless unless tomorrow's supply is also secure, and so on into the relevant future. The manager – every manager – has to be concerned with today and tomorrow. Every manager is concerned with long-term planning and corporate strategy. It is not reserved for boardrooms. Bad management can be recognised through operations with inappropriate time-scale perspectives.

The management situation for public organisations is no different from that for private organisations. Private businesses close down if they cannot obtain incomes and supplies. So do schools – and hospitals. Their income may come from government instead of individuals but the organisation still has to perform a function that enough people feel is sufficiently important to justify providing it with money.

The significance of government is no different in essence for government-owned organisations than for those privately owned. Government affects all organisations today and all of them have to accept government relations as a necessary task of management. Politics is part of practical management, not something to be embraced or avoided. The policies of government change, so organisations have to learn about government, not just the government of the day. Because policies change, organisations have opportunities to change them, but only if they learn how to. They have to understand the problems and needs of government if they are to have influence: it is not a simple problem of agitation or bluff.

The heart of the problem of management is recognising the networks that form its total organisation, in addition to its own unique, distinguishing specialisation. All organisations have accounts departments: only hospitals have medical technology. Management has to design and operate relevant networks so as to ensure that its special nucleus has the conditions needed for it to flourish effectively. That requires continuous study and frequent adjustment. Occasionally, it requires carefully prepared creativity and innovation designed to make the most use of its networks of inter-organisational relationships with the minimum avoidable disturbance. The supplier is an ally, not an enemy.

Future Research

It would seem sensible now to extend these studies beyond health service supplies into the general field of procurement in the widest business sense (now sometimes called 'materials management'.)

There are two primary mechanisms whereby relationships between firms and other economic organisations are activated—marketing and procurement. Marketing is the process of measuring, motivating, meeting, and maintaining the demand for an organisation's products or services. It is an unavoidable task of every organisation, carried out at a wide range of competence. It is now widely researched and taught, and there are close links between academic and business interests in marketing.

The aim of marketing is purchase by the customer. Much effort has been given to the study of consumer behaviour but largely confined to the consumer as private individual. The consumer as corporate purchaser is relatively neglected. Thus one reason for a study of business procurement is the need to complement the extensive but incomplete study of the marketing process, and particularly to understand this major form of inter-organisational relationship.

Procurement has several facets and each has to be studied in order to obtain a comprehensive understanding of its mechanism and optimum operational conditions. It is, first, part of the purchasing organisation and we need to know how decisions to buy are made and how the purchased goods and services are managed after the order is placed. That involves a study of ordering, storage, payment, and issue of purchases. The procurement process is likely to differ in organisations according to function and ownership. The experimental group thus needs to contain manufacturing and non-manufacturing firms, in private and public ownership, and both large and small in terms of numbers employed.

There is no simple dovetailing between marketing and procurement, and considerable efforts are made by buyers to discover all relevant sources of supply and to assess their appropriateness. The difficulties of linking buyers and suppliers has led to the growth of numerous intermediaries, such as sales agents, wholesalers, retailers, export merchants, advertisers, and trade papers. These confusing networks of link organisations need to be identified and traced in order to understand the full procurement process.

It is known that some organisations arrange purchasing jointly with others in order to obtain lower unit prices for larger total quantities, or to safeguard long-term supplies. Such joint purchasing is sometimes arranged by trade associations, but some appears to be undertaken locally and informally and needs to be investigated. Similarly suppliers regulate the quantities available from time to time in periods of scarcity, particularly through commodity markets, and a proper study of procurement must include these activities.

The procurement process clearly has many direct and indirect influences on the production of goods and services and consequently on employment. The organisation of procurement may provide a means of aggregating demand and hence maintaining or increasing employment if purchasing decisions can be consolidated and smoothed. Thus procurement has a potentially important and unique economic role that has been neglected in both research and policy. The optimum form of aggregated demand policy can only emerge from a thorough study of conventional procurement operations.

There is thus a significant political dimension that requires analysis and should lead to useful policy proposals. Recent attempts to stimulate investment, promote regional development, and reduce unemployment have had only small success, largely because the measures adopted have created artificial mechanisms that complicated and disrupted normal business activities. Procurement provides the only potentially powerful mechanism for stimulating and regularising demand within normal business activities. Procurement also provides painless opportunities for integrating purchasing decisions, and hence relationships, within the private and within the public sectors of the economy, and between the two sectors. It also offers opportunities for similar policies in respect of international trade, especially with developing countries.

These many facets of procurement can only be properly studied within a particular framework and period that (a) represents the whole economy, (b) allows for the study of inter-organisation relationships, (c) extends over sufficient time to permit the analysis of normal procurement cycles, and (d) ensures that the practices observed are not peculiar to one particular district.

Hence the following proposals for experimental and control groups:

(i) the study should be made in Portsmouth and within approximately a twenty-mile radius. A 1974 survey of employers by Hampshire County Council showed that firms from all 21 orders of the Standard Industrial Classification are to be found within that area;
(ii) the study should extend over three years;
(iii) the experimental group should comprise if possible 84 organisations – 4 from each of the 21 SIC orders, 2 of which should have fewer than 100 employees and 2 over 100. Two of the 4 should be privately owned and 2 publicly owned – preferably one small and one large organisation in each sector.

There are no grounds for assuming that the procurement situation in the Portsmouth region is atypical, but some form of control group is desirable to guard against that possibility. The control group could attempt to replicate the experimental group in another geographical area.

Notes

1. Cf. G. Tullock, *The Vote Motive*, Institute of Economic Affairs, London, 1976.
2. C. Turpin, *Government Contracts*, Penguin, London, 1972, p. 264.
3. 'Government Organisation for Defence Procurement and Civil Aerospace', Command Paper 4641, HMSO, London, 1971.
4. Most of this information was obtained from a series of articles in the January 1975 issue of *Procurement* and from an article by G.H. Green, Deputy Under-

Secretary of State (Policy), Procurement Executive, entitled 'British Policy for Defence Procurement' in *NATO's 15 Nations*, April-May, 1976.

BIBLIOGRAPHY

Abel-Smith, B., *An International Study of Health Expenditure*, World Health Organisation, 1967

——— *et al.*, *Accounting for Health*, King Edward Hospital Fund, 1973

———. *Value for Money in Health Services*, Heinemann, 1975

Ammer, D.S., *Purchasing and Materials Management for Health Care Institutions*, Lexington Books, 1975

Association of NHS Supplies Officers, *Members Reference Book and Buyers Guide*, 1976-7

Banham, J., *Realising the Promise of a National Health Service*, J. Banham, c/o McKinsey & Co., London, 1977

Beddard, F.D. *et al.*, *Positions, Movement, and Directions in Health Services Research*, Nuffield Provincial Hospitals Trust, Oxford University Press, 1974

Blanpain, J., *National Health Insurance and Health Resources: The European Experience*, Harvard University Press, 1978

British Airways, *A Supplies Organisation for British Airways*, Heathrow Airport, 1976

Brown, R.G.S., *The Changing National Health Service*, Routledge, 1973

Chester, T.E., 'Health Care in West Germany and France: A Comparative Analysis', *Three Banks Review*, Dec., 1976

Cochrane, A.L., *Growth, Effectiveness and Efficiency*, Nuffield Provincial Hospital Trust, Oxford University Press, 1973

Cooper, M.H. and Culyer, A.J. (eds), *Health Economics*, Penguin, 1973

Craft, I. *et al.*, *Specialized Futures*, Oxford University Press, 1975

Department of Health & Social Security, *Equipping a Hospital Building*, HMSO, 1970

——— *Nucleus Hospitals*, HMSO, 1976

——— *Health and Personal Social Services Statistics for England*, HMSO, 1974, 1975, 1976

——— *Regional Chairmen's Enquiry into the Working of the DHSS in Relation to Regional Health Authorities*, HMSO, 1976

——— *On the State of the Public Health for the Year 1974*, HMSO, 1976

——— *Annual Report 1975*, HMSO, 1976

——— *Annual Report 1976*, HMSO, 1977

Donaldson, R.J., *The New Health Service in Britain*, Royal Society of Health, 1977

Famery, P., 'Politique des Achats des Etablissements Hospitalier Publics', *Gestions Hospitalières*, Feb., 1978
Farmer, D.H. & Taylor, B. (eds), *Corporate Planning and Procurement*, Heinemann, 1975
Fulcher, D., *Medical Care Systems*, International Labour Office, 1974
Green, J. & Moss, R., *Hospital Research and Briefing Problems*, King Edward's Hospital Fund for London, 1971
Green, S., *The Hospital: An Organisational Analysis*, Blackie, 1974
Haslemere Group, *Who Needs Drug Companies?*, Third World Publications, n.d.
Hauser, M.M. (ed.), *The Economics of Medical Care*, George Allen & Unwin, 1972
Haywood, S.G., *Managing the Health Service*, George Allen & Unwin, 1974
HMSO, *Public Purchasing and Industrial Efficiency*, 1967
Hyman, S., 'Why the Supplies Service is in Need of a Transfusion', *Health and Social Services Journal*, Jan., 1977
—— 'Eine Einschätzung Medizinischer Einuregerzeugnesse', *Krankenhause Unschein*, May, 1977
—— *The Hospital Supplies Market for Disposable Products: Britain, France, West Germany*, Frost & Sullivan Inc., 1976
—— 'The Hospital and the Supplier', *British Hospital Journal and Social Services Review*, June, 1970
—— *Hospital Supplies and Suppliers*, Kingston Polytechnic, 1970
Institute of Health Service Administrators, *The Hospitals and Health Services Yearbook and Directory of Equipment and Supplies*, 1977
Iwai, Y., 'Development of Electronic Equipment – Co-operation between Hospital and Industry', *World Hospitals*, 1977
Kaihara, S., 'Optimum use of Electronic Equipment in Hospital and Community', *World Hospitals*, 1977
Klass, A., *There's Gold in Them Thar Pills*, Penguin, 1975
Levy, M.E., 'French Studies on Health Economics: A Survey' in Hauser, M.M. (ed.), *The Economics of Medical Care*
McKeown, T., *The Role of Medicine: Dream, Mirage or Nemesis?*, Nuffield Provincial Hospitals Trust, 1976
McLachlan, G. (ed.), *Positions, Movements and Directions in Health Services Research*, Oxford University Press, 1974
—— *Measuring for Management: Quantitative Methods in Health Service Management*, Nuffield Provincial Hospitals Trust, Oxford University Press, 1975
Maxwell, R., MP, *Public Sector Purchasing*, R. Maxwell, 1967

Maxwell, R., *Health Care: the Growing Dilemma*, McKinsey & Co., 2nd ed., 1975

Maynard, A., *Health Care in the European Community*, Croom Helm, 1975

Merrison, A.W., *Report of the Committee of Enquiry into the Regulation of the Medical Profession*, HMSO, 1975

Millard, G., *Commissioning Hospital Buildings*, King's Fund, London, 1975

National Economic Development Office, *Focus on Pharmaceuticals*, HMSO, 1972

Newell, K.W., *Health By The People*, World Health Organisation, 1975

Office of Health Economics, *Hospital Purchasing*, London, 1972

—— *Innovation in Industry: A Factor for Growth*, London, 1970

—— *Compendium of Health Statistics*, 2nd ed., 1977

Revans, R.W., *Action Learning in Hospitals*, McGraw Hill, 1976

Richter, Mrs H.B. and Barbosa Assumpção, T.E., 'Electronic Equipment – Supply and Servicing in Developing Countries', *World Hospitals*, 1977

Sainsbury Committee, 'Report of the Committee of Enquiry into the Relationship of the Pharmaceutical Industry with the National Health Service', Command Paper 3410, HMSO, 1967

Thorp, J., 'Economic Considerations in Adopting Electronic Equipment', *World Hospitals*, 1977

Tulloch, G., *The Vote Motive*, Institute of Economic Affairs, 1976

Turpin, C., *Government Contracts*, Penguin, 1972

Van Langendonck, J., *Prelude to Harmony on a Community Theme. Health Care Insurance Policies in the Six and in Britain*, Nuffield Provincial Hospitals Trust, Oxford University Press, 1975

World Health Organisation, *Health Services in Europe*, 2nd ed., 1975

INDEX